SOUTH PACIFIC

Geoffrey Block, Series Editor

Series Board

Stephen Banfield   Jeffrey Magee

Tim Carter   Carol Oja

Kim Kowalke   Larry Starr

"South Pacific": Paradise Rewritten

Jim Lovensheimer

SOUTH PACIFIC
Paradise Rewritten

JIM LOVENSHEIMER

OXFORD

UNIVERSITY PRESS

2010

OXFORD
UNIVERSITY PRESS

Oxford University Press, Inc., publishes works that further
Oxford University's objective of excellence
in research, scholarship, and education.

Oxford   New York
Auckland   Cape Town   Dar es Salaam   Hong Kong   Karachi
Kuala Lumpur   Madrid   Melbourne   Mexico City   Nairobi
New Delhi   Shanghai   Taipei   Toronto

With offices in
Argentina   Austria   Brazil   Chile   Czech Republic   France   Greece
Guatemala   Hungary   Italy   Japan   Poland   Portugal   Singapore
South Korea   Switzerland   Thailand   Turkey   Ukraine   Vietnam

Published by Oxford University Press, Inc.
198 Madison Avenue, New York, New York 10016

www.oup.com

Oxford is a registered trademark of Oxford University Press

Publication of this book was supported in part by a grant
from the H. Earle Johnson Fund of the Society for American Music
and through the generosity of the Blair School of Music at Vanderbilt University.

Library of Congress Cataloging-in-Publication Data
Lovensheimer, Jim.
South Pacific : paradise rewritten / Jim Lovensheimer.
p. cm. — (Broadway legacies)
Includes bibliographical references and index.
ISBN 978-0-19-537702-6
1. Rodgers, Richard, 1902–1979. South Pacific.
2. Hammerstein, Oscar, 1895–1960. South Pacific.
3. Musicals—United States—20th century—History and criticism. I. Title.
ML2054.L68 2010
782.1′4—dc22   2009041073

3 5 7 9 8 6 4 2

Printed in the United States of America
on acid-free paper

For
JOHN CALLIHAN

ACKNOWLEDGMENTS

• • •

This book is an outgrowth of the research I did for my doctoral dissertation, "The Musico-Dramatic Evolution of Rodgers and Hammerstein's 'South Pacific,'" which was completed in the spring of 2003. While this book differs greatly in content from the dissertation, the primary sources used for both are the same. Because of this relationship between the research and the two resultant studies, I would be remiss not to first thank the members of the musicology area in the School of Music at the Ohio State University, all of whom were the best mentors a developing scholar could hope to have. Arved Ashby, who advised the dissertation, Charles M. Atkinson, Graeme Boone, Margarita Mazo, and Lois Rosow, the last of whom reminded me more often than anyone else that good writing is hard work, all have my ongoing gratitude, as does Burdette Green from the music theory area.

At the Library of Congress, Mark Eden Horowitz was generous with his time and his guidance, and my access to the uncatalogued collection of Oscar Hammerstein II would have been far more difficult without his help. Everyone in the Performing Arts Reading Room was helpful, but Mark went several extra miles to ensure that I had what I needed when I needed it. Without him, the process might have been even more formidable than it already was.

At the Rodgers and Hammerstein Organization, Ted Chapin, Robin Walton, and Bert Fink have been interested, supportive, and generous. Their deep and cautious concern for protecting the published and unpublished works of Rodgers and Hammerstein is combined with an enthusiasm for new considerations of those works, and they were always encouraging.

I am grateful to Dean Mark Wait of the Blair School of Music, Vanderbilt University, for his support in all phases of my writing. Also at Blair, Associate Dean Cynthia Cyrus has been a wonderful mentor and listener, as have been Melanie Lowe, Chair of the Department of Musicology and Ethnomusicology, and my colleagues Greg Barz, Joy Calico, Dale Cockrell, Robbie Fry, Jen Gunderman, Michael Hime, Douglas Lee (Emeritus), Jimmy Maiello, and Helena Simonett. And I offer abundant thanks to everyone else at Blair and to Vanderbilt's Chancellor, Nick Zeppos, for providing an environment that is supportive and appreciative.

Special thanks to Erin Steigerwald, who calmly dealt with requests and changes to all the musical examples in the book. All professors should have such bright, positive, and selfless students.

Many thanks to the Society for American Music (SAM), not only for the generous Johnson Subvention Award that has defrayed publication costs, but also for being a professional society dedicated to diverse and wide-reaching areas of American music. SAM's interest in, and support of, wide-ranging scholarship in the field of American musical theater is consistent and unprecedented. Those of us who work in this specialized area are lucky to have SAM as a parent organization. While scholars from other disciplines who write about musical theater often comment on being treated by their peers as if their interest was somehow illegitimate, musicologists active in SAM feel no such outsider status. For that, we all are grateful.

Thanks to Tom Riis, for first suggesting Oxford University Press and for his interest and advice; to John Graziano, for his ongoing support and encouragement; to Karen Ahlquist, for convincing me that I needed to stay within the American music fold when I was tempted to stray into another area of research; to Graham Wood, for his insights into Richard Rodgers and his generosity in sharing them; to Jim Randall, Jessica Sternfeld, Anna Gentry, Tim Carter, Joe Horowitz, Wayne Shirley, Richard Mook, Tammy Kernodle, Bill Everett, Paul Laird, and everyone else who has read, listened to, and/or put up with me talking about this project for so long.

I deeply appreciate the time and effort taken by the peer reviewers, both anonymous and self-identified. Their expert and constructive comments and criticisms were applied in every instance. Seldom have so many critical observations been presented in such a supportive tone. I owe much to each person who took such careful time writing a response.

At Oxford University Press, thanks to Suzanne Ryan for her patience. A great deal of thanks to the copy editor, Jackie Doyle, whose keen eye saw nearly every opportunity to improve my style. Chris Dahlin has been tremendously helpful in guiding this first-time author through the process of turning a manuscript into a book. She has always been available and quick to respond to the most mundane of my questions (and I had many). I also owe profound thanks to Geoffrey Block, the editor of Oxford's Broadway Legacies series. Geoffrey played a crucial role in the timely acquisition of rights and permissions from several important sources, without which the appearance of this volume would have been greatly detained. Oxford University Press chose wisely when it picked Geoffrey to edit this series, and those of us who contribute to it are fortunate to have him leading the way. Long an important voice in musical theater scholarship, Geoffrey is now vitally important to the rest of us trying to be heard. And above all, thanks to Norm Hirschy. Norm was the first person I talked to about this project, and his guidance and support have made it possible. More than just an acquiring editor, Norm has become a friend, a sometime scold, a source of endless information to this first-time author, and the kind of nurturing editor most authors can only imagine. He has kept me going and shown inordinate patience when my other academic activities slowed my progress to a crawl, and he also is always the first to celebrate every accomplishment, no matter how small or seemingly insignificant. This book would not exist without him.

Finally, I must thank two people I have long, long since lost track of. When I was around three years old, a young couple named Jim and Jean Tidd used to babysit for me while my parents sought some time away from parenting. Among the entertainments they provided was the original cast recording of *South Pacific*, which was the first music I have any recollection of hearing. I quickly knew many of the songs by heart and was unembarrassed about singing and dancing to them. The score has had a special place in my life ever since. Although I also heard other cast albums during my evenings with Jim and Jean, it was always *South Pacific* that I asked to hear first. I can still recall the smell of the record, and if I no longer dance around the living room with the same kind of abandon that I did at age three, I still listen to the score of *South Pacific* with the same appreciative awe as always. This book, then, is an extension of that long-held love and appreciation for a show that continues to encourage us to dream of our own special island.

PERMISSIONS ACKNOWLEDGMENTS

• • •

The following have graciously granted permission to reprint copyrighted and unpublished material:

Excerpts from OKLAHOMA! used by permission of The Rodgers and Hammerstein Organization, an Imagem Company. © 1942 and 1944 by Oscar Hammerstein II. Copyright Renewed. International Copyright Secured. All Rights Reserved.

Excerpts from CAROUSEL used by permission of The Rodgers and Hammerstein Organization, an Imagen Company. © 1945 by Richard Rodgers and Oscar Hammerstein II. Copyright Renewed. International Copyright Secured. All Rights Reserved.

Excerpts from SOUTH PACIFIC used by permission of The Rodgers and Hammerstein Organization, an Imagen Company. © 1949 by Richard Rodgers and Oscar Hammerstein II. Copyright Renewed. International Copyright Secured. All Rights Reserved.

Excerpts from MUSICAL STAGES by Richard Rodgers. Used by permission of the Rodgers and Hammerstein Organization on behalf of the Family Trust u/w/Richard Rodgers. © 1975 by Richard Rodgers. All Rights Reserved.

Excerpt from "South Pacific in Concert from Carnegie Hall." © 2010 by Theodore S. Chapin.

Excerpts from unpublished materials in the collection of Oscar Hammerstein II, Library of Congress. Used by permission of the Rodgers and Hammerstein Organization on behalf of the Estate of Oscar Hammerstein II. © 2010 by Hammerstein Properties LLC.

Excerpts from "A Wonderful Guy." Music by Richard Rodgers, Lyrics by Oscar Hammerstein II. Copyright © 1949. Copyright Renewed. WILLIAMSON MUSIC owner of publication and allied rights throughout the World. International Copyright Secured. All Rights Reserved. Used by Permission.

Excerpts from "The Bright Young Executive of Today." Lyrics by Oscar Hammerstein II. © 2008 Hammerstein Properties LLC. International Copyright Secured. All Rights Reserved. Used by Permission.

Excerpt from "My Friend." Lyrics by Oscar Hammerstein II. © 2008 Hammerstein Properties and Trustees of the Family Trust u/w/o Richard Rodgers, (deceased) renewed. International Copyright Secured. All Rights Reserved. Used by Permission.

Excerpts from "Suddenly Lucky." Lyrics by Oscar Hammerstein II. © 2008 Hammerstein Properties LLC and Trustees of the Family Trust u/w/o Richard

CONTENTS

• • •

FOREWORD

• • •

It is with great pleasure that I introduce Jim Lovensheimer's *"South Pacific":* *Paradise Rewritten* as the inaugural volume in the new series called Broadway Legacies, published by Oxford University Press. The series will offer engrossing books on Broadway composers, composer-lyricist teams, choreographers, directors, and other creative artists who have made Broadway one of America's most celebrated, recognizable, and popular cultural institutions. Other books in the series will be devoted to musicals, like *South Pacific*, that have made a major cultural and artistic impact on the genre. All volumes will present original research and new ideas by authors who understand the importance of telling their stories in engaging and accessible prose. Among the coming attractions are books on the great librettist and lyricist Dorothy Fields, who wrote the book for *Annie Get Your Gun* and the lyric "Pick Yourself Up," which inspired part of President Obama's 2009 inaugural address; *Oklahoma!* and *Carousel* choreographer Agnes de Mille; Jerry Bock and Sheldon Harnick (the composer and lyricist team that created *Fiddler on the Roof*); the American musical icon Irving Berlin; Charles Strouse, the composer of *Bye By Birdie* and *Annie*; and the pioneering Broadway classic *Show Boat* by Oscar Hammerstein and Jerome Kern.

Although *South Pacific*'s Broadway homecoming was delayed for nearly sixty years, not unlike other long-awaited revivals of 1940s classics like *Annie Get Your Gun* (1946) and *Kiss Me, Kate* (1948), neither of which were to officially return until 1999, millions were familiar with its amazingly rich score as once seen and heard and still heard on the magnificent and intimidating original cast recording starring Mary Martin and Ezio Pinza, and the work continues to be performed in thousands of regional theaters, high schools, and other theatrical venues. The unsettling garish color filters that pervade Joshua Logan's relatively faithful 1958 film adaptation inspired widespread and to some extent unfair disdain for the film as a whole. In any event, whether because of the film or despite the film, the show never disappeared from popular consciousness.

Nevertheless, *South Pacific* and the world it portrays remain problematic. In our efforts to move beyond where we were in 1949, Americans are less sure about how to characterize World War II (in fact, in filmmaker Ken Burns's recent documentary series, what historian Studs Terkel and others called the "good war" is now the "necessary war"). We might prefer that horny navy men would sing a tune less overtly sexist than "There Is Nothin' Like a Dame," and we might hope that the Tonkinese beauty Liat would have been allowed to do more than listen in silence to Lt. Joseph Cable's "Younger Than Springtime" or perform silent hand movements to "Happy Talk," sung to the lovebirds by Liat's mother, Bloody Mary. Our evolving social awareness on issues of race, gender, and colonialism does not, however, change the fact that *South Pacific* was forward looking and bold in its day and continues to engage contemporary directors, performers, and audiences.

Three years before the popular televised "*South Pacific* in Concert from Carnegie Hall" starring Reba McEntire (a staple airing on Public Broadcasting Services' pledge nights and also a best-selling DVD), and five years before the critically acclaimed current Broadway hit revival directed by Bartlett Sher (astonishingly, aside from several short engagements, this is the musical's first major return to Broadway since ending its long run from 1949 to 1954), I wrote a chapter on Rodgers and Hammerstein's *South Pacific* in the book *Richard Rodgers* (2003), in which I concluded that this landmark show "seizes a moment and reflects that moment honestly" and in the process "daringly confronts sex, race, and war in its own time, with a libretto that challenges its characters and its audiences." Despite my cockeyed optimism concerning the show's future, I did not anticipate how soon *South Pacific* would regain its popularity and acclaim on the concert and theatrical stage, nor did I foresee that this challenging musical would provide the subject for Jim Lovensheimer's provocative and important work on the compositional and creative process and cultural meanings of this provocative and important show.

Lovensheimer's unprecedented research into Hammerstein's papers and drafts for *South Pacific* reveals a more confrontational stance on the subject of racial tolerance, a stance that the librettist would soften in the course of the work's creation, both to avoid creating a show that would exceed the comfort zone of post–World War II audiences and to strengthen the work's dramatic qualities. In its final opening night on Broadway, the teachings in Cable's "You've Got to Be Carefully Taught" would provide most audience members with more than enough instruction for one hit show. Lovensheimer has also discovered how closely the ideals of *South Pacific*, with its plea for tolerance, can be traced to Hammerstein's writings for the Writers' War Board, an organization that evolved from generating war propaganda (to promote the sale of war bonds) to indicting America's failures to achieve racial tolerance on the home front. In "*South Pacific*": *Paradise Rewritten*, readers will learn the fascinating story of how Hammerstein, aided by Joshua Logan as colibrettist and director and Richard Rodgers's hit-studded score, transformed James A.

Michener's Pulitzer Prize–winning novel *Tales from the South Pacific* into a classic of the American musical and a vibrant reflection of American culture from its time to ours.

GEOFFREY BLOCK
Series Editor, Broadway Legacies

SOUTH PACIFIC

1

WHO CAN EXPLAIN IT?

• • •

Four days after the Lincoln Center revival of *South Pacific* opened on April 3, 2008, the classic musical celebrated its fifty-ninth birthday. Despite its age, the show was the hottest ticket on Broadway even before it opened. And once the almost unanimously glowing reviews came out, *South Pacific* was even harder to get into; months later it was still selling out. What about this war-horse of a musical so attracts twenty-first-century American audiences that they are willing to wait weeks and even months to see it? Frank Rich, formerly the principal theater critic for the *New York* Times and now a columnist in its Sunday "Week in Review" section, addressed this question and other related issues in an article devoted to the revival.[1]

Writing on Memorial Day weekend, over a month after the production's opening, he observed, "This old chestnut is surely the most unexpected cultural sensation the city has experienced in a while." He went on to note that contemporary audiences think "they've seen the genuine 'South Pacific' only because its songs reside in the collective American unconscious. . . . They expect corn, but in a year when war and race are at center stage in the national conversation, this relic turns out to have a great deal to say." What *South Pacific* has to say, Rich observed, was especially important during a presidential campaign that probed how far Americans have come toward an ideal of racial tolerance and to what extent we feel "optimism about the possibilities of healing and redemption that may yet lie ahead." Indeed, *South Pacific* reflects major issues confronting Americans today, not the least of which is an unpopular war that stands in stark contrast to World War II, the conflagration that Studs Terkel later called "the good war."[2] As Rich commented, "*South Pacific* isn't pro-war or antiwar. But it makes you think about the costs. . . . This is a more fatal-istic World War II than some we've seen lately." *South Pacific*, especially in its current incarnation, further challenges Terkel's suggestive name for World War II by emphasizing the irony of Americans fighting a war against racist enemies while their own racism remains unresolved. And it shows the tragic results that can come from that lack of resolution.

Audiences in the United States seem to have forgotten so much about this musical that its almost startling confrontation with homegrown racism catches them off guard. Recalling only images of Mary Martin and Ezio Pinza on an old original cast recording, or the overly produced Hollywood version of the musical made almost ten years after the Broadway production, audiences who expect only to be lulled by "Some Enchanted Evening" are jolted out of their reveries by "You've Got to Be Carefully Taught," perhaps the most confrontational moment in any of Rodgers and Hammerstein's work. In an era in which many Americans like to think of themselves as "post-racial," to borrow a term used without irony in the 2008 presidential primaries, the tragic consequence of Joe Cable's learned racism still draws gasps.

In his review in the *New York Times*, the theater critic Ben Brantley suggested that the production itself provided another key to the revival's popularity. This *South Pacific*, he noted, "feels too vital to be a museum piece, too sensually fluid to be square." He further observed that the production is infused with "the fire of daily life, with all its crosscurrents and ambiguities, underscored and clarified by music." The revelation of the revival is that *South Pacific* is an emotionally honest, thematically daring show whose power has been all but forgotten after innumerable high school, college, community theater, summer stock, and touring productions and countless routine performances of its songs, nearly all of which are masterpieces of the genre. "It's as if a vintage photograph had been restored not with fuzzy, hand-colored prettiness," Brantley later commented, "but with you-are-there clarity."[3]

Several aspects of the production demonstrate this restored clarity. When the thirty-piece orchestra begins the overture, for instance, the sound is stunning. While this was the size of the orchestra for the original production, Broadway pits have grown smaller over the years as amplification and electronic instruments allow for more sound from fewer musicians. Here, the strings soar and the power of the brass and woodwinds comes from the players, not from the sound engineer. To be sure, the pit, like the actors, is amplified, but the result is enhancement, not ear-shattering volume. The sensitively mixed sound seems to come from the pit and the stage, not from speakers on either side of the stage. (A concurrent revival of *Gypsy* also began with a full orchestra playing the overture—in this production, the orchestra was onstage—but when the percussionist's mallet hit the tympani on the downbeat, the sound came from speakers, not from the tympani. The moment was surreal.) When the overture reaches the chorus of "Bali Ha'i," the lip of the stage that has covered most of the pit slides back and the entire ensemble is revealed. The combination of the radiant song, the all-but-forgotten orchestral sound, and the sight of so many musicians in the pit generates appreciative and even awestruck applause. Many young people in the audience probably have never experienced such an acoustic event in the musical theater, which is also the first moment of the performance when many in the audience get teary.

Brantley pointed out another key reason the revival achieves such power. The director Bartlett Sher, Brantley commented, "puts his trust unconditionally in the original material."[4] Because Sher is never coy about the sweeping romanticism that is so integral to *South Pacific*, the production is completely believable; no one seems to have been told that the show is sixty years old. "Mr. Sher," Brantley continued, "and Christopher Gattelli, who did the musical staging, have reinvigorated the concept of the organic musical, in which song feels as natural as breathing." Confronted with a production that treats the musical with complete integrity, audiences are surprised, perhaps unconsciously, by the depth of their response to the story and the songs.

Although Brantley is correct to admire Sher's trust in *South Pacific*, his use of the words "original material" is a little more problematic. Sher, in reality, did not use the "original material," if by that term Brantley meant the musical as it first appeared on Broadway. Instead, the first rehearsal script for the show has been revisited, and passages of dialogue and a musical number cut from *South Pacific* before it opened have been restored.

WHICH SOUTH PACIFIC?

Although Rodgers and Hammerstein were not afraid of creating a show full of social criticism, all of which is found in James A. Michener's *Tales of the South Pacific*, the Pulitzer Prize–winning novel on which it was based, they also wanted *South Pacific* to be a hit, and they walked a fine line between commercial and critical success and political controversy throughout the creative process. As Rodgers, Hammerstein, and the director and coauthor Joshua Logan carefully refined their musical to achieve the balance of popular appeal and dramatic heft they sought, substantial material was rewritten or cut. Many of the passages reinstated by Sher originally were cut either for reasons of time—this is the reason for the original excision of the song "My Girl Back Home," for instance, which was reinstated both in the film version and in Sher's production—or to soften the show's criticism of U.S. racism and social injustice, which nonetheless remained powerful for audiences in 1949.

1.1. *Richard Rodgers and Oscar Hammerstein II (right) working on "South Pacific."*
Courtesy of Photofest.

The latter concern notwithstanding, the topics of race and social injustice had been in the postwar national consciousness since at least early 1948, when President Truman proposed an unprecedented civil rights program in a highly controversial public statement. "The Federal Government," the president declared, "has a clear duty to see that the Constitutional guarantees of individual liberties and of equal protection under the laws are not denied or abridged anywhere in the Union. That duty is shared by all three branches of Government, but it can be filled only if the Congress enacts modern, comprehensive civil rights laws, adequate to the needs of the day, and demonstrating our continuing faith in the free way of life." In the same statement, Truman requested that the secretary of defense put an end to discrimination in the armed forces.[5] Further, despite being in the first phases of the postwar boom, Americans were becoming increasingly anxious about the world around them, and not long after the show opened, some of their fears materialized: the Soviet Union tested its first atomic weapon in August, for example; China's communist revolution occurred in October; and an intensified cold war and the domestic fallout from McCarthyism were just around the corner. The social and political climate of 1949, in other words, was rife with tension despite the outward trappings of a booming economy and its general prosperity.

In light of the volatile political atmosphere, Rodgers and Hammerstein's attempts to keep controversy to a minimum are unsurprising. But the use in 2008 of material from the first rehearsal script invites the question of what is "original": is it the early script, or is it the script as it first opened on Broadway? And what about "original" material that was cut even before making it into the first rehearsal script? The reinstatement of dialogue and songs originally cut from *South Pacific* is an excellent introduction to the question of "definitive" versus "open" texts, a question that affects creative approaches to productions in addition to audience responses to them. For instance, original cast albums, with a few earlier exceptions, began in earnest with the recording of *Oklahoma!* in 1943. After this, audiences who experienced the recorded "definitive" performances of original casts expected replications of those performances from subsequent performers. This, in turn, led to productions that replicated the original production as closely as possible. But, as Bruce Kirle argued in his groundbreaking book *Unfinished Show Business: Musicals as Works-in-Process*, precise replication is not only difficult. It is impossible. "Musicals wed text, performance, and reception to create meaning within specified historical contexts," he began. "Works-in-process, they are open and fluid, subject to a great deal of variation, even subversion, in the way they are performed. As such, in their original productions or over time, they often assume lives of their own that can be quite independent from the original intentions of their authors."[6] By tampering with the formal aspects of *South Pacific*, Sher treats it as an "open text" and thus creates a "variation" on the original text. But he does this in order to reinvigorate the original authorial intent and strengthen it for an audience in a different historical and social context. Sher's success recalls Kirle's observation that "even the most popular of musicals is universal and timeless *only* in its willingness to adapt to the values, anxieties, and tensions of new audiences in new cultural moments."[7] Given the critical and popular response to the revival, Sher has succeeded in adapting *South Pacific* for this moment in the early twenty-first century.

South Pacific is a particularly interesting show for this revisionist approach. It is unique in the Rodgers and Hammerstein repertory in that it was already altered *during* its Broadway run: in 1950, more than a year after the show opened, music and lyrics were added for Emile de Becque in act 2, scene 4 (2.4) that created a musical transition between "You've Got to Be Carefully Taught" and "This Nearly Was Mine."[8] This passage is neither on the original cast recording nor in the original published version of the script, but it has been a part of the score since it went into the show. This addition was unusual, and it demonstrates that Rodgers and Hammerstein's refinement of the show continued well after its successful reception. (Generally, shows are "frozen," or kept unchanged, after they open and remain so throughout their original run. Many shows, however, have been altered in subsequent productions.) While audiences since 1950 have no idea that this passage was not part of the "original" version of the show, at least one audience member in June of that year noticed. Hammerstein received a letter that asked for the "new" lyrics after mentioning that they were not on the recording or in the script. Hammerstein obliged, commenting, "I'm glad you like this addition. I think it helps the scene a great deal."[9]

PARADISE WRITTEN AND REWRITTEN

The addition for de Becque and the restorations from the first rehearsal script in the 2008 production, in addition to changes, cuts, or restorations in the 1958 film; the 2000 version for American television; and Trevor Nunn's 2002 London production all suggest the lack of a "definitive" or final version of *South Pacific*. This both supports and demonstrates Kirle's thesis about musicals being "open," or ever-changing, texts. Stephen Banfield, another important scholar of the musical theater, has suggested that musicals, by their very nature, are never "finished" or meant to stand fixed and unalterable. His comments are pertinent to this discussion:

> Scholarly criticism must after all be based on the technical detail of the source material, and the source material for the musical theater is ill-grounded in "authentic" documents. A musical exists in no definitive form, and a performance is created from no single source. The vocal score and the script are separate, the orchestral parts separate again, and, as it were, invisible in the absence of an accessible orchestra score . . . , and the choreography and staging may not be fixed in notation at all. The original cast recording is widely considered a show's most authoritative source, fallaciously in view of the many ways in which it may differ from (let alone foreshorten) what was heard in the theater.[10]

The openness of a musical's text, as indicated by Kirle and Banfield, suggests the usefulness of examining all possible versions of a work from any given point in its evolution. These versions usually involve either sketches, which are incomplete or partial versions of scenes and songs—perhaps an added but later discarded verse or chorus of a song, for example—or drafts, which are complete versions of a scene or song that later underwent transformation, editing, or excision. The investigation of sketches and drafts was integral for this study of *South Pacific*, and it provides a previously unavailable insight into how the work reached the initial form that secured its status as a pinnacle of the Rodgers and Hammerstein repertory and its later and varied forms that have maintained that status. The preliminary versions of the show demonstrate what was important to its creators at each stage of its development and how that changed. In addition to revealing the musical and dramatic development of *South Pacific*, the authors' sketches provide insight into the working methods of two towering figures in the American musical theater. Indeed, to many theatergoers in the 1940s and 1950s, Rodgers and Hammerstein *were* the American musical theater.

The sketches and drafts for *South Pacific*, and their subsequent rewrites, underscore the three principal themes of this book. First, they demonstrate that Rodgers and especially Hammerstein continually refined and softened the polemics of their musical until its confrontational thematic content was thought acceptable for mainstream Broadway audiences. Sometimes they changed no more than one word in a scene, and sometimes they changed entire characters; but, in the end, they sought to edify without offending their audience, and they largely, if not completely, succeeded. Second, the early drafts and sketches reveal changes made for dramaturgical purposes apart from any thematic concerns. Characters emphasized in early versions virtually disappear, for instance; the storyline is trimmed and streamlined; and the show is gradually transformed into a musical play worthy of its creators' confidence. Finally, an examination of changes in the structural and thematic materials of *South Pacific*, and of alterations made to Michener's novel, provides insight into the postwar era in which the musical was created; it also shows how that era is reflected in the various stages of the work's development. Racial intolerance may have been in the foreground of *South Pacific*, but Rodgers and Hammerstein's unused or cut material reveals how they explored and were influenced by other widespread social issues. Prevalent among these issues are gender, postwar colonialism, and the changing image of U.S. business in the postwar era; the treatment of each was transformed or eliminated during the creative process.

The majority of materials consulted for this study are found among Oscar Hammerstein's papers at the Library of Congress. This collection has yet to be catalogued, although the plentiful boxes are categorized by show. The papers for *South Pacific* were somewhat organized—one box of scripts, another marked "correspondence," and so on—but for the most part, research involved going through each box paper by paper. Each sketch or draft referred to in what follows is listed by the box in which it was found. The *South Pacific* boxes also contained much fascinating information unused in this study: business transactions, letters about product placement of beer and cigarettes in the original production, and drafts of a letter written to Rodgers on the occasion of his fiftieth birthday and subsequently published in *Town and Country*, and so on. In spite of its being of interest, however, much of the material falls outside the scope of this work.

The Richard Rodgers Collection at the Library of Congress was also of great importance to this work. Many sketches for subsequently undeveloped numbers are in this collection, and a few of them are unmentioned in the extant literature on the show. On several occasions, nonmusical items were also found among Rodgers's papers, the unused opening of act 1 being among the most important for this study. While Hammerstein's handwriting is sometimes challenging, Rodgers's work was almost always neat; even his preliminary sketches are fairly easy to make out. And at least one bit of Rodgers's handiwork was among Hammerstein's papers and confirms the well-known story about the creation of "This Nearly Was Mine," which went into the show late in rehearsals. When Rodgers asked for a working title for a new song to follow "You've Got to Be Carefully Taught," Hammerstein suggested "This Nearly Was Mine." Rodgers went off and wrote the music.[11] Among Hammerstein's papers is a half page of music-manuscript paper with the melody of the song written in pencil. At every point in the song where the lyrics "This Nearly Was Mine" now appear, they are written in Rodgers's handwriting under the melody. The rest is blank. That half page is a treasure.

PRECEDENTS AND PARTICULARS

Until recently, scholarly literature about the American musical theater was rare, and serious students of the genre still endure the condescension of some musicologists and theater scholars. Perhaps because it is frequently classified as "middlebrow," the American musical has continued to lack respect. This is changing, however, due to the growing interest of a new generation of scholars, the increased acceptance of popular culture as a serious subject of discourse, and the support of many university musicology departments and scholarly presses. In particular, sketch studies and examinations of musicals' musico-dramatic histories are also becoming more prevalent.

Two early articles paved the way for this kind of work, and subsequent scholars owe much to both. In 1987 Charles Hamm explored the cuts and changes that George Gershwin made to *Porgy and Bess* between the score's publication, which preceded the first production, and the show's New York opening in 1935. Later productions prided themselves on performing the "complete" score without acknowledging that Gershwin himself had deleted a number of sections. Audiences for the initial Theatre Guild production saw a version of *Porgy and Bess* that subsequently went unperformed despite Hamm's article, which argued that the cuts should be restored. (A performance by the Nashville Symphony, conducted by John Mauceri in February 2006, was the first since the original production to reinstate Gershwin's cuts.) Hamm's article, which undoubtedly benefited both from Gershwin's acceptance as a "serious" composer and from the categorization of the work as opera, was published in the *Journal of the American Musicological Society*.[12]

Two years after Hamm's article, Geoffrey Block wrote a study of Frank Loesser's sketchbooks for *The Most Happy Fellow*. Block's research was inclusive—he investigated all 383 pages of Loesser's sketches—and his conclusions were revelatory. Block not only provided a creative history of the musical, something that had not been done previously by a musicologist in a scholarly journal; he also found many indications of Loesser's compositional methods, nearly none of which had been discussed in the literature up to that point. Appearing in 1989, Block's article provided one of the first moments of legitimacy to scholarship on the American musical. Along with Hamm's work, Block's is essential reading for anyone interested in the genre and its historiography.

Block's subsequent scholarship remains important to musical theater studies in general and to this work in particular. First, his book *Enchanted Evenings*, utilizing the title of perhaps the most famous of the many well-known songs from *South Pacific*, was one of the earliest, and is still one of the best, comprehensive discussions of the genre. Second, as editor of the Yale University Press Broadway Masters series, he was partly responsible for a collection of excellent and virtually unprecedented critical biographies of composers for the American musical stage. (He is the current editor of Oxford's Broadway Legacies series, of which this book is part of.) Third, and most important to this study, his critical biography of Richard Rodgers is insightful and appreciative without becoming hagiographic, and it contains a chapter titled "World War II: The Musical" that reveals the changes *South Pacific* underwent during rehearsals and tryouts. Using a copy of the script dated January 21, 1949, Block demonstrated that this early version of the script "makes it possible to note a number of changes made during the two months of rehearsals and tryouts leading up to the New York premiere on April 7."[13]

Block only occasionally ventured further back than this early script, however, which is understandable, given that he was writing a chapter and not a full-length consideration of *South Pacific*. But the earlier materials offer information about how the work reached the point at which Block began his well-documented consideration, and that material constitutes the core of this study. The earlier sketches and drafts indicate that while the musical still needed the later structural and musical reworking that Block explored, many decisions regarding its thematic content were made well before rehearsals began. The changes to that content and the results of those changes, in addition to what they reveal about Rodgers and Hammerstein, *South Pacific*, and the social, political, and cultural context of 1949, are the focus of this book.

What follows, then, is not a "biography" of *South Pacific*, to borrow the term bruce d. mcclung uses for his excellent volume on *Lady in the Dark*. Nor is it a "narrative of the show from its inception . . . through the rehearsals and tryouts up to the New York opening," as Tim Carter described his exhaustive history of *Oklahoma!*[14] Instead, this is an investigation of the work's thematic concerns and how they were developed or altered during the creative process, a process that also involved changes to the work's structure unrelated to the distillation of its message. This study also explores what *South Pacific* reveals about its theatrical, political, and cultural contexts. Before that process and its contexts are introduced, however, some background information is necessary in order to situate the musical within Rodgers's and Hammerstein's work before and after the formation of their partnership, and define the musical's relationship to its source. This is done in the next two chapters.

Chapter 2 explores works by Rodgers and/or Hammerstein that reflect political and social issues. This investigation includes a discussion of Hammerstein's membership in liberal political groups such as the Hollywood Anti-Nazi League that later marked him as a potentially controversial figure, especially to the House Un-American Activities Committee in the years immediately following the creation of *South Pacific*. The recent declassification and availability of FBI documents pertaining to the league has been helpful in reconstructing and interpreting this earlier phase of Hammerstein's political ideology. Rodgers's work before his collaboration with Hammerstein, and his work after Hammerstein's death, also suggests his comfort with leftist political and social satire. Representative works from both periods are explored.

Chapter 3 concerns James A. Michener's novel *Tales of the South Pacific*. Block also considers the book, as does Laurence Maslon, whose sumptuous volume *The "South Pacific" Companion* will be considered momentarily. Hammerstein's notes on the book, however, have not been explored in the literature, and the changes Hammerstein made to Michener's characters have not been adequately placed within their postwar social and cultural contexts. Both of these observations indicate that further consideration of Michener's work is important for gaining a fuller understanding of Rodgers and Hammerstein's adaptation and transformation of an already successful source. Beyond its relationship to the musical, the novel's structure suggests a sophistication of form that has remained unmentioned in the literature about Michener and for which he has received no credit. This chapter provides a discussion of that form.

The specific topics explored after these preliminary considerations demonstrate how Rodgers and Hammerstein altered and sometimes eliminated the emphases of various thematic concerns throughout the creation of *South Pacific*. For instance, a very early draft suggests that Hammerstein wanted to explore the postwar phenomenon of the rising young executive, a subject found nowhere in Michener's novel. The topic had no place in a musical about World War II, however, and it was excised early in the creative process. Early drafts also indicate several other subplots and characters that at first engaged Hammerstein but eventually proved to be dead ends.

Examining the depiction of race, gender, and colonialism in *South Pacific* provides another unusually rich insight into postwar U.S. culture. Care is taken, however, not to approach these issues as if early twenty-first-century perceptions of them were common currency in 1949. As Aldous Huxley once noted, "We have no right to argue from the present to the past."[15] Oscar Hammerstein II died only eleven years after *South Pacific* opened, and much of the social transformation he sought with his work and in his life was not accomplished until after his death. For instance, he never lived to see the passage of the Civil Rights Act or the Voting Rights Act, although his pleas for tolerance in *South Pacific* anticipated these events and are perhaps even more powerful when considered, or reconsidered, in relationship to them. And although the Pidgin English he wrote for Bloody Mary might seem culturally insensitive today, it nonetheless represents the language Michener heard in the South Pacific and painstakingly reproduced in his novel. Further, Hammerstein's representation of Mary as a crafty but compassionate capitalist survivor and loving mother is more complex than many other stereotyped Asian characters of wartime and postwar popular culture.

Nellie may at first seem to represent the postwar American woman reassuming a role of domesticity after the professional and economic freedom that wartime opportunities provided. But a closer examination reveals a character whose connection to a culture outside her own is as emotionally deep as it is problematic for her, and her ability to overcome her racial intolerance remains a pertinent issue in early twenty-first-century U.S. culture, even if that culture seems unwilling to admit it. Further, her presence in the musical's iconic final image also suggests an American postwar presence in the South Pacific that resonates throughout the last half of the twentieth century. And the alterations Hammerstein makes to Michener's prototypes of masculinity, especially with de Becque and Cable, display postwar constructs of gender that became the norm as the cold war era intensified.

All these issues are explored in what follows, and the result is a perspective of *South Pacific* that substantiates its importance as a postwar indicator of social, political, and cultural currents in American popular art and life. And besides its status as a critical historical artifact, *South Pacific* retains its value as a highly entertaining and memorably tuneful work for the stage.

STILL DREAMING OF PARADISE

In anticipation of the 2008 revival, Laurence Maslon wrote an impeccably researched and originally organized work titled *The "South Pacific" Companion*, which follows his *"Sound of Music" Companion*, and his documentary *Richard Rodgers: The Sweetest Sounds*, which was part of the PBS series *American Masters*.[16] A beautiful oversized volume that is richly illustrated and elegantly written, Maslon's work is a substantial contribution to the literature. His access to papers, scripts, and other source materials afforded him a substantial base from which to construct the story of the work. In particular, he provides an excellent consideration of the work's genesis within its creators' varied experiences during World War II: the book begins with the war and its effects on Rodgers, Hammerstein, Michener, and Logan, and proceeds to demonstrate how the musical evolved out of that momentous event in U.S. history.

Despite Maslon's obvious research and presentational skills, however, his work is of limited scholarly use because it lacks documentation. This is not surprising, since the book is intended for a mainstream audience more interested in learning the background of the show than in consulting notes and citations. And this in no way suggests that Maslon's scholarship is questionable: his acknowledgments demonstrate he consulted a wide breadth of materials and range of individuals during his research. My hope is that the present work can be used to supplement and reinforce Maslon's, and that between us we have provided two considerations of this great musical that will inform and guide anyone interested in exploring it further.

The 2008 Lincoln Center revival, which Maslon's book preceded and for which it provides a fascinating background, confirms the status of *South Pacific* as an important and still viable work for the musical stage. The musical and dramatic integrity of the show are intact, and the result is an experience that entertains, edifies, and surprises contemporary audiences. That its entreaty for racial tolerance is still necessary suggests that it will retain its dramatic relevance for years to come. Countless audiences have enjoyed and been moved by *South Pacific* over the past sixty years. My goal with this work is to encourage countless more to enjoy and better understand the work over the next sixty.

2
THE MUSICAL IS THE MESSAGE
• • •

In a 1958 interview with Oscar Hammerstein II, Mike Wallace asked what Hammerstein and Richard Rodgers were "trying to say" in *South Pacific*. Hammerstein explained that neither he nor Rodgers ever asked "now what've we got say?" before deciding to adapt a source, adding, "We've always chosen a story that we found attractive, and then we've gone ahead and written it." He then answered Wallace's question. "What we were trying to say was . . . just what Nellie says in one of her scenes, 'All that is piffle.' . . . This [racial] prejudice that we have is something that fades away in the face of something that's really important." Wallace pushed Hammerstein a bit further and asked, "Does that express your view as far as you're concerned with miscegenation? Intermarriage between races is perfectly sensible?" Hammerstein answered, "Yes."[1]

Richard Rodgers also addressed the "message" of *South Pacific* in his autobiography. After noting that "You've Got to Be Carefully Taught" has been criticized for being "propagandistic," he observed that the song, although subsequently appropriated by religious leaders nationwide, was never intended as a "'message' song." He explained that the song was simply the right number at the right spot in the show: "It was perfectly in keeping with the character and situation that, once having lost his heart, he would express his feelings about the superficiality of racial barriers. End of sermon."[2] Like Hammerstein, Rodgers insisted that the story and the characters took precedence in the process of creating a musical.

Later in the Mike Wallace interview, Hammerstein was asked about Ayn Rand's comment that "the public is being brainwashed by the so-called liberal or leftist philosophies which have a strangle-hold on the dissemination of ideas in America." Hammerstein stated that he did not believe that "all the liberals have got together in Hollywood and New York and said let's be very liberal and brain wash the people and make them think as we do." He also objected to Rand's "adding gratuitously the word 'leftist' right next to liberal, because you can be a liberal without being a leftist, and many, and most liberals are."[3]

As if to challenge Hammerstein's self-distancing from "leftist" politics, or at least politics that could be perceived as "leftist," Wallace, near the end of the interview, asked Hammerstein what he thought about Paul Robeson. (Two years before the interview, the controversial Robeson, who had played Joe in the London production of *Show Boat*, in the 1932 Broadway revival, and in the 1936 film version, was called before the House Un-American Activities Committee [HUAC] after he refused to sign a State Department document denying his membership in the Communist Party.) Hammerstein began by discreetly distancing himself from Robeson's politics. He then added that he was not accusing Robeson of being a Communist, although many people thought that Robeson was. Hammerstein continued, "It troubles me to sit as a judge upon Paul, because I think of myself and try to wonder how I would feel if I were the son of a minister, a Phi Beta Kappa student at Rutgers, an All American tackle, a tall handsome man, a singer, an actor, an athlete and could not live in the same hotel with the other members of my theatrical troupe—I would be good and sore and I don't know what I would do."[4] In this interview, Hammerstein reiterated several of his long-held political and social beliefs, in particular his commitment to civil rights and liberties, while skirting the issue of so-called leftist politics whenever possible. And yet he also unflinchingly defended interracial marriage and an alleged Communist at a time when supporting either, let alone both, could lead to government investigation and subsequent interrogation.

Rodgers, often perceived as less political than Hammerstein, also made his sympathies clear elsewhere. In 1947, for instance, when the HUAC intensified its ongoing investigation of the alleged Communist presence in Hollywood, Rodgers and other artists formally protested the proceedings. This resulted in the formation of an FBI file on his political activities, although, as Rodgers's biographer Meryle Secrest later found, about the only thing that was ever in the file was the information that "the Roosevelt reelection committee [which Rodgers supported] might or might not have become a Communist front organization and that he [Rodgers] had risen in defense of free speech and civil liberties."[5] Later, after initially supporting Eisenhower for president, Rodgers changed his mind, noting that he had "[become] increasingly disillusioned when he [Eisenhower] failed to take a stand against the contemptible behavior of Senator Joseph McCarthy." Rodgers switched his allegiance to Adlai Stevenson.[6]

Despite their political beliefs and activities, Rodgers and Hammerstein's consistent emphasis that the story of a musical dictates its content is unsurprising. One of the notable developments in their musicals was the innovative primacy of plot and characters over well-worn musical theater formulae.

The dialogue, the songs, and the dances all grow out of a specificity of purpose—telling the story—and that, while not completely unprecedented in previous works for the stage, became the dominant paradigm for almost three decades after 1943, the year in which *Oklahoma!* premiered. Rodgers later made the wry observation that, after *Oklahoma!*, "Everyone suddenly became 'integration'-conscious, as if the idea of welding together song, story, and dance had never been thought of before."[7] The composer also offered a succinct explanation of the so-called integrated musical, noting, "When a show works perfectly, it's because all the individual parts complement each other and fit together."[8] This focus on story and a seamless structure did not preclude an occasional attraction to stories with messages and/or political content. Moreover, earlier works by each man reveal that, even before their collaboration, both were unafraid of political and social topics. Hammerstein's serious treatment of racism in *Show Boat*, for instance, is virtually unprecedented in the musical theater of the time, while the political satire of Rodgers and Hart's *I'd Rather Be Right* is lighthearted, if sometimes biting. Such onstage topicality, in addition to offstage comments and activities, occasionally brought both men to the edge of political safety before, during, and after World War II and into the cold war era.

HAMMERSTEIN AND THE ANTI-NAZI LEAGUE

Because the literature on *Show Boat* is extensive and covers the musical's daring use of topical subject matter, racism and miscegenation in particular, the show does not warrant prolonged attention in this discussion.[9] What should be noted, however, is that among the reviews of the original production given in the *Rodgers and Hammerstein Fact Book*, none mention the treatment of race so integral to Hammerstein's book.[10] Few critics seem to have given a second thought to the emphasis placed on interracial relationships or the harsh treatment endured by the African American characters outside the world of the Cotton Blossom. Most of the reviews were more concerned with the high level of craftsmanship demonstrated by the Jerome Kern–Oscar Hammerstein II score and what was perceived as the new level of cohesion in the structure of the piece, particularly the unification of its musical and dramatic elements and its fusion of musical comedy and operetta. In 1927, the year *Show Boat* opened, people seem to have been less concerned with the social or political implications of musical comedies and operettas, or of anything else, than they soon would be after the onset of the Great Depression and the ominous rumblings in Europe and Asia.

Between *Show Boat* and Hammerstein's sojourn in Hollywood, which is where his political activity began in earnest, only one show needs to be mentioned. *Free for All* (1931), for which Hammerstein wrote the lyrics and co-wrote the book with Laurence Schwab, was a satirical and sympathetic story of a group of college undergraduates who, enamored with socialism, attempt to set up an experiment in communal living. In part because the show opened before the beginning of intense government scrutiny of leftist art, and because it was a critical and commercial disappointment that ran only for fifteen performances, *Free for All* disappeared from Hammerstein's political biography. That biography soon underwent a transformation.[11]

Because of the negative impact of the Depression on Broadway and the subsequent diminished number of productions—by the middle of the 1934–35 season, for instance, only two new book musicals had opened—Hammerstein, like countless other members of the Broadway theater community, went to Hollywood. Film production was abundant and well paying, even if the quality of what was being produced was uneven and unpredictable. After signing a contract with Metro-Goldwyn-Mayer, Hammerstein and his family moved to Hollywood in 1934. Although they all returned to New York in 1935, during which time Hammerstein wrote *May Wine* with Sigmund Romberg, they moved back to Hollywood in 1936.

Hammerstein made substantial money in the film industry, as his Beverly Hills address attested, but before long, as Hugh Fordin observed, "the work was unsatisfying and the fun had begun to pall."[12] Finding that his intellectual and creative stagnation was shared by others in the Hollywood community, Hammerstein, in June 1936, became a founding member and executive council member of a new group that called itself the Hollywood League against Nazism, later the Hollywood Anti-Nazi League for the Defense of American Democracy, which was founded in part to raise consciousness about the growing threat posed to the free world, and to the United States in particular, by Hitler and the Third Reich. The group's name was often informally shortened to the Hollywood Anti-Nazi League. Hammerstein, Dorothy Parker, Frederic March, Florence Eldridge, and Donald Ogden Stewart were cofounders of the League, with Stewart acting as president.[13]

The league was also a reaction to the organized Nazi sympathizers and Aryan supremacists who became active all over the United States as soon as Hitler came to power in 1933, three years before the league's formation. These groups produced vast amounts of written and broadcast propaganda accusing Jews of being Communists, Communist sympathizers, and/or threats to the physical and moral well-being of white Americans. Because Hollywood was eventually targeted as a Jewish-controlled industry attempting to subvert white America, an inordinate number of these groups infected the Los Angeles area. Their propaganda, which linked Jews to the threat of world Communism and represented them as depraved and immoral, was usually sensational and always tasteless. Hammerstein's sensitivity to this issue is evidenced by an unidentified carbon copy of a memo with the heading, "Nazi—in Los Angeles," which is among the few documents in his papers pertaining to Nazi sympathizers. This memo is concerned with the influx of Nazi thought, propaganda, and activity in the United States; it notes especially the involvement of the Friends of the New Germany and the American Labor Party: "The American Labor Party, with a strong anti-Semitic, anti-Negro, anti-communist program, and with a direct tie-up with the Friends of the New Germany, is preparing to drill as many men as possible for future enlistment into the National guard. The purpose being the establishment of a group of trained 'storm troopers' who can fight should the occasion arise."[14]

Many of the printed materials from this pro-Nazi movement were collected for a 1989 exhibit at the Oviatt Library of California State University, Northridge, titled "In Our Own Backyard: Resisting Nazi Propaganda in Southern California 1933–1945." The online site for this exhibit features more than two hundred items that are chilling and often shocking.[15] The opening pages, which provide a historical contextualization for the exhibit, explain Hitler's plan to divide the United States into Christian and Jewish "nations" and then "make a psychological connection between the words 'Jew,' 'Bolshevik,' and 'Communist' in the American mind." Once this connection was distinct and Jews were isolated "as a race to fear and hate," German Americans would help the Führer assume power in the United States. The seriousness of this claim is underscored again and again in the exhibit. Materials from the Ku Klux Klan, the German-American Bund, the Militant Christian Patriots, William Dudley Pelley's Silvershirts, and Father Charles Coughlin's Christian Front, among others, figure prominently in the collection. In 1934, as this activity attained increased visibility, the Jewish community in Los Angeles formed the Jewish Community Committee to bring these pro-Nazi groups to the attention of the population at large. Two years later, the Anti-Nazi League was formed.[16]

The vehemence of the attack on the film industry and, eventually, on the league is demonstrated by a particularly odious flier from the late 1930s. The graphic is a profile of an Aryan woman in the foreground and a hook-nosed older man behind her, both of whom are superimposed on a Star of David. Beneath them is the word "Hollywood," out of which a snake rises. The copy shouts, "Christian Vigilantes Arise! Buy Gentile, Employ Gentile, Vote Gentile. Boycott the Movies! Hollywood is the Sodom and Gomorrah where International

Jewry controls vice-dope-gambling where young Gentile girls are raped by Jewish producers, directors, casting directors who go unpunished. The Jewish Hollywood Anti-Nazi League controls Communism in the motion picture industry. Stars, writers and artists are compelled to pay for Communistic activities."[17] The sordid character of the flier is typical of materials in this disturbing collection, one of which is a booklist from the Aryan Bookstore in Los Angeles that features, among other titles, "Anthems of the Third Reich." The response of Hammerstein and his colleagues, both Jews and non-Jews, is understandable, and the attacks on the league and the film industry reveal a domestic brand of paranoid anti-Semitism that is often overlooked in discussions of U.S. political movements in the 1930s.

Another memo, this one dated November 7, 1936, also suggests that the innuendo connecting the league to Communist activities began very early, as did its change of title. Henry Meyers, a writer and lyricist at Paramount studios, wrote to Hammerstein, imploring that the league's name not be changed in the face of accusations of Communist Party affiliations. Meyer observed, "I do not believe that very many people really have an idea that the League is communistic; all those who have said so, would say so anyway." He added, "I find that there is *not* a general feeling that we are communists" and that "it is impossible to stop the malicious few from continuing the charge of communism, no matter what name we select. . . . Also, it is not possible to avoid being called a Red, if you belong to what is mistakenly called the intellectual class."[18] Meyer's seeming lack of concern about the league's perceived "Redness" was rather naïve, as later developments attest. But his conviction that the league's primary focus should be combating Nazism was shared by Hammerstein.

Hammerstein became head of the cultural commission for the league and organized broadcasts, newspaper articles, and short informational films about the menacing threat posed by the Nazi regime. Within six months, the cultural commission was broadened to create an "interracial commission," which Hammerstein also chaired. The mission statement of the second commission notes that it was created to "combat racial intolerance and thus combat Nazism, which uses intolerance to attain power."[19] Hammerstein's work with the interracial commission demonstrates how he combined his passion against racial intolerance with his anti-Nazi beliefs. In January 1937, for instance, the interracial committee hosted what it called an "Inter-Racial Mass Meeting against Nazism" at Los Angeles's Philharmonic Auditorium. W. E. B. Du Bois was the principal speaker, although a pamphlet announcing the event adds that there would be other unspecified speakers "representing all races"; Hammerstein was billed as chairman.[20] Du Bois's presence on such a program in early 1937 is especially interesting. During the previous year, Du Bois had visited Nazi Germany and, immediately upon his return, began to speak out against the Nazi treatment of the German Jewish population, which he found reprehensible.[21]

Despite his political activism, however, Hammerstein was unhappy in Hollywood. Fordin observes that Hammerstein later noted that he "just didn't fit in" there, and when Dorothy Hammerstein suggested that they were starting to "rust," the decision to return east was made. By early fall of 1938, Hammerstein was back in New York.[22] In August of 1939, slightly less than a year later, the Soviet Union and Germany signed the Nazi–Soviet Act, more officially known as the Molotov–Ribbentrop Pact, in which the countries forswore military action against one another. They also agreed not to join with any other power(s) to undertake aggression prohibited by the pact. The pact outraged many Western liberals and Communist sympathizers, most of whom were appalled by Nazi Germany and shocked that the Soviet Union would align with Hitler's government. (The pact lasted only until Germany invaded the Soviet Union in June 1941.) Around this time, Hammerstein withdrew from the league, which by then was known as the Hollywood Peace Forum, an organization closely scrutinized by the FBI. Hammerstein's distancing and finally removing himself from the league and from Hollywood at this time was a politically wise move, as it turned out.

A report made by the FBI in 1940 at J. Edgar Hoover's request and submitted to Hoover in February 1941 reveals much unsettling information covering the time Hammerstein was active with the league. The tone of the report, and especially of the testimony from friendly witnesses to various grand juries, also recalls the sense of anti-Semitism that informed much of the anticommunist fervor of the late 1930s, and early 1940s. The residual effect of that ugly trait eventually reached Hammerstein. The report's "synopsis of facts" reads as follows:

> Hollywood Anti-Nazi League founded about 1937 in effort to unite Jewish people and others in Hollywood movie colony into organization to combat Nazism on local scale. Approximately 3,000 persons became members. League published paper, "Hollywood Now," which exposed Nazi influence in this country and supported various projects identified with Communist Party. . . . Communistic influence clearly discernible in League from organizations supported by it and its program. Majority of officers and many prominent members have been identified with Communistic activity. In Dec. 1939, shortly after Russian-German agreement, Hollywood Anti-Nazi League changed name to Hollywood League for Democratic

Action, a clear reflection of the change in Communist Party line. . . . Review of the files indicates that the League operated as a Communist front organization.[23]

This report demonstrates that the FBI scrutinized liberal and leftist organizations during the prewar and postwar eras and reveals that information gained through informants was often contradictory. It also suggests that innuendo and suggestion could contaminate the innocent.

The FBI's confidence that the Anti-Nazi League reflected Communist ideas, granted membership to party members, and had connections with or served as a front for Communist organizations is based on the testimony of many unnamed sources. Some of these sources provided names of suspected Communists, most of which are blacked out in the declassified document. (A reference to John Steinbeck and his "salacious writings" remains, however.) The FBI report notes that, in 1940, an informer "furnished a list of Communist front organizations, which . . . includes the Hollywood Anti-Nazi League."[24] Another unnamed witness who, according to the report, was an "admitted former county organizer of the Communist Party in Los Angeles [and] former Dies Committee witness" testified in 1940 that "the Communist Party conceived and organized the Hollywood Anti-Nazi League with the assistance of movie notables." This witness then noted that "only a small minority of the members were Communists."[25] Even so, "the report of the California Peace Officers Association for 1937 points out the interrelation between the Communist Party and the Hollywood Anti-Nazi League."[26] And in 1940, according to the report, an unnamed witness before a Los Angeles grand jury testified that "one of the methods of the Communists to dominate the movie industry was . . . the formation of the Communist-dominated Hollywood Anti-Nazi League, which the Communist Party hoped to use to capitalize upon the fear that was held by people of Jewish origin of Fascism and Nazism."[27]

Despite the sometimes conflicting implications made by the report, and despite how they were later exploited to connect former members of the league with Communist activity, the conclusions are straightforward. For instance, the following summary comes from the introduction to the report:

On the whole, I would say that whatever the inner plan was, in order to get a following they had to play up the anti-Nazi angle and consequently did much good in quickening the entire country against the Nazi menace. Since this propaganda necessarily reached the general public and the subtle pro-communist ideology only reached a handful of the members they at least did more good than harm. Their energies now seem bent on paralyzing us with unpreparedness and a false peace.

The Hollywood Peace Forum [which was the name of the group after it was the Hollywood League for Democratic Action] seems to be a more definitely pro-communist (and by implications pro-Hitler) off-shoot.[28]

The report's final statement further notes, "Since the Hollywood Anti-Nazi League for the Defense of American Democracy and the Hollywood League for Democratic Action have been out of existence for approximately two years and have engaged in no subversive activities *under those names* during the past two years, this investigation is being closed with the submission of this report."[29] However, the FBI continued to track the activities of the Hollywood Peace Forum, and members of the earlier phases of the group were not free from suspicion by association.

Among the more interesting items in the report is a lengthy passage from the league's publication *Hollywood Now*, which, the report says, "appears to be an issue during the early part of August 1940."[30] Based on passages in the publication that refer to the conscription laws that President Roosevelt eventually signed into law in early September 1940, that dating seems possible. However, the report later indicates that if this edition of *Hollywood Now* was from August 1940, it was probably one of the last to be printed: "This publication was discontinued about the middle of 1940, at which time the Hollywood League for Democratic Action was discontinued under that name and was, *to some extent*, succeeded by the Hollywood Peace Forum and later the American Peace Crusade."[31] The timing is hazy, but one section of the *Hollywood Now* passage is not: "We . . . denounce as a lie that we have in any manner had any connection whatsoever with the Communist Party. Our independence of action is our most treasured possession, and we would no more take the dictation of the Communist Party than we would of the Democratic or Republican Party. Our membership has at all times approved our actions by its vote." The accusations obviously were having an effect.

A 2005 essay, published on the opinion page of the *Los Angeles Times*, argued that the Communist influence on Hollywood had been stronger than post–cold war era revisionist thinking wanted to admit. In this essay, Ronald Radosh and Allis Radosh suggested that the party exploited leftist sympathizers, and that the eventual testimony given by some of them was admirable even if it has earned them a reputation as informers. They also mentioned Dalton Trumbo, a party member who was an unfriendly witness before the HUAC in 1947 and who was subsequently blacklisted and imprisoned. Trumbo, they noted, "ultimately realized that he and his comrades had been used by the party leadership," and they offered a statement that Trumbo made when accepting the Writers Guild award for career achievement in

1970: "It will do no good to search for villains or heroes because there were none. There were only victims." Further, the essay sympathetically, although not uncritically, observed that the Hollywood blacklist "extended not only to actual party members but, in some cases, to the well-meaning who joined party-controlled 'popular front' organizations."[32]

While Hammerstein was certainly never a party member, his membership in the league came back to haunt him four years after the opening of *South Pacific*. When he sought to renew his passport in 1953, Hammerstein was told by the Passport Division of the Department of State that they had information "that reflected on his loyalty to the United States." He was told that in order to be given an unlimited passport—he was approved for only a six-month passport—he would have to write and file a personal statement refuting the charges against him and demonstrating his loyalty to the United States. At first enraged, Hammerstein eventually wrote the document. Among the charges he had to confront were those implicating him with the Hollywood Anti-Nazi League and, thus, with Communism. One of the statements Hammerstein wrote in his rebuttal to the charges against him resonates as powerfully in the early twenty-first century as it did in the mid-twentieth: "You do not protect rights by abrogating them."[33] Hammerstein got his passport.

RODGERS AND THE POLITICAL MUSICAL

By the end of 1931, the year that Hammerstein's *Free for All* made good-natured fun of undergraduates' socialist leanings, Richard Rodgers and the lyricist Lorenz Hart had already been to Hollywood and completed their first original score for a film, *The Hot Heiress*. Their second feature, *Love Me Tonight*, was filmed the same year and released in 1932. *Love Me Tonight*, directed by Rouben Mamoulian, was an innovative commercial and critical success. Rodgers, Hart, and Mamoulian, as Rodgers recalled, were in agreement that "dialogue, song, and scoring should all be integrated as closely as possible so that the final product would have a unity of style and design." They also wanted to expand the use of musical scenes. As Rodgers explained, "There was no reason [that] a musical sequence could not be used like dialogue and be performed uninterrupted while the action took the story to whatever locations the director wanted."[34] The film's success was also aided by the charming performances of its stars Maurice Chevalier and Jeanette Mac-Donald. Rodgers and Hart's next film project, which was their first foray into political satire, was a different experience altogether.

Released just a month after *Love Me Tonight, The Phantom President* was, as Rodgers described it, "a satirical musical concerned with political skullduggery during a presidential campaign."[35] One of the problems with this project was its star, George M. Cohan, who remained unenthusiastic throughout the filming and created what Rodgers called a "frigid atmosphere on the set."[36] Another problem was that the film followed on the heels of the Broadway hit *Of Thee I Sing*, a Pulitzer Prize–winning satire of presidential politics by George and Ira Gershwin, George S. Kaufman, and Morrie Ryskind. Given his enthusiasm for the Gershwins, his regular theatergoing, and the must-see status of the musical *Of Thee I Sing*, Rodgers's familiarity with the Gershwin show before composing *The Phantom President* is a safe assumption. Nonetheless, *Of Thee I Sing* opened on Broadway in December of 1931, and *The Phantom President* was made in "early 1932," according to Rodgers, which suggests that he and Hart were writing their score at approximately the time that the Gershwin show opened. This did not prevent the critics from making comparisons that were for the most part unenthusiastic: John Mosher of the *New Yorker* dismissed *The Phantom President* as the "latest outgrowth from *Of Thee I Sing*," and the uncredited review in *Time* noted, "a strange combination of serious flagwaving, savage political comment, pure comedy, farce and romance, it owes much to *Of Thee I Sing*."[37]

The "savagery" of the political comment is debatable, although the film's fate is not. While the premise of the plot certainly suggests satire—a bland presidential candidate is replaced by a lookalike snake-oil salesman who successfully cons most of the voters—the tone is more amusing than biting. The first number, for instance, anachronistically presents Presidents Washington, Jefferson, and Lincoln making a plea for a suitable candidate. The refrain of another number, "Somebody Ought to Wave a Flag," manages to be simultaneously satirical and patriotic. After observing that, because of the ailing stock market and the lingering war debt, "Ev'ry day we get a little more debt," the lyrics noted that "there are Reds in Russia, / There are Whites in Prussia, / There are blues just everywhere. / Let's string the three together / And fly them in the air."[38] While the score is full of social and political criticism, however, it also contains problematic representations of ethnicity. "The Convention," which is an extended musical sequence about the nomination of the faux-candidate, exploits stereotyped dialects for a "Harlem Band," a "Hawaiian Orchestra," and a Southern delegate. The dialects are completely in keeping with popular performance practices at the time—blackface performance was still widely popular, for instance—but over the years the sequence has become less satirical than tasteless. "The Convention" also contains the only line of Hart's that recalls *Of Thee I Sing*, although the recollection is fleeting. The ensemble sings of the candidate Blair, "He'll sweep the country everywhere," which brings to mind "Love Is Sweeping the Country" from Gershwin's score. Unfortunately, the presidential election in *The Phantom President* was upstaged by Franklin Roosevelt's election in 1932, and audiences stayed away. Rodgers later commented, "I think even Hoover was more popular than the film."[39] The dismissive reception did not stop Rodgers and Hart from soon pursuing another film with socially satirical content, however.

Hallelujah, I'm a Bum, which starred Al Jolson, was released in 1933 and dealt with homeless victims of the Depression who lived in Central Park. The score afforded Rodgers and Hart the chance to further develop a technique used in *Love Me Tonight* and *The Phantom President* that Rodgers called "musical dialogue." The composer compared this to operatic recitative, although these sections might be better described as arioso, or musical passages that demonstrate characteristics of both recitative and aria: "We simply used rhymed conversation, with musical accompaniment, to affect [sic] a smoother transition to actual song and to give the entire film a firmer musical structure."[40] Despite the artistic advances the film afforded Rodgers and Hart, and the happy experience they had working with the legendary Jolson, *Hallelujah, I'm a Bum* was another box-office failure. "The subject of homelessness at a time when it was such an urgent national problem didn't strike many people as something to laugh and sing about," Rodgers later observed. Although it was probably unnoticed by audiences, one aspect of the film reflected Hollywood's affluence during the Depression: the scenes of the homeless in Central Park were shot at the Riviera Country Club in Pacific Palisades.[41]

Rodgers and Hart left what Rodgers later called "the limbo of Hollywood" after two more films.[42] While they eventually provided songs for several other films, they were never again under contract to a studio as they had been at Metro-Goldwyn-Mayer, and both happily returned to New York and Broadway. They were well received: *Jumbo* (1935) and *On Your Toes* (1936) were hits, as was *Babes in Arms* (1937). The latter show, in addition to having one of Rodgers and Hart's most hit-strewn scores—"The Lady Is a Tramp," "My Funny Valentine," "Where or When," "I Wish I Were in Love Again"—also featured an original book by the team. They had collaborated with George Abbott on the book for *On Your Toes*, but *Babes in Arms* was completely their own creation. It also marked their return to politically and socially sensitive subject matter.

In her book *Making Americans*, Andrea Most provided a chapter that is essential to understanding *Babes in Arms*. Contemporary audiences know the show either from the classic 1939 film, which starred Mickey Rooney and

Judy Garland but which retained only two of the score's songs and none of the script, or from the drastically rewritten 1959 version, which is the only script and score currently available for production. Unlike these later versions, however, the original 1937 show, as Most noted, "is a rich and complex historical document." She added, "It offers a snapshot of attitudes of the era, and reveals a sensibility deeply informed by the cultural, political, and theatrical events of the decade."[43] It does this through a story about the children of unemployed vaudeville performers. When their parents are put to work by the Works Progress Administration (WPA), the young people resist being sent to a "work farm" and instead decide as a group to put on a show and raise enough money to ensure their independence. As they form a creative community, the relations within the group reflect social, political, and cultural conflicts and solidarities from the Depression era. Most summarized the show's political perspective as follows:

> *Babes in Arms* illustrates the basic features of American Jewish liberalism. The play presents an underprivileged group fighting for freedom and liberty. The optimistic leaders are intellectuals who rely on the open exchange of ideas to effect change. The group believes in equal opportunity, regardless of race, religion, or ethnicity, and in hard work as the ticket to success. They aim to create an inclusive, tolerant, and diverse community.... The play strongly emphasizes the group's power to effect social change, but represents that power as resistance, not revolution.[44]

Most's consideration of *Babes in Arms* is as thorough as it is groundbreaking, and she repeatedly demonstrated how Rodgers and Hart gave voice to what she has called their "moderate liberal views," which undoubtedly were shared by many New York audience members. These views are especially noticeable in the musical's approach to race. The show "makes open statements about black civil rights . . . [and t]he community of *Babes in Arms* is defined most overtly by its respect for diversity and tolerance of difference."[45] The community's tolerance is tested, however. A young white Southerner named Lee is the producer of the show within the show, and he is adamant that Ivor and Irving de Quincy, two young African Americans, cannot perform in it. Val, the director, argues passionately for the integration of the show and eventually wins out. But despite Rodgers and Hart's outspoken stand for racial equality onstage and offstage, as personified by Val, they are unable to reach beyond accepted stereotypes in representing their black characters. Unlike the other characters that, as Most observed, "speak in the political language of the day," the young African Americans "can speak only from within in the language of stereotypical black performance: minstrelsy and

Dixie songs."[46] The lyrics to their song "All Dark People" recall the problematic lyrics of "The Convention" from *The Phantom President* in their use of dialect and racial stereotypes. For instance, "All God's chillun got buck-and-wings. . . . All dark people are light on their feet."[47] The young African American dancers "appear as performers in stereotyped roles that are enclosed within the world of the stage," Most revealed. "Ivor and Irving cannot move outside or even within their stereotypes. . . . The black kids could only play black."[48] Problematic representations of ethnicity and race in shows with liberal sensibilities continued to be a sporadic but recurring problem for Rodgers, notably in *South Pacific*.

Despite its depiction of race, however, *Babes in Arms* demonstrates what Most defined as "a uniquely American theatrical form which demands that the American musical, and implicitly America itself, live up to the ideals of liberal capitalism."[49] Those ideals were important to Rodgers and Hart, and their next project for the stage, after another brief and unsuccessful fling at the movies, again demonstrates their liberal political stance. Rodgers contextualized *I'd Rather Be Right*, the show that followed *Babes in Arms*, satire within the tradition of contemporaneous "topical" revues and book musicals that reflected the Depression era. He added that "the best of these never went in for preaching or propaganda but managed to make their comments on the conditions of the world without forgetting that the basic function of entertainment was to entertain."[50] This perfectly describes *I'd Rather Be Right*.

For their second spoof of presidential politics, Rodgers and Hart collaborated with George S. Kaufman and Moss Hart, the coauthors, with the Gershwins, of *Strike Up the Band*, *Of Thee I Sing*, and *Let 'Em Eat Cake*. Hart, with Irving Berlin, also wrote the book for the musical *Face the Music* and the revue *As Thousands Cheer*, both of which were also political in content. The four collaborators upped the stakes somewhat in their new endeavor by taking on the sitting president, something that had not been done before. Rodgers has insisted that all four "were ardently pro-FDR," but they saw great comic potential in the varied and sometimes controversial programs of the Roosevelt administration, not least of which was "the outlandish idea that Roosevelt would dare break with tradition and run for a third term."[51] Although the New Deal offered many targets for satire, few of which were overlooked by the writers, the result was a spoof that was good-natured, sympathetic, and always within the creators' liberal social consciences. Rodgers later commented that "every song was written to express some viewpoint on major topics of the day."[52] Roosevelt's appearance even took place in an extended dream, which created further distance from political reality.

Garrett Eisler has argued that, in this one work, Kaufman, Moss Hart, Rodgers, and Lorenz Hart somehow subverted their own moderate liberal political beliefs to create "a fundamentally right-wing cultural project."[53] While Rodgers and Hart's old nemesis George M. Cohan, the star of the show, was widely known to be considerably less than sympathetic to Roosevelt (Rodgers states flat out that "Cohan hated Roosevelt"[54]), the authors, composer, and lyricist remained loyal supporters. Further, Eisler misreads the work's lampooning of many figures and policies of the New Deal as a "consistent rejection of 1930s progressivism."[55] After establishing that, by 1937, Rodgers and Hart had entered the upper socioeconomic tier of U.S. society, Eisler suggested that, "as their own prosperity and interests distanced them more and more from the leftward shift in the government and in the country, maybe they wondered if even such liberals as themselves might have more in common—and do better business—with those on the 'right' after all."[56] Rather than cater to the politics of some of their wealthy audience members, however, Rodgers and Hart continued to satire them in subsequent works. For instance, Hart's 1940 lyric to the song "Disgustingly Rich," which was an ensemble number in *Higher and Higher*, is a spot-on send-up of the privileged that also mentions Roosevelt. After revealing that they shop at Saks and cheat on their taxes, the singers add, "I will buy land / Down on Long Island / And as a resident / I will pan the President."[57] Despite Eisler's misreading of the musical, Hart and, more important to this discussion, Rodgers retained their "moderate liberal views," to recall Andrea Most's term, before, during, and after *I'd Rather Be Right*, and Rodgers's comments that the show was "political satire" full of "topical wisecracks" should be taken at face value.[58]

RODGERS AND HAMMERSTEIN

South Pacific was the fourth Broadway musical by Rodgers and Hammerstein, and it was the first to contain any kind of overt political message. While their criticism of racial intolerance is embedded in stories that are plot and character driven, as Rodgers and Hammerstein have insisted, it nonetheless is a powerful element of the musical. Unlike *South Pacific*, two of their three earlier musicals contained no such overt messages; but like *South Pacific*, they told stories that resonated strongly with the times in which they were presented. If the result of that resonance was a "message," it was not the goal. In the Mike Wallace interview, for example, Hammerstein noted, "*Oklahoma!* has no particular message except that it has a flavor which infects the people who see it."[59] The people who originally saw it lived in a country at war, and much about the show spoke to that context. As Rodgers wrote, "People said to themselves, in effect, 'If this is what our country looked and sounded like at the turn of the century, perhaps once the war is over we can again return to this kind of buoyant, optimistic life.'"[60] The creators and producers of the show thought this optimism important enough to give more than forty free matinees for those serving in the armed forces. (The performers also donated their performances.) But Rodgers and Hammerstein are right about *Oklahoma!* not containing a message. The whole show was the message.

Carousel, which opened near the end of the war, worked in a similar way. Its story concerns the ability of unconditional love to transcend the problems of life and the seeming finality of death. After nearly four years of war, many Americans had lost loved ones, and the final scene of *Carousel* spoke to that loss and to the ability to endure it. That scene, in which the specter of Billy tells his surviving wife that he loves her as the chorus swells with the reprise of "You'll Never Walk Alone," had a power that it perhaps has never had since. Although it came at the end of a terrible period of loss and grief, this, too, was optimism, and the finale demonstrates what the critic John Chapman called the show's "inner glow."[61]

Allegro was the team's third show, and it was the first to meet with widely mixed critical and commercial reception. That reception may or may not have been due to the show having a "message," but Hammerstein later admitted to Mike Wallace that it did indeed have one. Wallace revealed that, in a pre-interview discussion with a reporter, Hammerstein said the show was concerned with "a sickness that infected modern society as a whole." Hammerstein explained that the "sickness" he referred to was caused by "trying to do too much, availing ourselves of all the inventions, the improvements in communications, of all the things we're able to do[;] and being able to do them, we do them all and we should just be content not to avail ourselves to such an extent of modern science."[62] The sometimes frenzied pace of trying to do too much in too little time, which gives the show its title, brings about the main conflict of the story, which concerns a doctor who gets caught up in the superficial world of high society after becoming the head of a hospital; what he really wants to do is practice medicine. Hammerstein, using the show's plot as an example, observes that this is a dilemma many people face: "The discovery that after you're successful . . . there is a conspiracy that goes on in which you join, a conspiracy of the world to render you less effective by bestowing honors on you and taking you away from the job of curing people. . . . You're better off if you remain a doctor."[63]

Hammerstein remained politically active while writing these shows with Rodgers. Although he left the Anti-Nazi League in Hollywood, for instance, he became active in the wartime Writers' War Board (WWB) within days of the attack on Pearl Harbor. The WWB was founded to promote the sales of war bonds, rationing, and other war-related activities. The WWB was also especially aggressive in its attack on domestic social conditions that its members viewed as antithetical to the ideals that Americans were fighting, and dying, to preserve. In short, their propaganda was intended not just to boost wartime morale but also to change the social conditions of the United States in general. The following passage from a WWB annual report makes this clear:

> The Writers' War Board was founded on December 9, 1941, at the request of the Treasury Department to enlist the help of writers in selling war bonds throughout the country. Within a short time the board broadened its scope to meet requests from other government agencies and from patriotic organizations. . . . Throughout 1944 the Board's basic function has continued to be the fulfillment of requests for all kinds of writing required to win the war. The Board has also continued to concern itself with the nature of the Japanese and German enemy, and with the *rising tide of prejudice against racial, religious, and other groups here at home*. We believe our military success must not be jeopardized by sentimental illusions about our enemies or bigoted notions about our Allies and fellow-citizens.[64]

Other WWB articles among Hammerstein's papers state unequivocally that U.S. citizens harboring racial prejudice against other Americans are enemies of the United States. Hammerstein's drafts and sketches for 2.4 of *South Pacific*, in which the characters climactically confront their racial intolerance, are especially reminiscent of these equations of American bigotry with the attitudes of the enemy. Indeed, much of what Hammerstein and others wrote for the WWB is noticeably similar in content, and sometimes in phrasing, to Hammerstein's preliminary versions of this powerful scene, thus indicating the lingering effect of the WWB on Hammerstein's first postwar work.

Christina Klein provided further information on Hammerstein's political and social activities at about the same time he was writing *South Pacific*. Klein cited a little-known letter that Hammerstein wrote in 1948 to the *Daily Worker*, a popular Communist Party newspaper. The paper had criticized the way African Americans were represented in the 1946 revival of *Show Boat*, arguing that what it called the "Uncle Tom business" and the presentation of "the Negro as the object of patronizing ridicule" should be removed from the show. The response, which was credited to Rodgers and Hammerstein, who produced the revival, but which almost certainly was written by Hammerstein, defended the show by insisting that it was "pro-Negro and anti-Jim-crow [sic]" and that the ideas about race expressed in the show agreed with those of the *Daily Worker* and, subsequently, of the party. As Klein observed, "This public pledge of agreement with the Communist Party newspaper is significant because it took place . . . after the Truman Doctrine had established anticommunism as an ideological foundation of U.S. foreign policy, after Truman had instituted loyalty tests in the State Department . . . after HUAC had begun its investigation of communism in Hollywood, and after the Hollywood Ten had been convicted."[65] It is also significant given Hammerstein's earlier activities with the Anti-Nazi League. The criticism of Hammerstein's depictions of African Americans is somewhat ironic in that, from the late 1940s until the end of his life, Hammerstein was a member of the NAACP and active on its board of directors.

POST–*SOUTH PACIFIC*

While Rodgers and Hammerstein's political activities after *South Pacific* are technically outside the scope of this study, a few points nonetheless seem relevant. Hammerstein, for instance, remained active in several organizations in addition to the NAACP in the decade following 1949, and they all reflected his vision of internationalism. Hugh Fordin asserted that "*Oscar Hammerstein II* on an organization's letterhead meant that the group was helping to promote understanding between people of different races and nationalities and that more than a 'name' was being contributed."[66] Hammerstein's principal activity was the world government movement, and the first group that he was associated with was the Writers' Board for World Government, which was a 1949 outgrowth of the former WWB. Soon after the formation of this new group, Hammerstein wrote a guest editorial for the *Saturday Review of Literature* in which he explained his point of view. "The world government I am talking about here is *limited* world government, limited to the objective of peace. . . . The nations are not to give up their form of government, their customs, their songs, their games—only the right to make war."[67] The group was in part a response to the 1946 publication of essays collectively titled *One World or None*, which was subtitled "A Report to the Public on the Full Meaning of the Atomic Bomb." This anthology, which was assembled by the Federation of American Scientists, contained essays by Albert Einstein, J. Robert Oppenheimer, Niels Bohr, and Walter Lippmann, and was a best-seller. The United World Federalists later named their newsletter after the book.

By 1958 Hammerstein had written two chapters for a proposed book on racial prejudice that was also to contain work by James A. Michener and Pearl S. Buck, both of whom lived near Hammerstein in Bucks County, Pennsylvania. Buck was the founder of Welcome House, an adoption agency that found homes for Asian and part-Asian children who, although born in the United States, were shunned by most established adoption agencies. Hammerstein was more than a good neighbor: he served on the board of Welcome House for seven years. Although the book was never completed, Hammerstein's chapters, which are in typescript with pencil corrections, reveal his ongoing concern. The first chapter is titled "Progress," and it begins with the lyrics to a "coon song" from around 1910 titled "St. Patrick's Day Is a Bad Day for Coons." After citing the racist lyrics, Hammerstein observed, "For a long time few people realized how much traditional comedy was creating and perpetuating slander about various kinds of Americans, discrediting them and causing untold damage to their reputations as groups and individuals." He continued by noting that this kind of comedy, while still in existence, was less prevalent: "[Its] decline has been hastened by a very conscious movement on the part of groups of Americans who awakened to the evil and did all they could to discourage the continuation of these damaging stereotypes." Hammerstein modestly refrained from including himself in this last group.

The second chapter, "Dear Believer in White Supremacy," is far more confrontational than the first. "The race problem is serious," Hammerstein began. "You and we must build some kind of bridge of understanding so that we may join together in a sincere effort to avert the ultimate world tragedy that must ensue if we do *not* join together." Hammerstein enumerated supremacist arguments for the inferiority of African Americans and then refuted each argument. Within his refutations, he made the sly observation that "the popular concepts of religion seem to point strongly toward the equality of all men in the sight of God." He was especially sensitive to the unique position of the United States in regard to race, commenting, "The question of race equality or inequality, of integration or segregation has caused great disunity in the United States, and great misunderstanding of us abroad. . . . It is high time that we approached this question with reason rather than passion."[68] The book, which never seems to have advanced beyond the preliminary stages, would have contained some of Hammerstein's most succinct and pointed writing about this issue.

After *South Pacific*, Rodgers and Hammerstein dramatized some of their worldview in *The King and I*, another critical and commercial hit. Hammerstein told Mike Wallace that this musical was "best symbolized" by the song

"Getting to Know You," the tune for which was originally composed for *South Pacific*. (It was replaced by "Younger Than Springtime.") Sung by the British governess Anna Leonowens and the many children of the King of Siam, whom she was instructing in Western ideas and customs, the song represented to Hammerstein a situation in which "all race and color had faded in their getting to know and love each other."[69] Hammerstein's book was based primarily on the novelist Margaret Landon's retelling of Leonowen's story, and the 1946 film based on Landon's book. He altered the narrative somewhat, however, as Christina Klein observed: "In keeping with his own liberal racial politics, Hammerstein excised much of Leonowens's and Landon's ethnocentric and racist language and bypassed the 'yellow-peril' characterizations of the 1946 film. He downplayed the notion of unbreachable cultural differences and heightened the message of tolerance and mutual understanding."[70] Rodgers wrote in his autobiography that he, too, was drawn to "the theme of democratic teachings triumphing over autocratic rule," and that the story "was a project that Oscar and I could really believe in."[71]

The song "Getting to Know You," in addition to demonstrating Rodgers and Hammerstein's approach to intercultural relations, was also appropriated by several internationalist groups of the time as their theme song. The People-to-People program of the Eisenhower administration used it, for instance, as the theme song for Project Hope, a hospital ship that provided medical services for countries in Southeast Asia without adequate facilities.[72] Although it was a recycled tune that was rewritten and added to the show during previews, "Getting to Know You," in addition to becoming one of the best-known songs of a rich score, provided a succinct statement of what its creators thought their show was about, and it provided Hammerstein's biographer with an appropriate title for his work.

The only Rodgers and Hammerstein show after *The King and I* to deal with cultural exchange was *Flower Drum Song*, which concerned Chinese and Chinese Americans and the problems of acculturation. The team, despite Hammerstein's early work on *Show Boat* and his lifelong dedication to promoting racial tolerance, never wrote a work that addressed the problematic relations between whites and African Americans in the United States. Rodgers's first show after Hammerstein's death, however, deals with that very issue, and it takes such a matter-of-fact attitude about an interracial relationship that it almost seems like a nonissue.

No Strings, for which Rodgers provided his own excellent lyrics, is an original story. The initial idea for the show came to Rodgers after he saw Diahann Carroll perform on the Jack Paar television show. Her beauty and sophistication struck Rodgers, and he later wrote that Ms. Carroll's performance inspired him to create a role in which she could play "a chic, sophisticated woman of the world." Rodgers believed that the unprecedented presentation of a black female character as glamorous and intelligent would shatter more racist stereotypes than a work that was "strident or preachy."[73] The plot, which was developed with the playwright Samuel Taylor, concerned an affair between Ms. Carroll's character, an American model in Paris, and a white American author, played by Richard Kiley. When the author decides that he must return to his home in Maine to finish his novel, both realize that she cannot go back with him because of racial prejudice in the United States. While some critics found the ending unconvincing, the presentation of an interracial relationship in 1962 was nonetheless daring. Rodgers downplayed this in his autobiography, arguing, "Simply having a black actress in the starring role would . . . demonstrate our respect for the audience's ability to accept our theme free from rhetoric or sermons."[74] Nonetheless, preview audiences in Detroit walked out in silent outrage over the onstage relationship. Reviewing the New York opening, which was met with no such hostility, the critic Harold Clurman wrote, "There is something real in this story. . . . I liked the fact that the affair between the lovers of two 'races' (or colors) is taken as a matter of course; it is socially fraudulent but healthy in terms of our stage."[75]

Rodgers never returned to the issue of race in his subsequent works for the commercial stage, but *No Strings*, which also featured strikingly innovative staging by Joe Layton and which had a successful Broadway run, was a brave statement. While Rodgers's distancing himself from "preachy . . . sermons," terms that had been among the criticisms Hammerstein received for *South Pacific*, is interesting, his daring approach to race in *No Strings* suggests his ongoing sympathy for one of Hammerstein's greatest concerns. While Taylor's book received most of the criticism aimed at the show, Rodgers's score was critically acclaimed and demonstrated the depth of his ongoing commitment to the issue of race. It also showed that, like Hammerstein, Rodgers thought that interracial relations were "perfectly sensible."

3

AN ADAPTABLE SOURCE
• • •
Michener's *Tales of the South Pacific*

In his 1992 memoir *The World Is My Home*, James A. Michener tells of an event that occurred in his second tour of duty late in World War II.[1] Sent by Commodore Richard Glass, an aide to Admiral William Calhoun, on four investigative trips to various areas in the then-quiescent eastern theater of the war in the Pacific, Michener found himself in a particularly unpleasant village in the Treasury Islands that was inhabited by "scrawny residents and only one pig." Michener's final observation from this trip was to resonate later in his life and career:

> On a rude signboard attached to a tree, someone had affixed a cardboard giving the settlement's name, and it was so completely different from ordinary names, so musical to my ear that I borrowed a pencil and in a soggy notebook jotted the name against the day when I might want to use it for some purpose I could not then envisage: Bali-ha'i.[2]

Perhaps the musicality of the village's name increased with hindsight and because Richard Rodgers eventually set it to such memorable melodic and harmonic effect. After all, Michener wrote his memories approximately fifty years after the beginning of the war, and he had not yet decided to write commercially about his experiences in the South Pacific, or anything else, when he encountered the village. Whatever the reason for the notation, however, it later resulted in the memorializing of a place name that came to represent paradise and private dreams for thousands of audiences.

Tales of the South Pacific, published in 1947, is the work that Michener eventually wrote about his experiences in the Pacific theater of the war and in which he used the name Bali-ha'i. A discussion of Michener's book is important at this point for several reasons. First, *Oklahoma!* and *Carousel* were based on plays (Lynn Riggs's *Green Grow the Lilacs* and Ferenc Molnar's *Liliom*, respectively) and *Allegro* was based on an original concept; *South Pacific*,

3.1. *American soldiers in the South Pacific. Courtesy of Photofest.*

therefore, is the first nondramatic work that Rodgers and Hammerstein adapted for the musical stage. Second, because they later adapted other prose works for the stage—Margaret Landon's *Anna and the King of Siam*, John Steinbeck's *Sweet Thursday* (for *Pipe Dream*), and C. Y. Lee's *Flower Drum Song* principal among them—Rodgers and Hammerstein's first joint adaptation of a novel demonstrates a technique that would be repeated and refined in their later adapted works. Third, the nonlinear structure of Michener's collected tales challenged easy adaptation. Knowledge of the book's structural, thematic, and narrative elements, therefore, illuminates the creative choices involved in the pursuit of a manageable storyline. These choices also determined the musical's thematic message. While "Our Heroine," which is about Nellie Forbush and Emile de Becque, and "Fo' Dolla'," which is about Joe Cable, Bloody Mary, and Liat, provide the show's principal romantic story lines, they also strongly reflect the issue of racial intolerance that resonated with Rodgers and Hammerstein. Finally, the existence of Hammerstein's handwritten notes, made while reading the novel, provide insight into his first response to the book, and they reveal the initial stage of the creative process that led to the musical.

While the present study is the first in the literature on *South Pacific* to discuss these notes, the director Trevor Nunn had access to Hammerstein's copy of the book, which also had notes and comments in the margins that Nunn consulted in preparation for the revised 2001 London production of *South Pacific*. Nunn has commented on the usefulness of that volume in preparing his production: "What's wonderful about having Hammerstein's copy, with all the pencil marks, is you can see from his markings: 'I'm interested in that bit of content. I'm interested in those things because they're tough and contemporary and ask questions.'"[3] While Hammerstein's copy of Michener's book is not currently available, the notes found with his papers at the Library of Congress provide similar insight.[4]

The following discussion of *Tales of the South Pacific* is in three sections. The first briefly explores the author James A. Michener's World War II background and his origins as a writer, which are integral to the creation of the novel. Michener has written at length about his intentions in this book, his first, and these intentions are closely related to the thematic content of the novel and, subsequently, the musical. The second section analyzes the novel's structural, thematic, and narrative elements. The third section is concerned with Rodgers and Hammerstein's attraction to the work, and eventual decisions about adapting it. This section includes a discussion of Hammerstein's notes and also relates the conflicting accounts of how Rodgers and Hammerstein came to the work in the first place.

MICHENER AND HIS TALES

James A. Michener was thirty-four years old when the Japanese attacked Pearl Harbor. Although his upbringing as a Quaker would have enabled him to register with the draft as a conscientious objector, he enlisted in the United States Navy in October 1942. Michener's friend Wilbur Murra relates that Michener "became an ardent advocate of the war as a moral imperative to stop Hitler and the Japanese aggressors; and he was determined to have a part in it himself."[5] An active role in the war was not immediately forthcoming, however, and Michener spent almost two years stateside in various clerical and personnel positions before getting a commission to go to the South Pacific in April 1944.

Michener spent his first tour of duty in the South Pacific in or near battle zones "as a kind of superclerk for the naval air forces," as he later put it, adding that he "usually got to the islands three days after the fighting was over."[6] If his job description seems irregular, his authorization for it was even more so. Shipped to the South Pacific on a troop transport that was manned by merchant seamen, Michener noticed early in the voyage that the captain never appeared to his crew or his passengers; for the duration of the month-long journey, "no one saw him, or heard him speak, or had any kind of communication with him."[7] The army colonel in charge of the transported troops was equally reclusive, and Michener learned that the crew thought both officers were in their cabins drinking for the entire voyage. He also learned from the four Marines who manned the ship's one and only piece of artillery that the ship made the same two-month-long trip, over and over, transporting troops across the Pacific, and that the captain's reclusive nature was the norm. At the end of the trip, Michener and a friend went to bid farewell to the phantom-like captain, but that, too, was thwarted by the captain's already having left the ship. Michener's friend, angered by this final demonstration of the captain's lack of professionalism, broke into the captain's office and soon spied some forms that were used for the writing of duty assignments. He promptly forged a form giving Michener "a set of orders . . . that gave [him] authorization to travel pretty much as [he] wished throughout the military zones of the South Pacific on what [his friend] designated 'tours of inspection.'" Michener added, "Rarely has a forged document been put to livelier use."[8]

Michener also assured his readers that these forged documents were later replaced by authorized orders, which were responsible for his traveling all over the South Pacific.[9] On several occasions, he accompanied pilots on night missions, and he witnessed troops landing on enemy islands. The latter experience provided him with the opportunity to see firsthand the action, and the casualties, of the war in the Pacific. When his first tour of duty ended, Michener, who could have returned to the States, instead accepted a stimulating second tour. Because his master's degree in history qualified him for it, he was offered a job writing a history of the navy in the Pacific. Michener accepted this extended tour for many reasons, most of which were personal and had to do with his lack of desire to return to the United States. He also liked the increased freedom he would have to move about the Pacific islands. "I would spend two full tours of duty, nearly four years, in the tropics," Michener observed, "the first two often in battle areas, the last two in paradise."[10] The work that became *Tales of the South Pacific* was produced during the years in paradise. Part of that work led him to the Treasury Islands and the village of Bali-ha'i.

Michener did not enter the war a professional writer. Before the war, he taught social studies at several universities, including Harvard, and worked as an editor of textbooks at Macmillan. His urge to write anything other than his assignments occurred after he survived a near plane crash on New Caledonia. This experience provided Michener with an insight that in turn prompted him to refocus his life, and he "began to listen with attention as men told stories at night." Listening to these stories personalized what Michener called "the human terms" of the war in the Pacific and suggested to Michener that, in later years, "the men who complain most loudly out here will want to explain to others what it was like." This led him to the decision "to write down as simply and honestly" as he could "what it was like."[11] Soon after this realization, typing at night in a shed lit by a lantern that also kept away the mosquitoes, Michener began telling the stories that, in 1948, earned him the Pulitzer Prize.

MICHENER'S STRUCTURAL, THEMATIC, AND NARRATIVE TECHNIQUES

Michener thought of *Tales of the South Pacific* as a novel even though the book has no linear narrative. Instead, Michener used an arch structure that peaks with "Fo' Dolla'," the central, and longest, story, and also creates a palindrome out of the order of the stories.[12] For instance, the first and last (nineteenth) stories are each reflective; the second and eighteenth describe battle action; the third and seventeenth concern preparation for battle, and so forth. The tenth, and central, story is "Fo' Dolla'." (This structure is demonstrated in Appendix 1.) While its symmetry and balance are unmentioned in Michener's discussions of the novel, or in extant critical studies of it, they are unmistakable, and the palindrome also suggests a carefully planned formal structure for the stories. Further, "Fo' Dolla'," the story at the apex of the arch and thus central to the structure, is the story that first appealed to Rodgers and Hammerstein as a potentially adaptable source.[13] It is also a story that Michener has singled out as one of four from his collected works that he holds "in high regard."[14]

Since the plot of "Fo' Dolla'" is referred to in some detail in the following discussion, a brief summary at this point will be helpful. The story concerns Marine Lieutenant Joe Cable, a Princeton graduate from a Philadelphia Main Line family, and his ill-fated romance with a young Tonkinese girl named Liat. Engaged to a girl at home, Cable nonetheless is encouraged by Bloody Mary, Liat's mother, to marry Liat and live on Bali Ha'i, her island home. Realizing that he could never take her back to Philadelphia society, and both unwilling and unable to stay, Cable rejects Mary's offers and Liat's love, and, at the end of the story, leaves for battle. The central conflict of the story is within Cable. While he partially overcomes his racial intolerance through the depth of his feelings for Liat, he eventually succumbs to it because he is unable to reconcile his feelings with the societal pressures of his upbringing, pressures that also bring issues of class into the story.[15] Liat accepts her mother's alternate plan for the future and becomes engaged to an older, but well-off, French planter.

In addition to demonstrating its importance to the book's structure, the story's placement at the center of the novel also reveals its thematic centrality to the overall work: "Fo' Dolla'" contains plot elements from nearly all the other stories, except those that describe battle action. For instance, Cable's indecision about what to include and what to withhold from his letters home reflects his growing confusion over his relationship with Liat. "Dry Rot," "Passion," and "Our Heroine" also concern letters to and from home, what the writer does or does not include in his or her letters, and the effects of letters on those who receive them. "Alligator" and "Wine for the Mess at Segi" both end in preparation and departure for battle, as does "Fo' Dolla'." "The Milk Run" and "The Airstrip at Konora" are concerned with individualism and the honor of a social group, and "An Officer and a Gentleman" and "The Strike" are concerned with individualism in opposition to a group. Similarly, in "Fo' Dolla'," Cable's relationship with the other soldiers and with the society he grew up in is contrasted with independent and even antisocial actions that conflict with his military and social background. And the secret island of Bali-ha'i, where Liat lives and where Cable cannot stay, provides a symbol of the private and sometimes internalized refuge from the war that Michener emphasizes in "The Cave" and "Those Who Fraternize."

The stories with which Michener surrounds "Fo' Dolla'" are also connected by recurring characters, plots, and the themes of waiting and racial intolerance. For instance, one of the most important recurring plot elements is the preparation for a mammoth military mobilization known as "Alligator," the purpose of which is to capture the fictional island of Kuralei. The action of "Alligator," which occurs near the book's end, is the battle toward which most of the stories point, and many of the characters from earlier stories meet their fates in this climactic fight. Its aftermath is recounted in the elegiac final chapter set in the cemetery at Hoga Point. Michener's handling of the key battle scene, however, is almost perfunctory. While the mention of "Alligator" throughout the book creates anticipation for the actual event, its presentation is succinct and not especially dramatic. This supports what Michener said about his goal in writing the book: "Rigorously I adhered to my commitment: to report the South Pacific as it actually was. . . . I had none of the excessive romanticism that had colored the works of my predecessors in writing about the Pacific."[16]

Michener also emphasizes the effects of the tropical island settings on all the characters and on the "Alligator" operation. The use of evocative settings, such as the islands of the South Pacific, is an essential element in almost all of Michener's work after *Tales of the South Pacific*. He also often details the physical challenges that these settings create for the humans inhabiting them. As Marilyn Stevenson noted in her overview of Michener's books, "Even in the shorter novels, he creates a sense of place that situates the reader directly in the world where the narrative takes place. And in all his fiction, there is the impact of a view of life, of certain values that are promoted."[17] Principal among these values are racial tolerance and personal courage, and these in turn provide Michener's thematic emphases. While the style of his books changed after *Hawaii* in 1959—with that work, Michener began creating the lengthy historical panoramas for which he is best known—his thematic concerns remain consistent. Michener's entertaining didacticism is also a critical element of Rodgers and Hammerstein's adaptation of *Tales of the South Pacific*.[18]

The effect of the setting on the characters is intensified by the seemingly endless waiting they endure. Indeed, each of Michener's stories is in some way evocative of the agonizing wait between the battles that he calls those "flaming things of the bitter moment" that occur around great stretches of inactivity, boredom, and restlessness.[19] The author is more concerned with individuals waiting for action than with the actual action most of them eventually experience. Michener's biographer George J. Becker observed, "It is no qualification of heroism that the novel gives an initial warning that all a man did in the Pacific theater was 'sit on his ass and wait.'"[20]

In addition to telling stories during their long periods of waiting, the men and women in the South Pacific, like Cable, also encountered, reacted to, and reflected upon cultures other than their own. This cultural exchange, which was often problematic, was of particular interest to Michener, and while the story "Fo' Dolla'" is central to Michener's exploration of this theme, nearly all the stories deal with it. As early as "Mutiny," the third story in the book, the problem of cultural relations between indigenous peoples and Americans is a critical issue. In "Mutiny," the conflict is between Americans and the inhabitants of a small island, all of whom are descendants of the surviving mutineers of the famous eighteenth-century English ship HMS *Bounty*. The Americans urgently need to build a strategic airstrip on a site occupied by a row of trees revered by the islanders. Originally planted by the mutineers, the trees are the predominant remaining symbol of the islanders' heritage. In the end, however, the airstrip is built. "A Boar's Tooth," which is used in the musical, concerns a native ritual attended by several Americans for reasons ranging

3.2. *Kamikaze fighter pilot, World War II. Courtesy of Photofest.*

from sexual curiosity to the hope of acquiring artifacts to sell to other soldiers and sailors. The American perspectives on the event are revealing. A chaplain comments, "The appurtenances of the religion are slightly revolting," to which an entrepreneurial lieutenant responds, "I feel that way myself, sometimes on Sunday in Connecticut."[21] Two references to race in the story "Those Who Fraternize" are typical of other, sometimes more fleeting, examples of the theme in the stories. Referring to a woman of mixed French and Javanese ethnicities with whom he had an affair, the pilot Bus Adams comments, "She looked like all the beautiful girls you've ever know. But darker." Later in the story, Tony Fry suggests that the struggles for power in the region will prove long-lasting. "We'll all be out here again," he comments. "Asia's never going to let Australia stay white."[22] Although the book is set in a war between two opposing cultures—American and Japanese, Western and Eastern—the stories repeatedly personalize the issue, demonstrating Americans' response to the different world in which they find themselves.

The military men and women in *Tales of the South Pacific* generalize with ease about the racial and cultural differences of the Japanese enemy, referring to the evil "other" simply as "the Japs." But their daily encounters with the equally "other" peoples of the occupied islands are more personal and specific and less easily defined. This contrast between the general and the specific, the global and the personal, permeates the stories. If the war presents a binarism, "us" versus "them," the individuals caught up in that conflict also encounter a more complex construct, one that is new to them and to which the clear-cut binarism does not apply so easily. Edward Said observed this trend somewhat later in the twentieth century:

> Gone are the binary oppositions dear to the nationalist and imperialist enterprise. Instead we begin to sense that old authority cannot simply be replaced by new authority, but that alignments made across borders, types, nations, and essences are rapidly coming into view, and it is those new alignments that now provoke and challenge the fundamentally static notion of *identity*.[23]

Michener reflects the "alignments" referred to by Said. Indeed, as Christina Klein observed, Michener's early work "tried to shape what Americans saw when they turned their gaze toward Asia and to teach them how to think about themselves in relation to what they saw." Michener wanted Americans to think about themselves in terms of race and racism, and because this concern was shared by Oscar Hammerstein, it became central to the content of *South Pacific*. If Michener, as Christina Klein thought, "popularized the link between domestic racial practices and foreign policy and insisted that questions of race belonged at the center of foreign policy discussions," Hammerstein insisted that they belonged at the center of a Broadway musical as well.[24]

Since the most intimate examinations of racial intolerance in *Tales of the South Pacific* are in "Fo' Dolla'" and "Our Heroine," Hammerstein's choice of the two stories to provide much of the material for the musical's two principal plots is unsurprising. Michener's nurse Nellie Forbush, who became the principal female character in the musical, and her confrontation with her own bigotry are the focus of "Our Heroine." While Nellie is introduced earlier as a secondary character in "An Officer and a Gentleman," her discovery of her own prejudice, and her overcoming it, is the main concern of "Our Heroine." Further, the conflict and its resolution recalls the earlier quote from Said: Nellie's notions of identity are challenged and ultimately overcome only when she casts her gaze outside herself and begins to make what Said called "alignments." Early in the story, for instance, she recalls telling her fiancé in Arkansas that she desired to experience more of the world and encounter more of its diverse population. "Then," she adds, "when the war's over, I'll be back."[25] Looking outside herself and her culture, she finds more than she anticipated.

After falling in love with Emile de Becque, a French planter in his mid-forties, and accepting his proposal of marriage, Nellie learns that he has eight illegitimate daughters, each with a different Javanese, Tonkinese, or Polynesian mother. (The musical makes de Becque's progeny legitimate and fewer, although they are no less problematic for Nellie.) Perhaps knowing of her discovery, de Becque introduces Nellie to the two daughters still at home, whom she finds enchanting, and tells her of the others. Nellie's acceptance reaches a temporarily insurmountable obstacle when she learns that de Becque had lived with a Polynesian. The Javanese and Tonkinese women, to Nellie's mind, were still acceptable as white or yellow, but the Polynesian was different, and her response is startling. Describing Nellie's reactions as coming from what she was taught growing up in Arkansas, Michener observes that, for Nellie, "any person living or dead who was not white or yellow was a nigger. . . ." Further, Nellie feels that her "revulsion" of other races is something beyond de Becque's ability to understand. Yet despite this reaction, and the "surge of joy" she feels when she learns that the Polynesian woman is deceased, Nellie nonetheless thinks, as she watches the two young girls during dinner, "I would be happy if my children were like that."[26] Nevertheless, she remains full of doubt and anxiety, and her assumptions that de Becque is incapable of understanding her prejudice are correct. In the end, however, Nellie overcomes her prejudice and accepts de Becque and his daughters, intent on marrying him and spending the rest of her days in the beauty of his island plantation.

In "Fo' Dolla'," the somewhat more complex racial conflicts do not end so happily. Michener creates in Bali-ha'i a secret and sensuous island where Joe Cable can momentarily ignore the prejudice that ultimately destroys his chance for happiness. The island is mysterious in part because it cannot be seen. Michener writes, "Like most lovely things, one had to seek it out and even to know what one was seeking before it could be found."[27] Its secrecy is why all the unmarried young women from nearby islands are kept there under the supervision of French nuns. Cable is led there by Bloody Mary, a Tonkinese so named because of the streams of red betel juice that run down the corners of her mouth.

Mary takes Cable to Bali-ha'i to meet her daughter, Liat, with whom he begins a physical relationship and eventually falls in love. Cable's troubled response to this relationship brings forth issues of colonialism, racism, and classism, in addition to his effort to overcome each of these prejudices, and his struggles are retained in the musical. Upon his arrival on Bali-ha'i, Cable's first sight of the half-clad women creates a mixed reaction. He did not think the women ugly (although by American standards they might have been), but he did not think them beautiful, as an artist might have. "Cable," notes Michener, "had no consistent thoughts as he looked up to the dark faces with their gleaming teeth."[28] Throughout the story, Michener sets Cable apart from the other Americans by emphasizing his sensitivity to his surroundings and to individuals who are a part of those surroundings, although this sensitivity often causes him anguish. With Liat, in particular, he often tries to explain away his initial perception of her as "other."

After first making love to Liat, for instance, one of the thoughts that Cable has, and one that partially relieves his guilt, is that the colors of his tanned skin and Liat's are virtually indistinguishable. The next day, away from Bali-ha'i, Cable thinks of Liat and again rationalizes her otherness: "Tonkinese were in reality Chinese, sort of the way Canadians were Americans, only a little different." He even compares her to the girls at home, noting that "her teeth were white. Her ankles were delicate, like those of a girl of a family in Philadelphia."[29] Creating an image of Liat that fits within acceptable images from his own elevated stratum of society helps Cable justify his growing love for her.

Cable's conflict is demonstrated further by his ceasing to write home after he makes love to Liat, and before long he realizes that he is "tied to Bali-ha'i by chains of his own making." Michener refers to Cable's having "permitted a new world to grow within him," a world that takes on a dangerous importance to his priorities. Later, noting Cable's intensified turmoil, Michener reveals that Cable "felt involved in a net of two colors. . . . And no matter which way he twisted, he was not free."[30]

Eventually, the pull of Philadelphia's cultural exclusivity wins out, and Cable thwarts Mary's wish that he marry Liat. The girl is unsurprised and accepting, but Mary is enraged, calling on her arsenal of expletives to express her fury. Cable soon leaves to participate in the "Alligator" operation, and, in the story's last scene, Mary hurls invectives at Cable, who is riding off in the back of a truck. When another soldier asks her the price of a shrunken head she carries, however, her attention switches immediately to a potential deal— Mary makes her substantial living hawking souvenirs to soldiers—and Cable disappears, on his way to the fate that awaits him on Kuralei.

In the middle of this story, Michener introduces an extended dialogue among a group of military men that provides a counterpoint to Cable's sensitivity. The Marines deride Hollywood's presentation of island women, noting that in the movies white actresses such as Dorothy Lamour usually play the women. As the conversation progresses, a Marine notes that the island women were "getting whiter every day." When another Marine asks Cable if he would "sleep with a native girl," Cable lies and says no, after which the

Marine comments that "few self-respecting American men would attempt to knock off a piece of jungle julep."[31] The scene puts Cable's feelings of guilt in perspective, reminding the reader that the issues of race, and of what was and was not acceptable behavior, were on the minds of many men in this unique setting. Codes of behavior, although challenged, for the most part still win out over sexual tension, although Michener notes the "highly tense conditions" that caused many men to have thoughts well outside the boundaries of acceptability in their civilian lives. Both rape and homosexuality are specified among these thoughts that, on occasion, were acted out. Rape is especially prevalent in the stories.

While "Our Heroine" and "Fo' Dolla'" provided Rodgers and Hammerstein with their principal plots and thematic concerns, many of Michener's other stories provided characters who appear in the musical or who are conflated into composite characters. All the other stories that were used relate to the thematic emphases of these two stories, however, allowing Rodgers and Hammerstein to keep their show tightly focused.

FROM BOOK TO MUSICAL PLAY

How the team of Rodgers and Hammerstein was introduced to the then-unknown James A. Michener and his novel is not clear. Three versions of the story provide very different accounts of the musical's genesis. The first version, which appears in Rodgers's autobiography, Joshua Logan's autobiography, and Hugh Fordin's biography of Hammerstein, is the most commonly reported; James A. Michener's story, however, which he felt he had to include in his autobiography, is equally compelling. And a more recent version offered by Laurence Maslon adds to the mix. All three versions deserve attention.

Joshua Logan claimed to have first thought of the book *Tales of the South Pacific*, and, more particularly, the story "Fo' Dolla'," as an adaptable source for a musical. This is not surprising, given that he also claimed to have first conceived most of the successful elements of *South Pacific*; in his autobiography, at least, Logan is the star of every show he mentions. Nonetheless, his account of the "birth" of *South Pacific* is supported by other sources. According to Fordin, for instance, Logan and the producer Leland Hayward "had made an informal producers' agreement to acquire theatrical rights" from Michener and his publisher. Fordin noted, "Since no contract had been signed, Leland ordered the voluble Josh not to blab about it."[32] But Logan was not exactly a retiring sort, and when he ran into Rodgers at a cocktail party, he immediately mentioned to the composer that he had a story—"Fo' Dolla'"—that would be perfect for Rodgers and Hammerstein. Rodgers made a note and forgot about it. Only later, when Logan asked his opinion of the story, did Rodgers actually read it. Soon after, Logan also pitched the story to Hammerstein—Rodgers, it seems, never mentioned it to Hammerstein—who read the book and agreed that the story had dramatic potential. Rodgers and Hammerstein then talked to each other about the story and the book, after which they called Logan and Hayward. Rodgers and Hammerstein expressed their serious interest in writing the show but said they would do so only if they co-produced it and held 51 percent of it. This did not make Logan and Hayward happy, although they realized that holding the majority interest was the only way that Rodgers and Hammerstein would agree to the project. So Logan and Hayward agreed. "The next step," Fordin observed, "was to locate the author of the book."[33] An important aspect of this story is that *South Pacific* was the first of their shows in which Rodgers and Hammerstein had controlling financial interest. Their previous three endeavors had been with Theresa Helburn and the Theatre Guild, and Rodgers and Hammerstein were adamant about having complete artistic control over *South Pacific* and subsequent productions.

Michener recalled the initial trajectory of his book to Rodgers and Hammerstein rather differently. The author wrote in 1992 that *Tales of the South Pacific* was first pitched to Metro-Goldwyn-Mayer by Kenneth McKenna, the head of the studio's literary department and a friend of Michener's. The studio saw no cinematic possibilities for the book, however, and passed on the option. McKenna then told his half-brother Jo Mielziner, the noted Broadway set designer, about the book, suggesting its potential as a play. After reading the book, Mielziner—who had designed *Carousel* and *Allegro*, Rodgers and Hammerstein's previous musicals—agreed with McKenna about its potential. He later told Michener that, after reading the book, he "took it to Dick Rodgers and told him it was a natural for him and Oscar and [that he'd] volunteer to do the sets," which he did.[34]

Michener then noted, "In the meantime he [Hammerstein] and Rodgers had allied themselves with two other outstanding talents, Josh Logan, the director, and Leland Hayward, the charismatic producer."[35] This indicates that Rodgers and Hammerstein knew about the book before Logan said anything to them about it. Michener recalled how Hayward cornered him secretly and tried to buy all the rights for the book outright for five hundred dollars without consulting with Rodgers, Hammerstein, or Logan. Michener summarized this version of the story by noting, "I have not told this story before, and in later years when Hayward and I became friends we never referred to the fact

3.3. *The production team. From left, Richard Rodgers, Joshua Logan, Oscar Hammerstein II, and Leland Hayward. Courtesy of Photofest.*

that he had tried to slip behind his partners' backs and pick up all the rights to what turned out to be a bonanza."[36]

A third version, related by Laurence Maslon, conflates elements of the first two. In this version, Logan met McKenna (which Maslon spells MacKenna) at Sardi's, and McKenna suggested Michener's book to Logan as research for Logan's upcoming directorial duties for *Mister Roberts*, a play set in the South Pacific during World War II. In this version of the story, which Logan told to a publicist at 20th Century Fox in 1957, Logan in turn told Hayward about the book and "they set about discreetly getting the rights to the story from James Michener."[37] Not long after, Logan told Rodgers about *Tales of the South Pacific* and, more specifically, "Fo' Dolla'." This last part of the saga concurs with the first version, above. But the second version takes the book directly from McKenna to Mielziner to Rodgers, leaving Logan out of the initial picture.

The exact path the book took from its Hollywood pitch to its rights being owned by Rodgers and Hammerstein is probably unknowable—and, ultimately, it makes little difference to the authors' creative processes—but

Michener's version suggests a more direct path from author to composer and lyricist. Either way, once they had the rights to the work, Rodgers and Hammerstein and, eventually, Logan began the process of turning it into a stage-worthy vehicle.

In Los Angeles for the tour of *Annie Get Your Gun*, which starred Mary Martin in the role made famous by Ethel Merman and which Rodgers and Hammerstein produced, Rodgers and Hammerstein began discussing what to do with Michener's book.[38] While acknowledging their mutual attraction to "Fo' Dolla'," they also realized that it presented at least two major problems. First, they found the unhappy plot too reminiscent of *Madame Butterfly*, and they had no desire to re-create that work. Second, wrote Rodgers, they thought it not "substantial or original enough to make a full evening's entertainment."[39] After this, according to Fordin, Hammerstein returned to the book and spent months "carefully studying the other stories, marking characters and incidents with the thought of combining several tales."[40]

These "markings," or notes, are among Hammerstein's papers in the Library of Congress.[41] Written in pencil on yellow tablet paper now in serious deterioration, these notes provide insight into the response the librettist–lyricist had to the book. (No such notes by Rodgers are known to exist.) The notes consist of single words, names, or short phrases. The title of the noted story is written first, followed by the comments. The notes do not seem composed; instead, they appear to be informal quick jottings. A story-by-story discussion of these notes, which show Hammerstein taking the initial steps toward adapting parts of the book beyond "Fo' Dolla'," is a convenient approach to Michener's stories and Hammerstein's responses to them. This allows for a brief summary of the stories and gives information about which stories appealed to Hammerstein at this very early stage of the musical's development. In the discussion that follows, the stories are listed as they appear in the book.

"The South Pacific" is the first story of the book. Its first page contains the following three topics or characters that eventually appeared in *South Pacific*: (1) the experience of waiting for action in battle amid the beauty of the islands, (2) the character of Bloody Mary, and (3) the story of the so-called Remittance Man, who hid on an island and radioed news of Japanese troop movement to the Americans until his discovery and death. This third topic was used, without the character of the Remittance Man, as a plot device for Cable and de Becque's climactic mission in act 2 of *South Pacific*. None of these ideas appear in Hammerstein's notes, however, which begin with the story "An Officer and a Gentleman," the fourth tale of the collection.

The first three stories were nonetheless integral to Hammerstein's overall response to the novel, for they partially provide the tone of his book and suggest elements for the development of a linear plot. Just as the opening directions of Lynn Riggs's play *Green Grow the Lilacs* inspired Hammerstein's lyrics for "Oh, What a Beautiful Mornin'"[42] (the opening number of *Oklahoma!*), the opening pages of *Tales of the South Pacific* contain descriptions that inform the tone of much of Hammerstein's book. As if to underscore the importance of Michener's opening, the 2008 Broadway revival of *South Pacific* has the first paragraph of the book projected onto a scrim displayed before the beginning of the show, introducing the audience to the author's lovely images even before they hear Rodgers and Hammerstein's exquisite evocation of them. And then, after describing the vast ocean and the tiny coral islands, the palm trees and the secret lagoons, Michener introduces one of his central themes: "The timeless, repetitive waiting."[43]

Like Michener's story, Hammerstein's script makes continuous reference to the beauty and the waiting, both of which affect the characters and the plot, and he never strays far from Michener's opening images. Soon after Nellie enters, for instance, she comments to de Becque, "Gosh, it's beautiful here. Just look at that yellow sun! You know, I don't think it's the end of the world like everyone else thinks."[44] These comments suggest that Nellie's characteristic optimism, which after the above dialogue finds voice in the song "A Cockeyed Optimist," is reinforced by the beauty of the locale. Hammerstein's stage directions often mention specifics of setting that indicate the constant presence of beauty—the opening description of de Becque's plantation, for instance, or the description for the beach setting of act 1, scene 3, which calls for the presence of Bali Ha'i in the background. The theme of anxious waiting appears often in the dialogue or lyrics for Billis and the Seabees. Not long after Billis first appears in the third scene, for example, he mentions that he is "feeling held down again" and that he needs "to take a trip" to the neighboring Bali Ha'i.[45] Of course, his desire for that particular trip is also motivated by his desire to indulge in the Boar's Tooth Ceremony and its half-dressed women and to bring back souvenirs that he hopes to sell for a handsome profit. In "There Is Nothing Like a Dame," after listing the beauties of "sunlight on the sand" and "moonlight on the sea," among others, the men comment, "We fell restless, / We feel blue, / We feel lonely."[46] Their waiting is specifically focused on female companionship in the song, to be sure, but it is also connected to the equally powerful anticipation of military action.

"Coral Sea," the second story, focuses on a battle to prevent the Japanese invasion of New Zealand. Because it is specifically about a single battle, however, and because it does not relate to the romantic elements of the book, the story had little influence on Hammerstein.

The next story, "Mutiny," was described as "one of the best stories about the Pacific ever written" by the Michener scholar A. Grove Day.[47] It is a gripping tale of cultural conflict and introduces the character Tony Fry, who is a recurring figure in the book. But the story, discussed above, is primarily concerned with the problems of building an airstrip, and both the setting and the large number of characters made it an improbable choice for inclusion in the plot of a musical. The character Tony Fry was one of several in the book that made a lasting impression on Hammerstein, although he made no mention of Fry in this set of notes.[48]

Next is "An Officer and a Gentleman," which is discussed extensively in the following chapter, and this was the first story about which Hammerstein made any comments. It concerns Bill Harbison, a handsome navy officer who has affairs with Dinah Culbert and Nellie Forbush, two navy nurses who are also good friends. He wrote the names Harbison and Nellie after the story's title, but he did not mention Dinah, whose first name survives in *South Pacific* as one of the nurses but whose wonderful character did not make it into the final book of the musical. Despite her absence from these notes, however, Dinah, like Harbison, made a strong initial impression. Hammerstein also noted "song 45," probably referring to an undeveloped idea for a song for page forty-five of the novel. This page discusses the island's beauty and how that beauty could provide a romantic atmosphere for an officer and a nurse. The relationship between environment and romance became integral to the musical and to the song "Bali Ha'i," which is about the romantic lure of the islands.

While "The Cave" is lengthy, Hammerstein made only two notes about it. One simply says, "Remittance Man," and the other says "song 66." The song reference seems to be to a Marine's song found on page sixty-six; it is sung by a rescued injured pilot on morphine, and it was soon forgotten by Hammerstein. The plot of "The Cave," however, became critical to the plot of *South Pacific* when Hammerstein needed a device to bring together de Becque and Cable. Dangerously ensconced behind the Japanese lines, a British man known to the Americans only as the Remittance Man reports on Japanese fleet movements from a hidden cave. His reports come regularly, beginning with the weather and then proceeding to specific information about the fleet, and he ends his reports with the sign-off, "Good hunting." Eventually, after providing the Americans with much valuable information, the Remittance Man is discovered and executed by the Japanese, a fate the Americans had long feared was inevitable.

This story provided Hammerstein with several important ideas, of which the Cable-de Becque mission is only the most obvious. In "The Cave," Michener develops a central image—a cave—that he uses in two ways, both of which informed Hammerstein. First, he places the Remittance Man in a series of dangerous caves where he hides from the enemy while making his radio reports to the Americans. But the Americans who listen to him are also in a cave, a safe cave where the radio receiver is located. Michener contrasts the two caves and then expands the image to include figurative caves in addition to literal ones: "Each man I knew had a cave somewhere, a hidden refuge from the war. . . . When battle became too terrible or too lonely or too bitter, men fled into their caves, sweated it out, and came back ready for another day or another battle."[49]

Hammerstein transformed Michener's images of caves into islands. For example, early in act 1, Hammerstein established that, as a young man, de Becque killed a man in France and fled to the island that became his home. Later, he refused the Americans' request to join Cable's mission—Hammerstein's reworking of the Remittance Man's operation—stating that all he cares for is on his island. Later still, after Nellie has refused to marry de Becque and Cable has refused to marry Liat, Cable says to de Becque, "Yes sir, if I get out of this thing alive, I'm not going back there! I'm coming here. All I care about is right here." De Becque responds that when everything that matters to you is on the island, "this is a good place. When all you care about is taken away, there is no place."[50] While the story inspired few notes on Hammerstein's list, its influence was important.

The next story is "The Milk Run." Again, Hammerstein's notes do not reveal the full influence of the story on *South Pacific*. He noted only the name Bus Adams, the narrator of the story; for the musical, Hammerstein changed the first name to Buzz. Adams, a "handsome, blond, cocky" pilot who likes a good story, entertains an impromptu audience by relating how, after being shot down by the Japanese, he was the object of a massive rescue campaign that involved the U.S. Navy and the New Zealand Air Force. This manhunt to rescue one pilot eventually cost the American military approximately $600,000, although, comments Adams, "it's sure worth every cent of the money. If you happen to be that pilot."[51] This story appears in the musical, but with somewhat different details. Instead of Adams, the rescued sailor is Luther Billis, who falls from a transport plane piloted by Adams and is the one-man target of a Japanese attack. The expensive effort by the navy to save him acts as an inadvertent cover for Cable and de Becque getting to their mission from a surfaced submarine. Later, when Billis is berated by his commanding officer for costing the navy so much money, he has a moment of pride, noting that an uncle had once said he would "never be worth a dime."[52]

Regarding "Alligator," Hammerstein wrote a succinct reminder to himself to "study this." Perhaps because he had no military experience, Hammerstein found an insight here into how a major operation might be planned and anticipated. A. Grove Day referred to the story as "an interchapter with little story content" and noted, "It foreshadows the big push for which all the painful waiting is a prelude."[53]

The greater detail of Hammerstein's notes on "Our Heroine" is not surprising, as it provided him with the principal romantic interest of *South Pacific*. This is the second story featuring Nellie Forbush, and Hammerstein noted its relationship to "An Officer and a Gentleman." After observing that Harbison "disintegrates" in this story—he begins to date indiscriminately, drinks to excess, and gets fat—Hammerstein also noted that Nellie "lands up" while Harbison "lands down." Hammerstein further suggested "link Nellie-Harbison w/ Nellie de Becque," observing that Nellie will marry de Becque and that she was "not good enough" for Harbison. These notes, and some to follow, indicated Hammerstein's initial, and briefly sustained, interest in retaining Harbison as a central character. Hammerstein also made a note about the appearance of de Becque's daughters in the story.

In his only note on "Dry Rot," Hammerstein suggests combining the character of Joe (not Joe Cable, but a shoemaker from Columbus, Ohio, who is the central character of the story) and that of "Professor" Hyman Weinstein. Weinstein is the sidekick of Luther Billis, who also impressed Hammerstein; "Professor" is retained as a minor, although memorable, character in the musical. Hammerstein, of course, also kept Billis, although he added elements of other characters and plots to his character. The principal plot of "Dry Rot," which Hammerstein might have considered as a subplot for Professor, is about how, through correspondence instigated by Billis, the shy Joe meets a young woman stateside and pursues an epistolary romance that ends sadly when the woman is killed in a car accident. Hammerstein ultimately rejected the melancholy story.

The notes for "Fo' Dolla'," which from the beginning was the principal story under consideration for adaptation, consist only of a list of the characters. For the story "Passion," Hammerstein again notes Harbison's presence. Harbison is only a secondary character in the story, however. As the censor of letters from enlisted men to their spouses and family, he brings a particularly vivid—to his mind, almost pornographic—letter to Dr. Paul Benoway, the consulting physician on the island. Benoway discovers in the letter an expression of married passion that he envies; it is an expression that suggests to him that he is incapable of true passion, and this realization disturbs him. Later, after reading a letter by Harbison, Benoway goes so far as to copy a passage from it into a letter of his own only to recognize that, as an expression of himself, it reads false. But Harbison's letter reveals a passion otherwise missing from his character, and this quality might have impressed Hammerstein as he sought to create a three-dimensional persona as a foil for de Becque.

"A Boar's Tooth" provides more details of Luther Billis and reveals Americans' reactions to the islanders' religious practices at the Boar's Tooth Ceremony. Hammerstein notes that "Cable could go on [a] trip with Billis, [Tony] Fry to Boar's Killing." Hammerstein indeed sends Cable and Billis on the trip in *South Pacific*—Tony Fry is not in the musical—but only Billis attends the ceremony, which is offstage. Cable instead meets Liat, and their love story ensues.

No notes have been found for either "Wine for the Mess at Segi" or "The Airstrip at Konora." The first concerns a humorous Yuletide escapade by Adams and Fry to procure whiskey, and the second, the construction of an airstrip needed for the "Alligator" operation. While Hammerstein made no notes on either story, the second story has a subplot featuring Luther Billis, his status as a "big dealer," and his extremely loose relationship with military rules and regulations. This story almost certainly influenced Hammerstein's final characterization of the souvenir-seeking Seabee. But neither story lent itself to adaptation.

Michener briefly brings back Harbison in the story "Those Who Fraternize," and Hammerstein again noted Harbison's name, indicating his continued interest in the character. He also wrote "Harbison lower," referring to Harbison's appearance in the story, and he even drew a box around the phrase. Drunk, disruptive, and eventually violent, Harbison, by now a lieutenant, appears in the story waving a pistol and yelling rude comments. After a skirmish with Bus Adams, he disappears from the narrative, which is mostly concerned with de Becque's beautiful grown daughters, none of whom appear in the musical.

For the story "The Strike," Hammerstein simply noted the presence of Bus Adams. "Frisco" is another story that did not have notes. It is an atmosphere piece in which battle-bound soldiers reminisce about their various experiences on leave in San Francisco, and the short tale is Michener's last example of the waiting that occupies so much of so many stories in the book. Here, the soldiers entertain each other to prevent themselves from being overcome with fear. The story is extremely effective but does not lend itself to dramatization.

3.4. *Victory: American soldiers in the South Pacific, World War II.*
Courtesy of Photofest.

A. Grove Day called "The Landing on Kuralei" "Michener's full-dress battle piece," the result of all the waiting that has gone before.[54] Because it is concerned with the battle, it did not fit into the foreground of the stories Hammerstein initially considered for his musical. Hammerstein did, however, provide a brief, and familiar, note: "Harbison." In this story, a recounting of the battle toward which the book has moved, Michener informed the reader of Harbison's fate. After almost perpetually complaining about his noncombat assignment, Harbison quickly pulls strings to get sent back to the States when he finds out that he is actually about to face battle. Harbison's downward trajectory, already noted by Hammerstein, is complete. He has slowly but steadily fallen from golden boy to coward, his actions bitterly recalled by a shell-shocked unit leader. This recurrence and development of a character throughout the stories, which is one argument that the work is indeed a novel, as Michener maintained, also provided Hammerstein with a model of how to take a single character from one story and work it into other stories, creating a linear and developmental narrative. The irony is that Harbison, whose name appears more often than any other character's in Hammerstein's notes, barely survives the transition from book to musical.

While no notes for the final story, "The Cemetery at Hoga Point," exist, Hammerstein here learned the tragic fate that Michener had in store for many of the characters. Cable, for instance, dies a hero's death, haunted until the end of his short life by his affair with Liat.

After studying the book for several months and making these and no doubt other notes, Hammerstein, almost certainly in cooperation with Rodgers, decided that the Nellie Forbush–Emile de Becque romance should be the principal plot and that the Cable–Liat–Bloody Mary story should be secondary. Conflating these stories presented a problem, however. Both plots were serious, and this, as Rodgers later wrote, "was against the accepted rules of musical–play construction," adding, "If the main love story is serious, the secondary romance is usually employed to provide comic relief."[55] The earlier musicals of Rodgers and Hammerstein that were adapted from other sources adhered to this practice. In *Oklahoma!*, for instance, the principal story of Curly, Laurey, and the ominous Jud was offset by the comic story of Ado Annie, Will, and Ali Hakim, the "Persian" peddler. *Carousel* exploited a similar structure, as did the film *State Fair*. Even in these shows, however, the sets of characters are not as stereotyped as Rodgers's comment might imply. Curly and Laurey begin as a comically bickering couple, for instance; their romance takes on substance only as the musical progresses and Jud's threats intensify. And in *Carousel*, the secondary couple Carrie Pipperidge and Enoch Snow is indeed comic; but Snow also has a nasty edge that reveals a condescending classism. (*Allegro*, written between *State Fair* and *South Pacific*, was sui generis, following a structural path previously and subsequently unexplored by the team.)

The structural challenge posed by the two "serious" plots was overcome in the early stages of development. This was accomplished in several ways. First, Rodgers and Hammerstein connected the two principal stories with plot elements drawn from "The Cave." A mission that brought Cable and de Becque together worked to connect the plots and the characters specific to each. Second, Rodgers and Hammerstein used Bloody Mary as a figure not only in the Cable–Liat romance, as she is in "Fo' Dolla'," but also as a connection to the comic character Luther Billis. For this, they drew on elements of "A Boar's Tooth" and on additional material later provided by Michener, who commented, "I played no role in the adaptation, except for writing, at [Joshua] Logan's request, some narrative accounts of how the rowdy Luther Billis might operate as a wheeler-dealer, and as an afterthought I suggested that he would probably run a laundry of some kind, and maybe have a shower."[56] Michener's additional material, when joined to the story "A Boar's Tooth," made it possible to include Billis in both principal plots and to introduce comic elements into them. In addition to making Billis a comic foil for Bloody Mary, for instance, Hammerstein eventually has Billis infatuated with Nellie, which is both touching and comic. Finally, Rodgers and Hammerstein created serious characters that were also believable when caught up in the comic sub-plots. Ethan Mordden explained:

> Nellie is fundamentally a comic character who is put through a serious test, and, despite Emile's operatic grandeur, much of their story is the stuff of musical comedy, charm, and high spirits, from the pensively sunny "A Cockeyed Optimist" to the spoofy "Honey Bun." What R&H did to tradition was less to vary it than to neutralize it, finding the humor in the deep people and the tragedy in the light.[57]

Rodgers and Hammerstein's balancing of humorous and tragic qualities in their characters was made possible through the expert interweaving of the various plots retained from their source.

Primarily drawn to two stories that appeared in a book without a chrono-logical or linear structure, Rodgers and Hammerstein were forced to make critical choices concerning content and structure early in the creative process. These choices resulted in a work that was based on a source without being imitative of it. The process was not always smooth, and many paths proved to be wrong turns. But in the end, Rodgers and Hammerstein's first attempt at adapting a book for the musical stage was, and continues to be, a stunning success.

4

FALSE STARTS

• • •

The Disappearance of Bill Harbison and Dinah Culbert

While Rodgers and Hammerstein had some initial difficulty piecing together a linear narrative plot from Michener's plotless and episodic book, they were also challenged by the book's basically anti-theatrical theme of inaction: each of Michener's stories is in some way evocative of the agonizing wait between the battles that Michener describes as occurring around great stretches of inactivity, boredom, and restlessness.[1] This, they knew, was not the stuff of theatrical drama, and their challenge was to lift characters, relationships, plots, and subplots and reassemble them into a dramatic structure. In other words, deciding on two principal sets of characters and surrounding them with an array of other colorful characters was only the first step. Even after deciding which stories and characters to draw from, Hammerstein was left with the challenge of connecting those stories and characters in a newly constructed narrative. He also had to find opportunities for believably expressing the characters' emotions, inner thoughts, and relationships in songs central to the various dramatic conflicts. This was a slow process, and several of the important early sketches and drafts for *South Pacific* are false starts that emphasize characters of little consequence to the finished work. Two of these characters, Bill Harbison and Dinah Culbert, are important to Michener's novel and are among the principal concerns of this discussion, along with their dwindling importance to, and appearances in, the final script.

As demonstrated earlier, Hammerstein made notes about the character Bill Harbison throughout his reading of Michener's novel; however, he made no notes about the nurse Dinah Culbert. But early drafts suggest that she, too, initially impressed him as a character worth developing. The treatment of these two characters in early drafts for *South Pacific*, and their eventual reduction to little more than bit parts, offers an insight into Hammerstein's ability to narrow the focus of his work until it is excised of any superfluous material. While Harbison and Culbert at first seemed like promising secondary characters that could enrich and propel the primary plots, Hammerstein's notes demonstrate that he soon realized both were dead ends and fundamentally extraneous to his central concerns. In particular, an early draft for 1.1 demonstrates how the inclusion of Harbison pointed Hammerstein toward a path that was ultimately best left untaken. Nonetheless, examination of this early draft and others, unexplored in the extant literature on *South Pacific*, reveals at least one area of social criticism—the growing importance of the junior executive in corporate America—that was on Hammerstein's mind in the postwar era. And tracing the rise and fall of Harbison and Culbert as characters in *South Pacific* offers further insight into the process of adapting a wide-ranging source into a finely focused musical play.

HARBISON, DINAH, AND NELLIE

Hammerstein's initial interest in Bill Harbison is unsurprising. Harbison is the first character in Michener's book with leading-man potential, and this is apparent as early as the fourth paragraph of "An Officer and a Gentleman," the story in which he first appears. Michener tells the reader that, while in college, Harbison was an outstanding athlete and popular with his fraternity brothers and with sorority women; he was, "in short, the kind of man the Navy sought . . . an officer and a gentleman."[2] A few pages later, Michener reveals that the enlisted men serving under Harbison respect him and his athletic prowess and that they often demonstrate this by considerate and/or supportive gestures, bringing him fresh fruit for his breakfast, making a diving mask for him, and watching with pride as he leads his basketball teams to victories. When not demonstrating his athletic skills, he stays in touch with the world at home through reading *Time*, *Life*, and the hometown Denver *Post*, although his finding *War and Peace* "hard to follow" suggests to the enlisted men that perhaps he is no more highbrow than they are.[3]

In between playing basketball games, taking swims in the ocean, and reading and censoring letters from enlisted men to their loved ones at home, which is one of his principal duties, Harbison, like everyone else on the small island where he is stationed, waits. And waits. When he is introduced, Harbison has not seen action, and within three weeks of arriving on the island, he applies for a transfer, reminding his commanding officer that he joined the army to fight a war. He is denied the transfer, however, and spends most of each day exercising, reading, listening to the radio, and writing letters to his wife. After receiving repeated denials for a transfer, he stops asking and accepts the idleness and the frustration of waiting.

Up to this point, Harbison seems almost perfect. He soon makes junior grade lieutenant and is only nine months from being a full lieutenant. His principal contributions to his unit, apart from adequately doing his job as censor, were his trim appearance and exemplary self-discipline, and, perhaps most important, "the fact that he found a French plantation owner who would butcher steers at regular intervals." Yet throughout this portrait of what seems to be a nearly ideal officer, Michener repeatedly brings forth Harbison's one glaring character fault: he is smug and vain and, despite how the enlisted men perceive him, he thinks himself superior to all those around him. Further, he is envious of his brother-in-law, to whom he also feels superior, because the brother-in-law is rising faster in the army's ranks than Harbison is rising in the navy's. For a considerable time, this sense of entitlement and superiority remains concealed just beneath Harbison's tanned and trim exterior. One important event changes all that, however, and it soon puts Harbison on a trajectory that moves him further and further outside the range of a romantic leading man in a musical. As Michener reveals, "Everything would have turned out all right for Bill if a slight accident hadn't intervened."[4] That "accident" was the arrival of nurses on the island.

Harbison's relationship with the nurses begins magnanimously, and he continues to deport himself as a gentleman even as he flirts with the nurses. Although his behavior might suggest that he is married or, to use a term from the time, "a pansy," he nonetheless withholds information concerning his marital status.[5] Eventually, Harbison starts spending time with one particular nurse, Dinah Culbert. Although she holds Harbison in high esteem, Dinah is otherwise an unlikely candidate for his attention. She is not particularly attractive and she is forty-two—Michener's Harbison is twenty-three, although he is usually played older in the musical—so Harbison is able to ingratiate himself and still avoid the snares of romantic entrapment.

While Harbison and Dinah's ongoing togetherness inspires talk among the other nurses, the situation continues amicably until Harbison learns that his loathed brother-in-law has risen to the rank of major. This sets Harbison into a tailspin of anger and self-pity. "He was going nowhere," Michener notes, "and he had given up a good life in Albuquerque to do so." His perception of Dinah subsequently changes from benign to resentful. As a "safe" older woman, she now reinforces what Harbison perceives as his lack of stature. Harbison's change of heart toward Dinah is immediate and revealing: before long "it was common gossip at the hospital that Bill Harbison, the fine naval lieutenant, had joked about Aunt Dinah as his Grandmom."[6] Dinah is blithe and accepting of Harbison's less than gallant behavior, however, and she thinks, "I pity the next girl he goes with."[7] The next girl is Nellie Forbush, a twenty-two-year-old nurse from Otolousa, Arkansas (not Little Rock, as in the musical).

While Nellie eventually becomes the central female character in *South Pacific*, she is a secondary character in "An Officer and a Gentleman." Nonetheless, she made a strong impression on Hammerstein. Indeed, the relationship between Nellie and Harbison remained a part of Hammerstein's plan for the musical's plot well into the initial drafting of the script. To Harbison, though, Nellie is little more than a nice young catch that offers far more prestige than the older Dinah. Not long into their dating, Harbison attempts to rape Nellie, an act that she thwarts with a well-aimed coconut to his head. Somewhat surprisingly, the dating survives this. Shortly thereafter, on another outing, Harbison's physical advances are welcomed and Nellie allows him to begin undressing her. However, several things occur to prevent the consummation of their passion. First, as Harbison undresses Nellie, an islander appears on the usually deserted road and interrupts the action. The interruption gives Nellie a moment to reconsider, and she starts to put on her clothes with renewed resolve. She tells Harbison that she loves him, that she wants him, and that she is not afraid of him. Then, as he again starts to undress her, she offers what, at that moment, is the ultimate anti-aphrodisiac: she asks him if they might get married after the war. His thoughts in response to her query, which he sees as a proposal, reinforce his unsympathetic egotism. "He knew Nellie was his for the asking, but damn it all she was nothing but a country girl. Hell, he wouldn't look at her twice in the States." He reminds himself that he is an officer, after all, and the story ends with a smug Harbison pleased with himself for having turned down one of the most desirable nurses on the island. As he self-satisfactorily slaps himself in the stomach, however, he notices the first signs of fat. It is the beginning of his decline.[8]

Between Harbison's attempted assault on Nellie and their final encounter, Michener further develops Dinah and her friendship with Nellie. Nellie comes to her for advice about Harbison, confessing her love for him and asking Dinah if he is married. Dinah does not know, and she tells Nellie it never was of much interest to her. After acknowledging her awareness that Harbison had used her simply "to fill a need in himself," she is blunt with Nellie: "Bill is a snob. Nellie, you may not like this, but it would be as impossible for Bill to marry you as it would be for him to marry me."[9] She further notes that Harbison's feelings of superiority make his marital status irrelevant to her or to Nellie.

Later, in "Our Heroine," the story that provided Rodgers and Hammerstein with the romantic story of Nellie and the French planter Emile de Becque, Michener explores the growing closeness between the two nurses.

After the "proposal" to Harbison that ends their short relationship, Nellie thinks about why she enlisted and why she was excited to travel to the South Pacific. She also remembers telling her boyfriend that she would come home to him. But, Michener observes, neither she nor her boyfriend, who was 4-F and thus unacceptable for military service, believed what she said. [10]

In Dinah, however, she had a kindred spirit. Both women craved new experiences and shared "a lust for sensations."[11] When Dinah is ordered to a different island to help establish another hospital, she asks for Nellie to be sent to the new hospital as well, and they are reunited. Dinah remains Nellie's confidante, and when Nellie meets de Becque on this new island, Dinah encourages Nellie in her struggle against the prejudice that almost, but not quite, tears her away from de Becque. In short, Dinah, in Michener's book, has an important and influential relationship with Nellie, and it is understandable that Hammerstein would initially see it as a relationship worth preserving.

The next glimpse of Harbison's decline is also in "Our Heroine." While the romance between Nellie and de Becque is the focus of the story, it is enriched in part because Nellie still has feelings for Harbison. He has none for her, however. At this point, Harbison is drinking a lot and has lowered his standards in women, moving from Nellie to a not very smart but sexually available woman, and from her to a divorcée cognizant of his marital status. Another officer observes that Harbison is having "serious girl trouble in the South Pacific," and in a later story Harbison bursts into the salon of a plantation, firing a pistol and bellowing, "Where's the girls?"[12] When Nellie meets de Becque, her connection with Harbison is immediately severed, and the rest of Harbison's appearances in the novel are unrelated to Nellie in particular or to any romantic involvement in general.

In "The Cemetery at Hoga Point," the final story, Michener discloses that when Harbison was actually called to action his reaction was less than heroic. A unit commander recalls that Harbison, through the political machinations of his father-in-law, arranged to be sent back to the United States four days before his unit was to see combat for the first time: "when our orders came through he got white in the face. . . . Right now he's back in New Mexico. Rest and rehabilitation leave."[13] By the end of the novel, Harbison completely lacks any potential as a romantic figure. Harbison's early involvement with Nellie and her subsequent interest in de Becque initially suggested a romantic triangle to Hammerstein, as discerned from his notes about the book, and he was at first drawn to Nellie's emotional maturation as opposed to Harbison's disintegration. Certainly, Harbison's connection with Nellie brought him into the focal area of what became the musical's principal plot. Hammerstein was uncertain quite how to put Harbison into that plot, however, and his early attempts to do so are among the least-known stages in the development of *South Pacific*.

In the early draft for 1.1, Hammerstein demonstrates his initial interest in retaining the Harbison–Nellie relationship, although the draft also demonstrates that he was not quite sure what to do with it. This lengthy draft is unmentioned in any of the literature and reveals that, while Hammerstein initially planned to retain Harbison, he also intended to make considerable alterations to his character. Before exploring those alterations, however, a few observations are in order about how Hammerstein exploits the tension between Nellie and Harbison.

In the final version of 1.1, Nellie returns to the base at the end of a long scene with de Becque, after which de Becque has a quiet moment with his children. They reprise "*Dites-moi*," the number that opened the show, and the scene ends.[14] In the draft, however, Hammerstein's stage directions indicate that de Becque and Nellie are startled from their romantic reverie by the entrance of Commander Bill Harbison and Lieutenant Joe Cable. Nellie immediately greets Harbison, and de Becque comments that they must know each other. As Cable subsequently acknowledges Nellie without an introduction, Harbison, his gaze fixed on Nellie, responds caustically to de Becque that yes, he knows Nellie. He then adds that he was unaware de Becque and Nellie were on such good terms. After Nellie asks to use Harbison's jeep and driver to return to the base, and Harbison agrees, de Becque accompanies her to the vehicle, leaving Cable and Harbison alone. As Cable makes them a drink, Harbison impulsively calls after Nellie, "Give my regards to that 4F back in Arkansas—if you ever write to him again." Nellie responds, "Thanks, Billy Boy. And remember me to your poor wife back in Detroit, will you?"[15] Hammerstein's change of Harbison's residence from Albuquerque to Detroit is worth noting and was probably made because Detroit was more important as a center of business and industry. The importance of big business to Hammerstein's initial characterization of Harbison will soon be clear.

The ensuing dialogue between Cable and Harbison suggests they have known each other for a while. This, too, is at odds with the final script, in which Cable first arrives on the island in 1.2. In the draft, however, Harbison and Cable seem quite comfortable with each other. Indeed, Harbison is comfortable enough to comment that he has recently made moves on Nellie. Cable says he remembers, further establishing their acquaintance. Harbison continues, telling Cable that he was faring well with Nellie until someone told her he was married. He suggests that the information chilled their relationship, and that Nellie is now seeing de Becque to get back at him. At this point, the conversation turns to the spy mission for which Cable and Harbison have come to seek de Becque's advice.

Another demonstration of Hammerstein's intention to retain the Harbison–Nellie conflict, and the friendship between Dinah and Nellie, is in an important draft for 1.4, later 1.7.[16] This early draft for 1.4 is also informative because it challenges the previously accepted chronology of the musical's development. At the top of the first page, Hammerstein wrote "old" and underlined it. As in its revised version, the scene opens on the beach and reveals a homemade shower, indicated by signs as the property of Luther Billis. At the beginning of this version of the scene, we see a group of nurses, including Nellie and Dinah, exercising under the rather stern leadership of "Lieutenant" Harbison. The reference to "Lieutenant" Harbison suggests that either this draft is even earlier than the draft for 1.1 or that Hammerstein had a memory slip regarding Harbison's rank; in the draft for 1.1, Harbison is referred to as "Commander," and that is his rank in the final version of the script.[17] The stage directions reveal that as the nurses continue the demanding regimen, Harbison "is especially tough on Nellie, as a rejected boy-friend would be." After the exercises, Nellie and Harbison have a terse exchange regarding de Becque. Harbison sarcastically suggests that de Becque might be spying on Nellie through a telescope. (Hammerstein follows up on this comment later in the draft.) Ignoring the comment, Nellie asks him why she earlier had been interrogated about de Becque by a commanding officer. Harbison "stiffly" responds that he cannot tell her and exits with several admiring nurses. Nellie comments to Dinah, identified in the script as Nellie's best friend, that Harbison is a "stuffed shirt." Dinah responds that she likes the way his shirt is stuffed, adding, "I'm looking for an officer who isn't too much of a gentleman," thus providing a subtle reference to the Michener story that tells of their relationship.

Hammerstein's relaxed and intimate three-page dialogue scene for the two women after Harbison's exit is a clear demonstration that he initially planned to retain Dinah's importance to Nellie and to the story line. For instance, Nellie confesses to Dinah that de Becque has proposed to her and that she does not how what she is going to do about it. Recalling a scene in "Our Heroine" in which Nellie tells Dinah about her mother's advice concerning the romance,[18] Nellie says that her mother must have sensed from her letter that Nellie was serious about de Becque: her reply was uncharacteristically immediate. The reply was also intuitive. Although Nellie had made no mention of marriage in her letter home, her mother's reply clearly states that she has no objections to her daughter marrying an older man.[19]

Dinah's comments in this scene about Harbison, and about men in general, also suggest that Hammerstein saw in her the potential for a secondary comic character. For example, Dinah remarks that she thinks she scares men: "I think they're afraid if they start anything with me, I'll make them finish it. Nothing scares a man more than that!" Nellie then asks about the "little Seabee" who is love with Dinah, but Dinah replies that, as an officer, she cannot fraternize with enlisted men and that, even if she were willing to break the rule, "Billis has more respect for me than even the Navy requires." This is the first mention of Luther Billis in any of the drafts. In the final version, Nellie is the recipient of Billis's unrequited adoration, but this scene implies that Hammerstein might have been exploring Dinah and Billis's possibilities as a secondary, "comic" couple to contrast with the principal "romantic" couple. This is further suggested by the reference to Billis as "little" and by his subsequent appearance and brief dialogue scene with the two women.

Hammerstein's notes indicate that Billis's initial appearance in the story "Dry Rot" made an impression. By the time Hammerstein began writing the script, Billis had already become a composite of several characters from the novel. From the beginning, however, this composite was a comic character, and Hammerstein's exploitation of him in this draft as a foil for the man-hungry Dinah is consistent with his later use of Billis as a straight man for the comical side of Bloody Mary. (Cable and Liat, Mary's daughter, bring forth her maternal and more serious side.) Although he often appears to be a brash if generally unsuccessful con man constantly outsmarted by the shrewd Bloody Mary, Billis is shy around Dinah. He brings hot water from his laundry service, thinking that Dinah might use it to wash her hair. When she says she washed it the day before, Nellie immediately asks if she might wash hers. After setting up the shower, Billis leaves, shyly telling Dinah that her laundry will be finished that night.[20] The women continue discussing Nellie's relationship with de Becque as Nellie prepares to wash her hair in what was to become one of the show's most famous musical numbers.

"YEA, SISTER"

According to Joshua Logan, "I'm Gonna Wash That Man Right Out-a My Hair" was conceived approximately a week before rehearsals began and Rodgers "had an instant tune" for it.[21] Yet the sketch for 1.4 suggests that perhaps this isn't quite the way it happened. For instance, in the draft, Nellie begins washing her hair fifteen lines before the music begins.[22] During this, the dialogue between Nellie and Dinah continues. Nellie expresses her doubt

4.1. *"I'm Gonna Wash That Man Right Out-a My Hair." Mary Martin and members of the original Broadway cast. Courtesy of Photofest.*

concerning de Becque, arguing that she knows nothing about him and that he might be something other than the cultivated and romantic figure he seems to be. Dinah then suggests that Nellie terminate the relationship. She tells Nellie that if there is any doubt, Nellie should cut the strings sooner rather later. Nellie agrees, at which point *Dinah* begins a musical number that becomes a duet, not the solo with chorus that it is in its final version.

Quoting the advice of the cook from her high school, Dinah begins speaking, and then shifts into singing:

> If you ask the man right
> And his answer ain't right,
> If he don't look right
> And he don't love right,
> Then somethin' must be wrong.
> And nothin' can be wronger than a man who's wrong![23]

These lines, for which no music exists, are not in the final lyrics of "I'm Gonna Wash That Man Right Out-a My Hair." But Dinah's next lyrics are.

They introduce the contrasting "blues" section after the first full chorus of the finished number ("If the man don't understand you, / If you fly on separate beams," etc.).[24] Here, however, Hammerstein refers to them as the refrain. Dinah continues with words that again suggest the blues section of the finished number ("If he never buys you flowers / Or a box of chocolate creams," etc.). Only at this point does Nellie join the number. The stage directions note that she is "beating time with her elbows against the sides of the shower and stamping her feet rhythmically, ad libbing a chant that fits the spirit of Dinah's refrain," indicating the spontaneous nature of the song. (The reference to "Dinah's refrain" is worth noting. The number does not yet belong to Nellie.) Nellie's "ad libbing" consists of lyrics similar to those that, in the later version, end up as the bridge of the first chorus ("Don't try to patch it up, / Tear it up, tear it up!" etc.). Dinah adds, "Yea, sister! / Cancel him and let him go!" After this, Hammerstein noted, "Nellie, in the home stretch of her shampoo now ad libs an appropriate extension," which, finally, is the familiar, "I'm gonna wash that man right out-a my hair." The number then continues in its familiar form, the second eight measures stating, "I'm gonna wave that man right out-a my arms," followed by previous lyrics that here, and in the final version, serve as the bridge ("Don't try to patch it up," etc.). The final eight bars of the draft use lyrics not in the final version—"I'm gonna live that man right out-a my life." However, instead of ending the number with a big finish, which would generate applause, and following it with a reprise, as in the final version, Hammerstein has Nellie repeat the last eight bars as de Becque enters and catches her singing.[25] When she realizes his presence, her voice dies off and the song fades out without really ending.[26] After noticing de Becque at the end of the song, Nellie notes the "coincidence" of his "just happening to walk down the beach" while she was there. De Becque tells Nellie that his appearance is no coincidence. He explains that he saw her through his telescope, a comment that recalls Harbison's sarcastic reference to a telescope earlier in the scene. Dinah interjects herself into the conversation, and de Becque invites the two of them to dinner the next Friday. Dinah offers Nellie an out by suggesting that she will accept the invitation only if Nellie does, too. Nellie responds that she will talk to de Becque about it, and de Becque and Nellie leave.

Having Nellie and de Becque exit in order to continue the discussion of their relationship suggests that Hammerstein was uncertain about what to do with this scene, in particular the section between two numbers featuring Nellie. In this early version, Nellie's true feelings are revealed only after she reappears in the scene. By the January 21 draft, de Becque and Nellie at this point have an extended romantic scene in which she undergoes a change of

4.2. *Mary Martin, mid-shampoo. Courtesy of Photofest.*

heart suggesting that, instead of wanting to dismissively wash de Becque out of her hair, she feels a love for him that is transformative. Geoffrey Block provides an excellent analysis of this section's problematic development during tryouts and of the multiple musical transformations it underwent.[27]

Clearly, "I'm Gonna Wash That Man Right Out-a My Hair" did not burst forth already in its inspired final form, as Logan's recollections imply. Instead, it appears to have been one of the earlier numbers conceived by Rodgers and Hammerstein. Further, in the draft, "I'm Gonna Wash That Man Right Out-a My Hair" is at least as expressive of Nellie and Dinah's friendship as it is of Nellie's state of mind, and most of the song's original ideas are Dinah's. While the earlier version provides the excuse for the onstage shampoo, it also indicates that Nellie's ideas and feelings are as much influenced by Dinah as by her own self-conviction, thus diverting the emotional focus from Nellie and diverting the musical focus from Mary Martin, one of the stars of the show. Regardless of Martin's star status, however, the need to redirect the scene's dramatic focus is apparent—Nellie is not convincing as a parrot of Dinah's

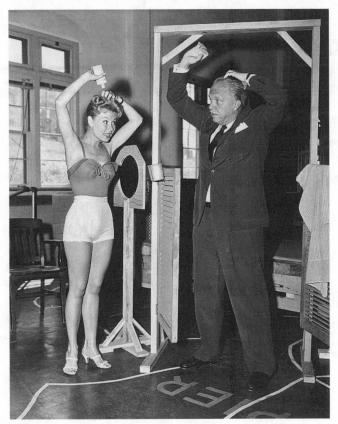

4.3. *The director Joshua Logan rehearses the famous shampoo scene with Mitzi Gaynor for the 1958 film. Courtesy of Photofest.*

advice. Unfortunately, their friendship became increasingly incidental to the plot as the writing continued. Hammerstein eventually realized that the decision to wash de Becque out of her hair had to be Nellie's. Only then did the scene have the dramatic potential for Nellie's emotional transition, and that transition is the core of the ensuing part of the scene that Hammerstein eventually wrote.

In the draft, the nurses enter as Nellie and de Becque exit. Hammerstein seems immediately aware of the contrived nature of this entrance: Dinah asks, "Say, where did all of you *come* from, anyway?" Inconsequential dialogue transpires during Nellie's absence; it ends when Dinah observes that relationships between people as opposite as Nellie and de Becque usually don't work, after which she again begins the verse of "I'm Gonna Wash That Man Right Out-a My Hair." Nellie's entrance interrupts the reprise and, after a brief bit of dialogue informing the nurses that she has changed her mind about de Becque, she begins "I'm in Love with a Wonderful Guy."

Joshua Logan recalled that this number was originally sung to the nurses, who remained onstage, and that it was turned into a soliloquy for Nellie when he realized that it wasn't working.[28] The draft supports this. However, the appearance of the song in the draft is somewhat problematic. The original typed pagination is 1–4-13, but a 4 is handwritten over the 3 in 13, indicating either that a page was added or that a simple typing error was made. (The previous page of dialogue during which Nellie enters is 1–4-13.) Further, 1–4-14 contains handwritten rewrites. At the top of the page, for instance, is a handwritten stage direction, "Nellie laughs," although what she is laughing at is unclear from the previous page. Beneath this, the draft has typed dialogue that is not clearly related to what is on the previous page. These two discrepancies perhaps suggest an added page is missing. A few lines later, the stage direction "Dinah puts her arm around Nellie protectingly" is crossed out and, in the right-hand margin, Hammerstein has penciled in an added speech for Nellie: "Go ahead and kid me. Nothing can make me mad now. I—I've got a feeling I'm all set." Dinah cracks, "You ought to see your hair, baby!" and Nellie begins to sing.[29] At some point, Hammerstein realized that Nellie, not Dinah, must be the emotional energy and focus of the scene, and he eliminated Dinah's protective quality. Nellie is on her own, and that includes acceptance and expression of her love for de Becque. Dinah still gets the last wisecrack, at least for the time being.

"I'm in Love with a Wonderful Guy" begins as it does in the final version and continues so through "Any fable I hear from a person in pants!" Then Nellie addresses the nurses still onstage with lyrics that are slightly different from those of the song's final version.[30] The chorus also scans somewhat differently; in the third and fourth lines, instead of the familiar, "No more a smart little girl with no heart," we find the somewhat awkward, "I'm no longer a smart / Little girl with no heart." Both versions are followed by "I'm in love with a wonderful guy!" The chorus draft continues with metrically awkward phrases that, like the original third and fourth lines, were rewritten to provide a much tighter match of words and music. The lyrics that finish out the chorus also contain discrepancies with the final version, perhaps suggesting that they, too, were eventually adapted to fit better with Rodgers's melody. At this point the nurses have a featured chorus, something unmentioned in any of the accounts of the number. After Nellie's chorus, the script indicates a section for "Dinah and the Girls (Imitating The Andrews Sisters)"; beside the indication, Hammerstein wrote "Interlude" in pencil. The lyrics, which, again, don't quite scan to any extant music for the song, are as follows:

> She's as normal as school in September
> Or an unattached leaf in November
> Or a snowflake that falls in December
> Or an ostrich's tail on a fan.
> She's as sweet and as dumb as [a] bumpkin.
> Any girl who is that kind of chump, kin
> Get as plump as a Halloween pumpkin,
> Sitting home every night with a man.

Nellie then begins the second refrain of the song and is joined by the nurses "in a vocal arrangement,"[31] after which Hammerstein wrote additional, and anticlimactic, dialogue for Nellie, Dinah, and the other nurses.

The awkwardness of the scene between the two musical numbers, the exit of Nellie and de Becque that creates the need for that scene, and the weak scene that follows the climactic "I'm in Love with a Wonderful Guy" support the argument for this being among the earliest drafts for the show. This argument is further strengthened by the drafts for the two musical numbers, both of which underwent extensive rewriting. Indeed, the presence of "I'm in Love with a Wonderful Guy" in the draft supports Joshua Logan's memory of "I'm in Love with a Wonderful Guy" as being among the first musical numbers written for the show,[32] but the presence of "I'm Gonna Wash That Man Right Out-a My Hair" in such an early incarnation challenges his dating of that number as a later creation.[33] This draft is also the most extended treatment of Dinah in the sketches and drafts for the show. As the script became more focused, Dinah was increasingly incidental, and by the time the show opened, she was little more than another one of the nurses. Curiously, even her last name was eventually changed from Culbert to Murphy. Hammerstein provided no mention of why this change was made.

THE BRIGHT YOUNG EXECUTIVE

Now that Hammerstein's initial explorations of Dinah and Harbison's respective relationships with Nellie have been examined, in addition to Dinah's possible comic relationship with Billis, an exploration of his treatment of Harbison apart from Nellie is possible. This also occurs in 1.1. The draft for this scene, which continues for twelve pages after Nellie's exit, introduces a target of social satire absent from the final script. While his aim is on the mark, Hammerstein eventually decided that it was an unnecessary extension of

4.4. *Discussing the mission. From left, William Tabbert (Cable), Martin Wolfson (Brackett), Harvey Stephens (Harbison), and Ray Middleton (de Becque). Middleton replaced Ezio Pinza in 1950. Courtesy of Photofest.*

a taut and well-made scene. The draft is illuminating on several accounts, however, and bears investigation. First, it is the only place in Hammerstein's work where he focuses his satirical skills on American business practices in such detail, and, second, it provides us the opportunity to examine a completed lyric to a song for which no music exists and that is previously unmentioned in the literature. The scene after this song also provides evidence that Hammerstein had created more script before Joshua Logan's input than previously realized, although little of it turns out to have been usable.

In the draft for 1.1, as noted earlier, Nellie and Harbison have a brief bickering exchange during her exit. When Nellie is gone, and Harbison comments to Cable on his earlier relationship with her, the conversation turns to de Becque. After revealing that he and Cable are visiting de Becque to discuss a "top secret job," Harbison questions de Becque's loyalty to the resistance. He bluntly asks Cable how they can be sure that de Becque is actually on their side. Cable is somewhat annoyed by Harbison's comment and tells Harbison that de Becque has been actively thwarting the Japanese since before the Americans arrived on the island; he adds that the Free French have weapons hidden throughout the hills in the event of an invasion. After Harbison asks if de Becque had been forthcoming with this information, Cable, taking maps out of his briefcase, tells him that U.S. intelligence made a thorough investigation of de Becque before considering him as a participant in the mission. At this point, Harbison steers the scene in an unexpected direction by commenting, "Well, I'm always leery of these European bozos. . . . They're always making a botch of their own affairs, and then calling us in to straighten them out."[34]

Ignoring a brief interjection by Cable, Harbison continues and, in doing so, reveals where Hammerstein is taking the scene. Harbison suggests to Cable that the problem with Europeans is their lack of American organizational skills. Cable responds with a sarcastic and rhetorical question—"Do you really think that's it, Bill?"—but Harbison pays no attention. Instead, he asserts that the war will be won by "the American executive type" that stands at the helm of U.S. industry. He continues, "And let me tell you something else you've got in your country! You've got a bunch of young men, coming up—fellows being trained to move into top executive jobs later." Harbison, whose reference to the United States as "your country" and not his own is a bit confusing, expresses his disappointment that Cable is a lawyer and not a businessman; he mourns that Cable will never know the thrill of working with a group of "live-wires" like the men in the company he works for. After Cable sarcastically comments, "Key men! Trouble shooters!" Harbison responds, "Funny, you're using that word. That's what the gang in our firm calls me—the trouble shooter." He then begins to sing.[35]

The song that follows is a complete, although untitled, draft for which no music exists. However, it possibly would have been called "The Bright Young Executive of To-Day," given the appearance and repetition of that phrase within, and at the end of, each chorus. But the surmised title is far less interesting than the song's content. Harbison begins the verse noting that, after the war, he will again be happily "working under the watchful eye" of Woodcock Nordlinger, his boss. Cable reiterates "under his watchful eye," and Harbison refers to Nordlinger's "piercing look" as he finishes the introduction. He then launches into the first chorus, which quotes Nordlinger:

> The hope of the world
> Is the well-trained, wide-awake,
> Bright young executive of to-day.
> The cream of the crop,
> Is the clean-cut, confident,
> Bright young executive of to-day.
> No feather-brained romancer,

Before he'll give an answer,
The facts and all the figures he'll survey!
So bet all you can borrow
On the man of tomorrow—
The bright, young executive of to-day![36]

De Becque returns during the beginning of the above chorus, and Joe exchanges glances with him, indicating that it might be fun to encourage Harbison's harangue. To that end, Cable begins a trio section in which he lists other occupations, all of which Harbison dismisses as trivial in comparison with the executive's job. The artist, for instance, is a "screwball and a bohemian." In what is perhaps a good-natured self-portrait, Hammerstein has Harbison observe that the writer "goes for walks in the country, / Plays with dogs and smokes a pipe."[37] After criticizing the farmer as "a rube," the actor as "a cad," and the teacher as "a boob," Harbison complains that the laborer is "money-mad!" Hammerstein emphasizes this final criticism—de Becque repeats it as a question, and Harbison repeats it yet again as an exclamation, to which de Becque sardonically quips to Cable, "The laborer, too?" Harbison responds, "I admit we need all kinds of men—" and Cable jumps in to complete the trio, "But not one tenth as much / As the peppy executive type / With the organizational touch!"[38]

Hammerstein gives the next chorus to Cable, noting that Cable "sings the refrain as earnestly as Bill [Harbison], and Bill is unaware of any satirical intent." Cable envisions a young executive in the exclusive Rainbow Room at the top of the R.C.A. building, where he makes quips about new cars and further demonstrates his business acumen. In this chorus, Hammerstein provides some mildly off-color humor as well; after Harbison notes that the young executive "Doesn't go off half-cocked! / His eye is on the ball," Cable responds, "And now and then, like mortal men, / He doesn't go off at all!" Hammerstein adds in parentheses that Harbison is oblivious to the humor as Cable picks up the chorus "con-spirito." Together, the three men continue the final chorus and bring the song to a rousing finish.

Harbison's song warrants inspection for two reasons. First, it provides a rare example of a completed Hammerstein lyric that can be read without any musical association. It reveals how much rhythmic and stylistic information Hammerstein provided in a lyric. For instance, the verse implies the feel of a march, and the chorus reinforces this feel. This march could be in 6/8 meter, the first "when" occurring on an anacrusis, or pick-up:

(beat)   6   / 1–2 3   4   5 6 / 1–2 3 4–5 6   / 1–2 3 4   5 6 / 1, etc.
6/8   When / I   get out of a / un- i- form Will / I   be hap-py a-/ gain, etc.

The same verse could also imply 4/4 meter, which, in turn, could also imply a march:

```
(beat) 4     / 1 2  3   4 + / 1   2 3    4   / 1 2 3    +   4 / 1, etc.
4/4    When / I get out of a / un- i-form Will / I be hap-py a- / gain, etc.
```

Rodgers wrote that he often deviated from the metrical suggestions found in Hammerstein's lyrics, however, so uncertainty exists as to what he might have done or how he might have altered the lyric to fit an altogether different musical idea.[39] (For example, the lyric also scans in 3/4 meter.) After indicating that he often changed Hammerstein's metrical suggestions, moreover, Rodgers added that, although Hammerstein "was not a musician, he did possess a superb sense of form"—the verse–chorus structure is apparent, for instance, as is the repetitive phrase "the bright young executive of to-day"— and that their working method created songs that "not only were right for the characters who sang them but also possessed a union of words and music that made them sound natural." Within the finished score for *South Pacific*, however, this song does nothing for the plot, and the character is one-dimensional, so, unsurprisingly, its musical content probably never got beyond the so-called dummy melody that Hammerstein created from bits of preexisting tunes while writing lyrics.[40]

The second interesting aspect of this song is that Hammerstein's lyrics for Harbison reflect a growing postwar concern with, and criticism of, the expanding executive class in American business. Hammerstein's inclusion of this social criticism, which is not found in Michener's work, indicates that he was aware of this concern and that he initially found it interesting and/or important enough to include in *South Pacific*. Although Hammerstein's response to this social issue was ultimately eliminated from the musical, its presence in his thinking at the time is worth exploring.

The three most important books that discuss this changing aspect of the American business world actually appeared after 1949 and therefore after the creation of *South Pacific*—David Riesman's *Lonely Crowd* appeared in 1950, and C. Wright Mills's *White Collar* and William H. Whyte Jr.'s *Organization Man* both appeared in 1956.[41] Several articles by Mills, however, anticipated the appearance of his, Riesman's, and Whyte's books. The most notable of these is his article "The Competitive Personality," which appeared in 1946 and which is the most relevant to this discussion.[42] Similarities between phrases found in Mills's article and in Hammerstein's draft, and some of the comments Harbison makes in the draft, suggest the possibility that Hammerstein was familiar with Mills's work and his concern with the new type of executive he called "the bright, young . . . new entrepreneur."[43]

"Executive" can be defined, as Mills and Hammerstein used the term, as (1) the presidents and vice-presidents of corporations who were in place before the war and, (2) the younger and highly driven group of men determined to rise from middle management.[44] In "The Competitive Personality," Mills provided an in-depth consideration of those middle managers rising to the status of executive; these are his "new entrepreneurs." He contrasted them with the old guard of business, already in power, and with those who remain stuck in the rigid structures of middle management. He found the future of the latter somewhat bleak: "At the center of the picture is business bureaucracy with its trained managerial staff and its tamed white-collar mass. And it is within these structures of monopoly that the bulk of the middle-class men and women must make their prearranged ways."[45] Against this "unheroic backdrop of big business and the white-collar mass," Mills began his discussion of the new entrepreneur:

> In contrast to the classic little businessman, who operated in a world opening up like a row of oysters under steam, the new entrepreneur must operate in a world in which all the pearls have already been grabbed up and are carefully guarded.
>
> The only manner by which the new entrepreneur can express his initiative is by servicing the powers that be, in the hope of getting his cut. . . . He gets ahead because men in power do not expect that things can be done legitimately, because these men know fear, because their spheres of operation are broader than their capacities to observe, and because they are personally not very bright.[46]

Mills's second paragraph, especially, recalls Hammerstein's Harbison, whose pleasure in serving Nordlinger is suggested by stage directions mentioning Harbison's eyes "gleaming in soulful recollection" as he begins the verse.[47] Harbison further sets up the chorus of the song by describing the pleasure he got when Nordlinger—"We call him W.N.," Harbison notes earlier—gave him "extravagant praise / And followed it up with a nominal raise."[48] Harbison's need for Nordlinger's approval—that is, from "the powers that be," as Mills puts it—is pronounced, and it supports Mills's further suggestion that, "as a competitor, the new entrepreneur is an agent of the bureaucracies he serves, and what he competes for is the good will and favor of those who run the business system."[49] This also recalls Harbison's mention of Nordlinger's gaze in the song's introduction. In other words, Nordlinger's "extravagant praise" (and "watchful eye") is more important to Harbison than the "nominal raise." Further, in the essay Mills observed, "he [the new entrepreneur] is a live-wire, full of American know-how, and if he does not invest capital, his success is all the greater measure of his inherent worth."[50] This is comparable to Harbison's comments that Europeans "haven't got our [American] know-how" and that he works with "a bunch of live-wires" at his firm. Harbison's increasing exuberance shows that he, too, is a "live-wire," thus demonstrating Mills's description of "the frenzy of the new entrepreneur."[51] Finally, Harbison's description of himself as "the trouble shooter" is not unlike Mills's repeated descriptions of the new entrepreneur as a "bureaucratic fixer" who eases the way for those above him.[52]

Harbison's dismissal of non-executive jobs in the song's trio demonstrates an attitude common to young executives in 1949. This attitude was among those discussed by William H. Whyte Jr. in his article "The Class of '49," which appeared only several months after *South Pacific* opened on Broadway. In a discussion of the "vocationalization" of higher education, Whyte observed:

> This vocationalized schooling has produced a class that on the whole has little regard for the arts—either as spectators or participants. The work of the artist satisfies few of '49's criteria for spiritual security; the artist is "too much wrapped up in himself" and his contributions to the community too obscure. Even for the intellectual of the class the creative role seems unrewarding.[53]

In partial explanation of this trend, Whyte also noted the drop in college students studying the humanities. In 1929, for instance, 27 percent of the college students surveyed by *Fortune* "majored in either English, philosophy, the classics, modern languages, or history; ten years later the figure had dropped to 17; today [1949], it is down to 10."[54] Harbison's values certainly reflect this trend.

Although *South Pacific* is set during the war, the characteristics Hammerstein attributed to Harbison are more reflective of the postwar type defined by Mills. While no known smoking gun exists to indicate that Hammerstein knew Mills's article, it appeared in the *Partisan Review*, a journal not outside the realm of Hammerstein's intellectual and political spheres.[55] Further, as Irving Horowitz later noted, Mills had "an extraordinary ability to communicate with professional and popular audiences alike."[56] What's more, Mills's approach is sympathetic with Hammerstein's liberal political and social beliefs, as Horowitz notes:

> For Mills, power as the realization of human will remains the critical axis about which the social commonweal spins. . . . The forms of power vary, the fact of power remains a constant. Because of this, one can objectively study the industrial power of employers over employees. . . . In short, the

settlement of the sociological question of how men interact immediately and directly entails research into questions of superordination and subordination, elites and masses, rulers and ruled, in-groups and out-groups, and members and non-members. This is the fertile ground upon which Mills' sociology proceeds.[57]

This is what Hammerstein, in a much more lighthearted way, was exploring in his song for Harbison. His interest in this matter is unsurprising, although his inclination to spoof it perhaps is. In *Allegro*, the musical preceding *South Pacific*, Joe Taylor is not a "bright young executive" like Harbison,[58] but his experiences with corporate organizations place him in a world similar to Harbison's, and he rejects it. In the end, Taylor does not conform to a corporate-determined image of success; he is a man who eventually remains true to his core values, which are also among the core values of Hammerstein's idealized America—personal integrity, a sense of community and a strong individual identity, and a desire to help others, to mention a few. These values were challenged in the postwar United States, and Harbison presented Hammerstein with the opportunity to comment on the situation. In his reflection on the 1950s, the historian David Halberstam noted, "This new threat to the human spirit came not from poverty but from affluence, bigness, and corporate indifference from bland jobs through which the corporation subtly and often unconsciously subdued and corrupted the human spirit. As they moved into white-collar jobs, more and more powerful people felt . . . that they had less control over their lives. Here was a world where individuality seemed to be threatened and the price of success might be ever greater conformity."[59] Hammerstein's sense of dramatic unity was stronger than his need to express this particular sociological observation, however, and the song, in addition to Hammerstein's exploration of its subject matter in the early stages of writing *South Pacific*, was excised.[60]

"A LABORIOUS PROCESS"

The draft for 1.1 does not end with Harbison's song. After the number, the focus returns to the mission mentioned earlier. Cable reminds Harbison of a top-secret plan to put Cable and some islanders ashore on a nearby Japanese-held island; from this vantage point, Cable can relay by radio the movement of the Japanese fleet, and the Americans can fire on the ships as if they were fish in a barrel. De Becque already knows the details of this mission. Cable indicates that de Becque has already lined up the islanders, for instance, and, a few lines later, Cable reveals to Harbison that he and de Becque have already talked through the initial plans. Reiterating his earlier suspicion of "European bozos," Harbison looks sternly at de Becque and asks if he is going on the mission. This is followed by "an awkward pause," after which Cable insists that de Becque is not going, and the discussion turns to how Cable will get onto the island. That is solved easily enough, but when Harbison inquires what the plans are to get Cable off the island, Cable responds that there are none. He observes that if he relays his position to a rescue team, the enemy will also learn his whereabouts. "We'll just have to take a chance on that part of it," Cable suggests. "See what happens."

At this point, despite Cable's protestations, de Becque decides that he will go along on the mission. Affirming that he knows the jungle almost as well as the natives do, and that he is a good shot, de Becque argues that a team could last longer than an individual. Cable and Harbison question his decision, and Harbison specifically wonders why de Becque would put his life in danger when he possesses such a beautiful plantation. "Yes, I have all this," de Becque responds. "To-day I have even begun to want—more than all this. But Joe wants what *he* likes in the world. And he must risk to lose it. It is the same for all who believe the same." This moves Harbison and, after he fumbles the pronunciation of "monsieur," de Becque insists on being called Emile. Harbison, referred to again by Hammerstein as the "usually articulate, bright young executive," replies that his coworkers refer to him as W. W., and Hammerstein noted that Harbison "can't help seeming proud of this, even at this time." The young man then tells de Becque that the Frenchman is "okay," they shake hands, and Cable and Harbison exit several lines later.[61]

After Cable and Harbison leave, the scene ends much as in the final version of the script, but without the return of de Becque's children.[62] The stage directions in the draft indicate that de Becque sings, "as in soliloquy," three lines of "Some Enchanted Evening," after which he picks up the demitasse from which Nellie had drunk her coffee. "Lipstick," he comments, as in the final version. "Three lumps of sugar! Three lumps of sugar in a demitasse!"[63] As he laughs softly to himself, the scene ends at the point where, in the final version, de Becque's children enter.

The draft for 1.1, as earlier suggested, and the draft for 1.4 contain several convincing indications of having been written very early in the musical's development. Hugh Fordin has written that Hammerstein found the initial work on the book for *South Pacific*, as he did for most shows, "a laborious process." Fordin continued, "This adaptation [*South Pacific*] proved particularly difficult and Oscar was finding it slow going during the summer [of 1948]."[64] Joshua Logan, who by the summer of 1948 was set to direct the show, recalled in his memoirs that, around that same time, Richard Rodgers suggested that Logan visit Hammerstein. According to Logan, Hammerstein "had only finished the first scene and an outline," although two pages later, Logan noted that Hammerstein had written the first scene, "a couple of exciting pages later, on the meeting of Cable and Liat," and "I'm in Love with a Wonderful Guy" for Nellie to sing "to her fellow nurses in an unwritten scene." He also suggested that Rodgers had composed the music for "I'm in Love with a Wonderful Guy."[65] If the music and lyrics for "I'm in Love with a Wonderful Guy" were indeed finished at this point, the draft for 1.4 indicates that they later underwent significant change. Nonetheless, all sources agree "I'm in Love with a Wonderful Guy" was one of the earliest numbers written.[66] But what of the scene that contained it? The reference to Harbison as a lieutenant in the draft is either a mistake, as noted earlier, or indicates that this is an early draft; the revisions of "I'm in Love with a Wonderful Guy" support the early dating; and the prominence of Dinah in both the scene and the eventually much-altered "I'm Gonna Wash That Man Right Out-a My Hair" further indicate the draft was an early endeavor.

Logan's mention of the first scene having been completed in the summer of 1948 is important, as is one of the reasons he and others give for Hammerstein having trouble with the script: Hammerstein knew nothing about the military. According to Logan, Hammerstein had confessed, "I hate the military so much that I'm ignorant of it."[67] Logan, on the other hand, was familiar with the military; he had served in the army during the war, and subsequently cowrote and directed the postwar military comedy *Mr. Roberts*.[68] He came on board as a cowriter, at first just to help Hammerstein with the military issues and, soon thereafter, to contribute to the dialogue. Hammerstein's self-proclaimed ignorance of the military is apparent in the draft for 1.1. For instance, early in the draft he uses the title "Commandant" for an officer in the United States Navy.[69] This error probably would not have occurred after Logan's contributions as writer. Further, the plan for Cable's mission, and certainly the lack of plan for his rescue when it was finished, does not sound like an actual military maneuver; Hammerstein is decidedly out of his element in the section of the scene where Cable presents the plan, whereas later versions of the script and descriptions of the mission reveal greater familiarity with military jargon and protocol.[70]

De Becque's premature decision to go on the mission with Cable further supports the early dating of the draft for 1.1. In the draft, for instance, de Becque decides to go with Cable on a virtual suicide mission because he has just fallen in love with Nellie, which makes little sense; in the final version, he decides to go when he thinks he has lost her, which is much more convincing.

At some point, Hammerstein and/or Logan realized that de Becque's decision would have greater dramatic effect if it occurred later in the story, where it could offer more psychological insight into de Becque.[71] In fact, the later scene is the turning point of the entire musical. De Becque's decision in 1.1 to accompany Cable indicates that Hammerstein had not clearly thought through the structure of his plot or the emotional conflicts of his characters.

Other problems exist with the draft of 1.1, apart from its superficial characterization of Harbison and its inappropriately timed introduction of the surveillance mission. After the romantic and intimate musical scene preceding it,[72] Nellie's exit is anticlimactic and, especially, unflattering; what's more, it gives Harbison the last word. The characterization of Nellie was never without apparent blemishes—her racism, for instance, is more blatantly drawn in several earlier drafts and sketches for the play and was later toned down by the creators—but this caustic and, to those in the audience unfamiliar with Michener's book, unmotivated banter is unnecessary and reveals nothing of any importance about Nellie. It is also a weak exit for the costar of the show. In the final version of the scene, Nellie tells de Becque that she will think about his proposal, after which, the stage directions read, "They are silent and motionless for a moment. Then she turns suddenly and walks off very quickly."[73] De Becque is left alone, at which point the children enter and the audience first learns they are de Becque's. It is a picture of tender domesticity, and it ingeniously gives a rounded feeling to the scene, which also began with the children. Having Harbison and Cable enter before Nellie's exit, and continuing the scene, destroys the memorable and romantic mood of all that goes before. And it is the romance of what goes before and the conflict that grows out of it that became the central focus of the entire work. Anything obscuring that focus was extraneous, and it ultimately disappeared.

5

YOU'VE GOT TO BE CAREFULLY REWRITTEN
• • •
The Distillation of Racial Intolerance

The overall exuberance of postwar U.S. society was tempered by increasing realizations of the country's institutionalized racial inequality, and some of the responses to this inequality were expressed in American musical theater. Indeed, while *South Pacific* is probably the best-known musical from 1949 to deal with race and racial intolerance, it was not the only such work. In the same year, for instance, the New York City Opera became the first major American company to perform a musical theater work—in this instance, an opera—created by African Americans. Featuring a score by William Grant Still and libretto by Langston Hughes (with additional text by Still's wife, Verna Arvey), *Troubled Island* concerned the Haitian revolution of 1791 and Jean Jacques Dessalines's subsequent rise to power. Dessalines served as independent Haiti's first ruler before crowning himself emperor for life in 1806. "For life" turned out to be a short rule, however, as Dessalines was assassinated that year.

Troubled Island received a generally favorable reception from audiences, but the critics were less enthusiastic, and the work was pulled from the company's repertory after three performances. Tammy R. Kernodle has observed that, after the withdrawal of *Troubled Island*, Still and his wife embraced several conspiracy theories regarding the reasons for its disappearance. For instance, Kernodle noted that Still and, especially, Arvey suspected the New York critics of writing bad reviews specifically to prevent the work of an African American composer from achieving critical success. Further, Still feared that some of the reviews might have been motivated by conservative critics' disapproval of librettist Langston Hughes's well-known leftist ideas. After noting the problems with these theories, Kernodle suggested that another reason for the work's mostly negative critical reception might have been U.S. critics' overall indifference to American opera.[1] Yet another possibility—one that was not mentioned by Kernodle—is that, in the racially charged postwar environment, an opera depicting a violent black despot's overthrow of a white

European colonialist government was somewhat unnerving to the United States' white cultural and social hegemony. Whatever the reasons, the opera disappeared.

A third work from 1949 that deals with race is somewhat better known, although Maxwell Anderson and Kurt Weill's *Lost in the Stars*, like *Troubled Island*, was a critical and commercial disappointment. Unlike *Troubled Island*, however, the musical has a connection, albeit once removed, with *South Pacific*: it was none other than Dorothy Hammerstein who, in 1947, first suggested Alan Paton's novel *Cry, the Beloved Country* to the playwright Maxwell Anderson. In March of 1948, she gave Anderson a copy of the book; he, in turn, introduced Weill to it.[2] Concerning Anderson's response to Paton's book, which is a powerful exploration and indictment of South Africa's particularly odious system of apartheid at the time, Ronald Taylor wrote, "Long before he put the book down, Anderson knew that here was something for him, something that not only raised fundamental moral issues in the conduct of human affairs but also had an immediate and painful relevance to the state of race relations in contemporary America."[3] Despite their similar themes, however, *Lost in the Stars*, unlike *South Pacific*, is almost unremittingly serious. Taylor commented that "the heavy morality in which Anderson shrouds the final scene . . . turns the work into nothing so much as a humanist sermon on a text of trust and optimism."[4] The word "shrouds" is telling: it suggests a show out of sync with the ebullient spirits of postwar American audiences. Those spirits were more receptive to Rodgers and Hammerstein's sermon on a similar theme, packaged as it was in a brighter wrapping. In mid-November of 1949, almost a month after *Lost in the Stars* opened, Weill wrote a letter to the critic Olin Downes, commenting, "It must be somewhat surprising indeed to find a serious subject treated in a form which (in this country at least) has been used so far only for a lighter form of entertainment."[5] Despite its serious message, *South Pacific* does not appear to have been weighty enough for Weill.

Notwithstanding their differences, all three productions reveal that race and racial inequality were very much present in American works for the musical stage in 1949. *South Pacific*, in particular, recalls the NAACP's 1947 petition to the United Nations declaring, among other things, "It is not Russia that threatens the United States as much as Mississippi."[6] This statement was especially ironic after World War II, given that the United States fought on two fronts to overcome regimes based at least in part on beliefs of racial superiority. As Wendell Willkie, the Republican nominee for president in 1940, noted during the war, "Our very proclamations of what we are fighting for have rendered our inequities self-evident. When we talk about freedom and opportunity for all nations, the mocking pathos in our own society becomes so clear they can no longer be ignored."[7] This irony was not lost on many others in the United States, and it remains prominent in writings about World War II. For instance, in his 2006 book *Choices under Fire*, the historian Michael Bess investigated moral aspects of World War II that, he argued, were more ambiguous than contemporary conventional wisdom acknowledges or remembers. "World War II," he suggested, "was not a race war, but it was—to an extent that is often overlooked—a conflict in which race played a central role, from start to finish and in every theater of combat."[8] Regarding race in the United States during the war, another of his observations strongly resonates with the thematic core of *South Pacific*:

> America's participation in World War II was supposed to be about fighting fascism and aggressions, and about defending the values of equality and freedom that the Western democracies had written into their constitutions and their way of life. But in the cases of Japanese-Americans and African-Americans, we find a profound contradiction between these ideals in theory and their actual enactment in practice. Both these groups faced pervasive forms of injustice and discrimination.[9]

To be sure, Americans were primarily fighting to prevent further Japanese attacks on their country and to thwart German aggression in Europe. But the enemies on both fronts were also overtly racist, and Americans' confrontation with their own racial intolerance while fighting those enemies, particularly the Japanese, provides the underlying conflict in *South Pacific*. Bess's comments reinforce that it was also an underlying conflict in the United States during and after the war.

As postwar anticommunist fervor grew more strident, however, expressions of any sentiment that challenged the status quo, racial or otherwise, had to be carefully worded; difficulties awaited those who spoke without caution. For example, in his 1949 Paris speech at the Congress of World Partisans for Peace, the African American singer and a ctivist Paul Robeson suggested that the racial policies of the United States were "similar to that of Hitler and Goebbels."[10] This was enough to get Robeson's passport declared invalid when he returned to the United States, thus preventing him from again leaving the country. A few years later, the teacher and author Jonathan Kozol was fired from the Boston public school system for teaching the Langford Hughes poem "Ballad of the Landlord," a bitter criticism of the imprisonment of an African American for challenging an unfair system.[11] In other words, while the movement for racial equality was present in 1949, its voice was often hushed by the cold war agenda. Mary Dudziak summarized this situation as follows:

> The Cold War would frame and thereby limit the nation's civil rights commitment.... By silencing certain voices and by promoting a particular vision of racial justice, the Cold War led to a narrowing of acceptable civil rights discourse ... [and] kept discussions of broad-based social change ... off the agenda.[12]

Of course, civil rights discourse in the United States was mostly framed in terms of blacks and whites, an observation that is pertinent to *South Pacific*. The "black/white paradigm," noted Dudziak, "renders other racial groups invisible."[13] But the opposite also proves correct: when that paradigm is removed and other racial conflicts are emphasized, the power of the dominant discourse is refocused. Their attention to a racial binarism other than black–white enabled Rodgers and Hammerstein to make general points about racial intolerance without directly involving the most inflammatory intolerance—that between white Americans and African Americans—and thus made their message "safer" in the postwar political climate. The conflicts between an American and an unseen Polynesian (Nellie and de Becque's first wife), or an American and a young Tonkinese girl (Cable and Liat), seem removed from the principal racial conflicts in the United States and therefore are more acceptable to a mainstream audience. Further, Michener was concerned with the Americans' racial intolerance of the islanders, not of each other, and the stories most critical of that racism—"Our Heroine" and "Fo' Dolla'"—were the stories that Rodgers and Hammerstein used as the principal sources for their adaptation.

As work on *South Pacific* progressed, Rodgers and Hammerstein were not oblivious to the possibility of being criticized for their thematic choices, and they were not blind to a growing public suspicion of social criticism. They were also confident that their social commentary was critical to the work. But during the out-of-town tryouts, Rodgers and Hammerstein were approached by what Hugh Fordin referred to as "a group of 'experienced theater people'" suggesting removal of the song "You've Got to Be Carefully Taught." Fordin also mentioned that, concerning this incident, James A. Michener remarked, "The authors replied stubbornly that this number represented why they had wanted to do this play, and that even if it meant failure of the production, it was going to stay in."[14]

Rodgers and Hammerstein's commitment to "You've Got to Be Carefully Taught" notwithstanding, several New York critics unfavorably singled it out. Wolcott Gibbs referred to "something called 'You've Got to Be Taught,' a poem in praise of tolerance that somehow I found just a little embarrassing,"[15] and John Mason Brown noted that he was "somewhat distressed by the dragged-in didacticism of such a plea for tolerance as 'You've Got to Be Taught.'"[16] The controversy continued. On Sunday, March 1, 1953, during the national tour of the musical, an article in the New York *Herald Tribune* reported that "two Georgia legislators, who denounced the musical *South Pacific* as propaganda, vowed to introduce bills to outlaw movies, plays and musicals having 'an underlying philosophy inspired by Moscow.' . . . Rep. Jones said their charge of propaganda referred particularly to the song 'You've Got to Be Taught' which, he says, urged justification of interracial marriage." Hammerstein is quoted as responding that he did not think the legislators were "representing the people of Georgia very well."[17]

Despite the team's attraction to the theme of racial intolerance, however, and perhaps in anticipation of critical and popular discomfort with that theme, Hammerstein repeatedly subdued the play's criticism of prejudice throughout the creative process. He tempered the overtly confrontational tone of early sketches and drafts into a more moderate and, for the audience, less abrasive presentation of the thematic material. The changes in tone do not alter the message, however, and *South Pacific* remains a powerful indictment of what both men viewed as a flaw, albeit a fixable one, in U.S. society. The process of softening the impact of the show's theme reveals Rodgers and Hammerstein in complete control of all aspects of their art, including and, perhaps, especially the commercial element, which surely must have been behind much of the distillation of controversial material. The result is a work that, while somewhat restrained, nonetheless confronts the serious issue of racial intolerance at a time when that issue was largely absent from the commercial musical stage and other popular American art. While the 2008 Broadway revival reinstated some of the confrontational dialogue that made it as far as the first rehearsal script, other passages never got beyond earlier drafts and sketches.

Michael Bess suggested that this issue continues to challenge U.S. society, especially when it recalls World War II, and he provided an excellent entrée into the discussion that follows. He wrote, "The racism that marked the United States during these years [1941–45] was of a different order from that of the Germans and Japanese. . . . Yet it was there in all its ugliness—an important part of our history, which we must face and acknowledge."[18] Fifty-seven years before Bess wrote that, Rodgers and Hammerstein "faced and acknowledged" the issue in no uncertain terms. How they did so, and how they softened the presentation of their controversial "message" while maintaining its integrity, is the focus of what follows.

At the beginning of the story "Our Heroine," James A. Michener briefly let the reader think that Nellie Forbush is from Little Rock, Arkansas, when she is mentioned in a newspaper article from there. But, he added in the next sentence, the article was in a section of the paper containing "rural news."[19] This detail is important: the prewar South, in particular the rural south, was a unique region of the United States with unique problems. In his masterly work *Speak Now against the Day*, the author John Egerton provided a useful thumbnail description of the area and the time:

> The prewar South was still a peasant society. Barely one out of every six or seven farms had tractors to plow with or electricity to light their houses when the forties began. Half the nation's farm population lived here—and got by on a fourth of the farm income. . . . The region's primary industry was still textile manufacturing—an enterprise dominated by absentee ownership and characterized by hazardous, small-scale, low-wage sweatshops in which white women did most of the work. Double-digit unemployment plagued white men, and the job picture was twice as dismal for blacks.[20]

Just in case his readers think the conditions in urban areas were better, Egerton used equally bleak terms to describe Atlanta in 1935, by which time it was "widely regarded as a showcase of the progressive South." Despite this status, Egerton wrote, "More than a third of its households in 1935 were without indoor plumbing or electric lights or both, and the generally wretched living conditions caused thousands to suffer and die of illnesses now virtually unknown to us."[21] Prewar Little Rock was even more backward than Atlanta.

More specific to Nellie and her background are comments by the former Arkansas governor Sidney S. McMath, a progressive and pro-integration Democrat who governed from 1949 until 1953. Regarding Arkansas in the prewar years, McMath observed that much of the state had no electricity or water-development programs (which needed electricity) until several years after the war. Governor McMath added, "We had about twelve counties in the northern part of the state that didn't have a single hard surface road." McMath talked further about the corruption, political bosses, and blatant disregard for the rights of African Americans in prewar Arkansas. And yet, McMath continued, in language that recalls the theme of *South Pacific*, "after the war, we were motivated by the fact that we'd been fighting against this kind of thing [racial intolerance] that exists in, say, Garland County [Arkansas] and a

5.1. *Mary Martin and Ezio Pinza at the end of act 1. Courtesy of Photofest.*

lot of places over the country. If we're going to fight for it [racial equality] in the world, we want to fight for it at home."[22] McMath's observations about Arkansas provide a useful background for Nellie's struggle with her prejudice and her eventual triumph over it; they also suggest, as Michener does, how deeply that prejudice was rooted in the racist culture of Arkansas, in the South, and in Nellie.

Hammerstein removed the Otolousa connection and establishes that Nellie is from Little Rock. While to New York audiences in 1949 Little Rock still might have seemed remote and backward, it was a step up from rural Arkansas. Hammerstein also subdued the force of Nellie's racism, which is first demonstrated by an alteration to 1.12. This alteration is critical to how the audience perceives Nellie and her racism, and Hammerstein's rewrite put her in a decidedly less unflattering light. (This was probably with the blessing of Mary Martin, whose positive tomboy-next-door image might have been

5.2. *Richard Kiley (de Becque) and Meg Bussert (Nellie) harmonize at the end of act 1. From a 1985 Los Angeles Civic Light Opera production. Courtesy of Photofest.*

negatively affected by the scene's original language.) Only one small bit of dialogue was cut, but its absence from the script alters Nellie. The cut's effect is best observed by introducing its context within the scene.

The scene, which is the finale of act 1 and contains one of the work's most dramatic moments, reveals Nellie and de Becque slightly tipsy on champagne after a dinner party. They playfully sing some of Nellie's songs and harmonize for the only time in the show, after which they reprise some of the more serious "Twin Soliloquies" from 1.1. The mood again lightens, and, as de Becque parodies Nellie's "I'm Gonna Wash That Man Right Out-a My Hair," his children enter. This is the first time Nellie sees them or even knows of their existence. "You're the cutest things I ever saw in my whole life!" she exclaims. De Becque introduces them and sends them off to bed. Again alone with de Becque, Nellie calls them "adorable," noting their "big black eyes" and asking if they belong to Henry, de Becque's indigenous house servant. De Becque replies that they are his, and Nellie thinks it is a joke. She comments sarcastically,

5.3. *Mary Martin and Ezio Pinza at the end of act 1. Courtesy of Photofest.*

although playfully, that they look just like him and then asks, "Where do you hide their mother?" De Becque tells her that the children's mother is dead, and Nellie realizes he is telling the truth. He again states he is their father, and Nellie responds, "And—their mother—was a . . . was . . . a . . ." De Becque finishes the sentence for her with the word "Polynesian," and Nellie is literally stunned. "But you and she . . ." she says. De Becque remains calm, explaining that he wanted Nellie to know and that he has no apologies. Nellie, showing the combined effects of alcohol and shock, immediately starts trying to make her exit. She is graceless and hurried, and she begs de Becque not to accompany her to her jeep. Mumbling about how she will be too busy to call him in the coming week, she exits quickly as de Becque twice tells her that he loves her. When she is gone, and the sound of her jeep fades, he reprises the final four lines of "Some Enchanted Evening."[23]

In the first rehearsal script, Nellie's reaction is less evasive and comes closer to the reaction of Michener's character, although it is already greatly subdued. The dialogue in the rehearsal script is virtually the same through de Becque's response of "Polynesian." But then Nellie says, "Colored," to which de Becque replies that, yes, she was darker than either of them but that she was nonetheless beautiful.[24] Nellie's use of the word "colored" is jolting, which is unquestionably the effect Hammerstein wanted. Yet her response is far more restrained than that of Michener's Nellie. In "Our Heroine," Nellie learns of de Becque's children before he tells her and after she has already agreed to marry him and has informed the navy of her intention to do so. At a dinner, the pilot Bus Adams, not knowing of Nellie's romance with de Becque, regales the company with a bawdy story about a grown woman of somewhat loose morals who, by story's end, he identifies as de Becque's daughter. In the course of the story, he also reveals that de Becque has three other grown daughters by a different woman and four younger daughters who still live with him, each of a different mother. Nellie is stunned. At her next visit to de Becque's plantation, he introduces her to his four youngest daughters and tells her of his others, remarking, "I had to tell you first."[25]

At this point, trying to put her feelings into some kind of context, Nellie reminds herself that she left home to meet new people and have new experiences. Yet she is nonetheless revolted by de Becque's having lived with a Polynesian who, as we have seen, Nellie perceives as "a nigger." Further, she also describes de Becque's children with the same despicable term, reminding herself that "if she married him, they would be her step-daughters. She suffered a revulsion which her lover could never understand."[26] Because Nellie is convinced that de Becque cannot understand her feelings, she decides not to marry him. By the end of the story, and with the understanding support of her good friend Dinah, she changes her mind and decides to marry him, as in the musical. The strength of her prejudice is immense, and the expression of it is jarring in a character so likable. Her ability to overcome it makes her the true "heroine" of the story's title—the term, which has been bestowed upon her by the newspaper article mentioned above, is ironic until this point, in that she has done nothing even remotely heroic—and she ends the story triumphant.

Hammerstein obviously wanted to retain the power of Nellie's revulsion. While he had used the word "nigger" in *Show Boat* in 1927, the postwar racial climate in the country was quite different. Despite the word having been used in *Show Boat* by blatantly racist characters (or as a term that one African American character used for another, or for him- or herself), it has been problematic in all productions of the show since its premiere. (Hammerstein excised the word from the 1946 revival.) While the word "colored" was an appropriate and even polite term for African Americans in 1949—it had been part of the full name of the NAACP since 1909—within the context of a Rodgers and Hammerstein musical (and coming out of Mary Martin's mouth), it was still a surprise. The way Nellie uses the word makes her, for at least that moment, very unsympathetic.

Although Hammerstein's changes to the scene are understandable, especially considering the number of people who urged Rodgers and Hammerstein to cut "You've Got to Be Carefully Taught" even before the show opened, 1.12 is more powerful with the word "colored" and the more blatant presentation of Nellie's racism, as its reinstatement into the 2008 Broadway revival demonstrates. Frank Rich, writing in the *New York Times* soon after the revival opened, noted that the line "lands like a brick in the theater," adding, "It's not only upsetting in itself. It's upsetting because Nellie isn't some cracker stereotype—she's lovable. . . . But how can we love a racist?"[27] While the use of the word makes Nellie's transformation in the latter part of act 2 even more effective, it also reflects attitudes in U.S. society that many people were trying to ignore in 1949, attitudes about which Hammerstein felt very strongly and that American society eventually would be unable to avoid.[28] Of course, those also are the probable reasons that the word was excised from the script.

SOFTENING THE RHETORIC IN 2.4

The turning point of *South Pacific*'s plot is 2.4. It is not unlike the *anagnorisis* in a Greek tragedy, which is the moment of discovery or recognition at which a character, usually the protagonist, has a realization concerning some aspect of his or her life.[29] This scene contains, in varying degrees of intensity and detail, four such moments of discovery and self-recognition, and they all coincide to alter the lives of the characters and, subsequently, the course of the plot. Of course, *South Pacific* is not a classical tragedy, so the term, while useful, is used guardedly. Nonetheless, Nellie, de Becque, Cable, and, less dramatically, Billis are each propelled toward a self-awareness by the scene's end.

The scene was not always so rich with revelation, however. The development of 2.4 reveals its transformation from a highly polemical dialogue scene, rather perfunctorily followed by a song, to a less polemical and more tautly constructed bipartite scene that is the work's dramatic hinge. Part of Rodgers and Hammerstein's creative intent in *South Pacific* was to edify the audience without offending it, and 2.4 demonstrates how they partly succeeded with this intent—letters to Hammerstein suggest that people were indeed edified—and how they also partly failed—other letters and the reviews mentioned earlier suggest that the scene offended a substantial number of audience members. The scene's development also suggests a connection between Hammerstein's work for the wartime Writers' War Board (WWB) and the thematic content of the scene. Much of what was written during World War II by members of the WWB, including Hammerstein, was noticeably similar in content, and sometimes in phrasing, to what Hammerstein would subsequently write for *South Pacific*. The preliminary drafts for 2.4, a scene in which the characters climactically confront issues of racial intolerance, are especially reminiscent of WWB statements. Indeed, as Michener recalled, Hammerstein was attracted to the work partly because of its expression of ideas concerning racial intolerance, ideas sympathetic to those earlier espoused by the WWB. Before exploring the development of this scene, however, a familiarity with the 1949 version is necessary.

The second act up to this point has shifted between an onstage performance of the Thanksgiving Follies and backstage where, in 2.2, Cable has told Bloody Mary that he cannot marry her daughter, Liat. The third scene is again onstage and features the comic number "Honey Bun." The fourth scene returns backstage. After a brief dialogue scene between Billis and Nellie—he gives her a note from de Becque that obviously affects her—Billis exits, and Cable, who is still onstage from 2.2, speaks to Nellie about Liat, saying, "I love her and yet I just heard myself saying I can't marry her. What's the matter with me, Nellie?" Nellie replies that he's fine, that he's simply a long ways from home. She then adds, "We're both so far away from home."[30]

De Becque enters and confronts Nellie. (They have not spoken since the end of act 1.) Nellie tries to explain her feelings and why she has them. When she desperately argues that she was born prejudiced, de Becque angrily shouts his disagreement. She then asks Cable to explain how they feel, but he offers no support and she rushes off. When she is gone, de Becque asks Cable why he (Cable) and Nellie have such a feeling and why they believe it is born in them. "It's not born in you!" Cable responds. "It happens *after* you're born."[31] He then sings "You've Got to Be Carefully Taught."

Considering the importance of this number, both in terms of Cable's character and the show's principal message, and the controversy it subsequently provoked, its brevity is surprising. Fifty-two measures in all, its brisk tempo moves it by even more quickly; on the original cast recording, it takes all of one minute, seventeen seconds. The song's character—its quick tempo and nervous energy—reflects Cable's physical and mental condition: earlier in the scene, Nellie reveals that Cable has been in the hospital with malaria, and

5.4. *John Kerr (Cable), Mitzi Gaynor (Nellie), and Oscar Hammerstein II at the recording session for the 1958 film soundtrack. Courtesy of Photofest.*

throughout the scene he is agitated, unfocused, and, by the end of the scene, described as "delirious";[32] the stage directions also indicate that Cable sings the song "as if figuring this whole question out by for the first time."[33] Formally, "You've Got to Be Carefully Taught" is a variant of the familiar AABA structure common to many popular songs of the time. This form, and its variant, is what the musicologist Graham Wood calls "lyric binary" form, and its variants are what he calls "extended limbs." Because Wood's insightful classifications of Rodgers's song forms are used throughout the rest of this discussion, they should be introduced at this point.

Wood has created a typology of song forms used by Rodgers up to and including *Oklahoma!* The two principal forms are the lyric binary form (AABA, with the first two A sections acting as antecedent-consequent) and what Wood calls parallel period form (ABAC or ABAB, with the A sections acting as antecedents and the B and/or C sections acting as consequents). Further, many songs have "extended limbs," meaning that one or more sections may be longer than usual or that a coda is added; Wood listed other variants on the two principal forms, and they will be referred to as they are encountered.[34]

"You've Got to Be Carefully Taught" is an altered lyric binary form exhibiting expanded limbs—the first two A sections are sixteen measures long; the contrasting B section is eight, and the final A section eight plus a four-bar extension. Despite the length of the A sections, however, each is basically made up of one four-note, two-measure motive (a descending minor third, an ascending half step, and an ascending whole step: G-E-F-G) and a subsequent, and related, three-note, two-measure motive (a descending minor third followed by an ascending minor third: F-D-F).[35] The three-note motive lacks the passing tone between pitches two and four of the four-note motive. The rest of the song repeatedly recalls these motives, which are sometimes altered.

The constant repetition of, or reference to, this simple motive gives the song a singsong quality reminiscent of children's songs. This childlike simplicity is reinforced by the completely diatonic melody and simple harmony—the A section is accompanied solely by tonic and dominant ninth chords until the penultimate measure, at which point a supertonic chord replaces the dominant. This simplicity undergoes a subtle subversion, however. The straightforward triple time of the melody is set off by what initially could be heard as a duple pattern in the bass, reinforced by the offbeats in the string parts. Once the melody enters, the pattern is heard less ambiguously as triple. This contrasting relationship of duple and triple patterns recalls "Happy Talk," the childlike song that Bloody Mary sings several scenes before "You've Got to Be Carefully Taught," and it indicates Cable's confusion and uncertain emotional state.

The lyrics to this song refer to childhood and the lessons of racial intolerance carefully and successfully drilled into the minds of the very young. The melodic suggestion of a children's song is especially effective and ironic in this bitter context: Cable realizes that the lessons of his—and perhaps his country's—childhood, drilled and learned by rote, were full of bigotry and resulted in an intolerance he only now realizes. Like his earlier song, "Younger Than Springtime," "You've Got to Be Carefully Taught" is a song about discovery, the first sung in an almost childlike, if rapturous, awe, and the second in a bitter realization of lessons learned in childhood.

When Cable finishes the song, de Becque, after a line of dialogue, sings the bridge that was added to *South Pacific* after the show's Broadway opening. As noted in an earlier discussion, this was unusual, and it demonstrates that the refinement of 2.4 continued even after the show had been running for a while. An addition in the Hammerstein Collection is marked "4/10/50 'SOUTH PACIFIC—Insert immediately 'Carefully Taught" and contains de

Becque's line, "When I came here I was running away from ugliness . . . It has caught up with me." This is followed by lyrics that are now a part of the published score. They begin, "And the one chance for me / Is the life I know best," after which de Becque adds that he will stay on his island alone and "to hell with the rest!"[36]

After the song, Cable affirms de Becque's feelings, and then adds that, if he survives the war, he is returning to the island instead of going home. "All I care about is right here," he says. And then, echoing de Becque, "to hell with the rest." This rejection of, or turning against, society is a harbinger of Cable's fate: in Rodgers and Hammerstein's works up to this point, and in some that came after, the antisocial outsider, or the character who puts selfish interests above group interests, is treated with varying degrees of harshness. Cable's decision to leave the group—that is, American society—after the war is the kind of antisocial and anti-group act that, in a Rodgers and Hammerstein musical play, rarely occurs without some kind of a strong social reaction.[37]

Following Cable's speech, de Becque reveals that he, too, has had a change of heart. Unlike Cable, who wants to return to the island and to what he treasures most, de Becque realizes that, without Nellie, the island has no more meaning for him than does anywhere else. He walks away from Cable and muses aloud about how close he came to fulfilling his dreams. De Becque then sings his second solo song in the play, a slow waltz and trio titled "This Nearly Was Mine." This number is as reflective and elegant as "You've Got to Be Carefully Taught" is impetuous and edgy. Rodgers's use of contrasting songs in three-four meter for both characters is ingenious. Cable, the American, expresses his realization in a quick waltz that is complicated by the accompanying insinuation of duple rhythm. De Becque's waltz, however, is a straightforward and lyrical expression of an Old World sensibility that would not be out of place in an operetta from an earlier era.

After de Becque's song, Cable, sensing that de Becque has nothing to lose, again proposes the mission to him, and this time de Becque accepts. The tempo of the scene builds as they start to plan the details of the mission, and the two men run off to inform Captain Brackett that they are ready to undertake the challenge. After they exit, Billis appears. He has been listening to the two men, and, after taking a few moments to think it over, he runs off after them. His decision, the audience later learns, is to steal away on the flight taking Cable and de Becque to their mission; he thinks this is a way to reach Bali Ha'i and acquire souvenirs that he can subsequently sell to the soldiers and sailors on the base island. His totally self-serving actions actually, if inadvertently, contribute to the success of the mission. More importantly, this is the first time he is able to get to another island without the participation of an officer. Before, his ability to get to an island and its material goods (and women) was limited by his ability to get an officer to take him there; now, he is in charge of the situation and he is able to act independently.

The decision each man makes in this scene alters the course of his destiny and, the audience later learns, the war. And each man's decision, in addition to being based on an important new self-realization, is also related to American attitudes about race: de Becque is responding to Nellie's racism, Cable is responding to his own racism, and Billis's racism is apparent in that he sees the island inhabitants as little more than sources of material goods he can in turn sell.

There are seven sketches and/or drafts for 2.4 in the Hammerstein Collection. They will be referred to as 2.4A through 2.4G, and a brief description of each will be useful before closer examination. Sketch 2.4A is undoubtedly the earliest sketch, a simply constructed scene in which confrontational dialogue is followed by a parenthetical indication for a song. Sketch 2.4B is a so-called extra lyric for the song "My Girl Back Home"; it is dated January 22, not long before rehearsals began. Sketch 2.4C contains extra dialogue, later removed, before the song "You've Got to Be Carefully Taught." Sketch 2.4D, dated February 22, begins with a section of "You've Got to Be Carefully Taught" that was sung by de Becque and later cut. This sketch ends with the first and last sections of the song "Now Is the Time," which was also eventually replaced. Of particular interest is 2.4E, which is the scene as it appears in the first rehearsal script;[38] in this draft, the scene is already somewhat polished. Sketch 2.4F begins with new dialogue to follow "You've Got to Be Carefully Taught." This dialogue was kept in the final version of the scene. This sketch is also notable in that it contains the first reference to a song between "You've Got to Be Carefully Taught" and "Now Is the Time," which at that time ended the scene. After a speech for de Becque in which he tells Cable that one "cannot hide from life," the script simply indicates "Song." This song was eventually "This Nearly Was Mine." Finally, sketch 2.4G consists of a sung transition for Cable that leads into what was to be de Becque's intro to "This Nearly Was Mine."

In sketch 2.4A, the principal elements of the scene are already in place: the prejudice of Nellie and Cable; the argument whether this prejudice is born in an individual or learned; de Becque's feelings of loss and, subsequently, his arousal to action; and Cable's enthusiasm over de Becque's change of heart.[39] While it is undated, 2.4A contains no reference to any of the songs that eventually became important structural and dramatic elements of the scene; it refers only to one song at the end of the scene—"When a Man Makes Up His

Mind"—for which no music or lyric sketches are found. The similarity of the title to that of the subsequent "Now Is the Time," a song about making up one's mind, also suggests that this sketch predates the composition of that song. Another indication that this is an early sketch is the tone of de Becque's dialogue with Nellie, which is more confrontational than the final version of the scene.

For example, after Nellie admits that she cannot marry de Becque because of his having been married to a Polynesian woman, she acknowledges, as she does in the final version of the scene, that her reasoning is emotional, not rational. She argues, her voice rising, that these feelings are born in her and that she cannot help them. Emile angrily protests, and Nellie then admits that maybe these ideas were taught to her. What follows is unique to the draft. De Becque asks what Nellie is doing in the war. This throws her, and de Becque continues, asking why Americans are fighting and getting killed "by people you seem to agree with." He suggests that they all return to the United States and sing themselves to sleep with songs about people being "created free and equal." Nellie seeks support from Cable, but none is forthcoming, and she exits.

The first difference between the final version of the scene and this early version is that, in 2.4A, the revelation that prejudice is learned is Nellie's, not Cable's. Her line, "Bred in me then—taught to me since I learned to walk," anticipates Cable's speech that begins, "It's not born in you," which introduces his song. Each version makes the connection between learned prejudice and childhood. Hammerstein ultimately took these observations away from Nellie and, instead, gave her a solo scene later in the act (2.10), in which she realizes the error of her thinking.[40] Hammerstein retains Nellie's acknowledgment that her prejudice is emotional and not rational, however, and her exit in both versions is prompted by Cable's lack of support.

The second and more powerful difference between the sketch and the final version, and between the sketch and Michener, is de Becque's angry speech. In the sketch, de Becque criticizes not just Nellie, but also U.S. society and its prejudices. He attacks the hypocrisy of bigotry in a society that prides itself on freedom and equality, and the harshness of his words stuns Nellie. The equating of America's racism with the enemy's undoubtedly would have shocked an American audience as well. In the final version of the scene, this speech was eliminated, and de Becque's protest is reduced to two sentences arguing that prejudice is not born in people.

The initial version of de Becque's speech, and the idea stated by Nellie (later by Cable) that perhaps children learn prejudice, is similar enough to the content of several items written for the WWB—items found in the Hammerstein

Collection at the Library of Congress—to warrant closer inspection. The first passage is from the "Third Annual Report of the Writers' War Board" and is a continuation of the quote given earlier:

> The Writers' War Board believes that the sense of superiority harbored by large sections of American people toward smaller groups on the basis of skin color, religion, or national extraction is closely lined with native American fascism. These distinctions, which tend to create groups of second-class citizens, are often perpetuated by well-meaning persons who do not realize that they weaken the fabric of democracy.[41]

The term "native American fascism" is especially powerful at a time when the United States was fighting fascist regimes on two fronts.

De Becque's line about Americans killing people they seem to agree with, which clearly equates Americans with the enemy, recalls an unpublished book review from the WWB also found in the Hammerstein Collection. (This review, on official WWB paper, is a suggested newspaper editorial; the WWB supplied such editorials for local newspapers across the country.) Its presence among Hammerstein's papers, and its similarity in tone to de Becque's speech, suggests the possibility that the anonymous review was written by Hammerstein. At the very least, its presence in his papers argues for his familiarity with it. This review not only equates prejudiced Americans with the enemy but also suggests Nellie's, and later Cable's, lines about the influence of adult prejudice on the young. The similar emphases of the sketch and the following passage from the review are worth noting:

> [Prejudice is] the most virulent enemy that has appeared on the home front. It is impossible to read this book without realizing that any citizen who either speaks or acts out of prejudice against fellow citizens belonging to minority groups is warring with the United States as truly as are Goebbels, Goering, and Hitler. . . .
>
> It has been our observation that *the minds of young people are not apt to be poisoned by prejudice unless the poison has been prepared by adults.*[42]

These passages from the WWB are from a time when Hammerstein's work for the stage—specifically, *Oklahoma!* and *Carousel*—was not directly concerned with such issues. Hammerstein's first two postwar theater works, however—*South Pacific* and *The King and I* (1951)—are about problematic relations between cultures and races, and they both vividly express Hammerstein's wartime concerns. Moreover, after *The King and I*, Hammerstein's concern with matters of racial understanding and interracial tolerance appears less frequently in his works for the stage.

The exchange between Nellie and de Becque in the final version of 2.4 can be reduced to four briefly stated points: (1) Nellie's admission of the prejudice that prevents her from marrying de Becque, (2) her belief that this feeling was born in her, (3) her plea that she cannot help her beliefs, and (4) de Becque's refusal to accept this. De Becque makes no recriminatory comments about her beliefs, apart from doubting that they were inborn, and he does not place Nellie's beliefs into any larger context. Nellie's prejudice is left within the confines of the personal. But the addition of Cable's song of self-discovery moves prejudice into a broader context. "You've Got to Be Carefully Taught" argues that society in general is to blame for prejudice. Cable's realization, which causes him to reject the society that taught him his prejudice, explains his subsequent actions and fate. The removal of de Becque's criticism of U.S. society, and his added romantic song, also give him a less discordant role in the scene.

Sketch 2.4A continues after Nellie's exit. Cable suggests that de Becque has no right to criticize the principles of Nellie or any other Americans since he, de Becque, is unwilling to fight for anything. Cable refers to an earlier comment by de Becque about living on his own private island, at which point de Becque quickly notes that things have changed in a week's time. De Becque then mentions going with Cable on his mission, and from this point on the scene builds in intensity as the two men talk with increasing excitement about the mission. Cable is afforded no insight and undergoes no transformation in this version of the scene, and he is provided with no song. De Becque's decision to accompany Cable is abrupt and unconvincing; almost immediately after accusing the Americans of hypocrisy, he agrees to participate in a virtual suicide mission in support of their cause. Cable is left without an important dimension that was added later with the addition of his song, and de Becque lacks the introspective moment that, when added, convincingly propels him into action. In fact, no reference to anything musical occurs until the very end of the sketch. After agreeing to go with Cable, de Becque observes, "It is good to be a useful man again!" This is followed by the directions, "From here cue to song: WHEN A MAN MAKES UP HIS MIND Emile and Cable."[43] The development of this musical afterthought into an extended musical scene is the most important change in the structure and thematic tone of 2.4.

While much of 2.4A is retained in the scene's final version, the song indicated at the end of this sketch was never written. A reprise of "Now Is the Time," which first appears in 2.4D, eventually filled the spot. De Becque initially sang the song in act 1, between "I'm Gonna Wash That Man Right Out-a My Hair" and "I'm in Love with a Wonderful Guy," and the reprise of this song provides an interesting irony. In the first act, de Becque sang "Now Is the

Time" to convince Nellie to marry him. The song was an argument for Nellie to stay with de Becque on his island, far from the worries of the world. In the second act, rejected by Nellie, de Becque in turn rejects his previous idea of living in isolation. "We will not sit back and wait for the future to take care of us," he asserts to Cable before beginning the reprise.[44] Further, the reprise of "Now Is the Time," and "When a Man Makes Up His Mind," the title from 2.4A that it replaced, both raise a question that was solved only in the final version of the scene: once two characters have made an irreversible decision to act—in this case, a decision made in response to a confrontation with racial intolerance—what is the point of a musical number in which they sing about that decision and/or action? This question seems to have become an issue only after the musical was in rehearsal, for no mention of another number in the scene appears until sketch 2.4F, which contains a substantially rewritten version of the last part of the scene and a shortened reprise of "Now Is the Time." The rewrite introduces Cable's idea of not returning home after the war, and the new dialogue was kept in the final version of the scene. De Becque responds with a speech in which he warns Cable not to fool himself, that he cannot hide from life. Life will find him, he tells Cable, and when it does, he will embrace it anew, "facing life as it is and all that is wrong with it."[45]

De Becque's introspection in 2.4F is a new addition to the scene, a heretofore unexplored dimension of de Becque brought forth by his resigned acceptance of Nellie's rejection and his inability to understand her racism. This sketch is the first time the scene, like de Becque, turns its focus inward. Instead of singing about and eventually taking action, as in earlier sketches, de Becque is now reflective, and instead of immediately thrusting his characters forward into action, Hammerstein takes a moment to explore the emotions that motivate the action. This exploration sets up the reflective song that eventually appears in the scene, and it softens the impact of the scene's earlier confrontational elements concerning race. A song is first mentioned at this point in 2.4F; it would have preceded the reprise of "Now Is the Time," although Hammerstein provides no specifications for the song.

De Becque's resignation in turn gives Cable a motivation for mentioning the mission, and, following the spot for the new song, Cable asks de Becque if he would reconsider going on the mission. (In the right margin of 2.4F, after the indication for a song, Hammerstein wrote in pencil, "not so much to lose.") Cable's dialogue after the song cue is also retained in the final version of the script. While 2.4F still uses a partial chorus of "Now Is the Time" to end the scene, the added dialogue and the indication of an added song at an earlier moment for de Becque emphasize the uselessness of the reprise to the plot and to the development of both characters. At this point of the scene's development, the elimination of the reprise seems almost imminent.

Sketch 2.4G was written after the composition of the new song, "This Nearly Was Mine." Hammerstein's lyric sheet, and 2.4G, reveals that the song went through some formal adjustments before reaching its final structure, however, and these adjustments improve the overall effect of the developing musical scene. In the lyric sheet that accompanies Rodgers's manuscript copy of the song, for instance, the song begins with a verse consisting of what later became the trio of the waltz ("So clear and deep were my fancies . . ."). This is followed by the refrain ("One dream in my heart . . ."). The lyrics for the verse introduce the refrain, as is customary, but they address an absent Nellie: "I'll keep remembering evenings / I wish I'd spent with you," which is dramatically weak in that the song grows out of a dialogue with Cable. To solve this problem, in 2.4G Hammerstein added three lines of dialogue and a new introduction to the song that are not on the final lyric sheet. After de Becque ends his speech by implying that one must face what is wrong with life, Cable responds that plenty is wrong with it. De Becque then comments, "One doubts if it is worth fighting to save. And yet . . ." Cable responds bitterly to this and then sings, "The world's a lousy dish, / You may quote me if you wish." De Becque responds by singing, "But in this same world I was very glad to be, / When the soft eyes of beauty nearly smiled on me."[46] At this point, 2.4G indicates "go into refrain," which would have been "This Nearly Was Mine." The introduction was eliminated in the final version, and a short transitional speech for de Becque was written that led directly into the refrain of the song. The "verse" became a trio that allowed for a repeat of the refrain, and this repeat assured a second-act solo of substance for the leading man.[47]

Sketch 2.4B is dated January 22 and is marked "extra lyric." This lyric is for "My Girl Back Home," a song for Cable and Nellie in the early part of 2.4 that was later cut; the sketch also includes a short speech for Cable, following the song.[48] "My Girl Back Home" is also in the first rehearsal script, where it is the same as in 2.4B. In the sketch and the script, 2.4 begins with Nellie discovering Cable lying prone on a bench outside the women's dressing room. She scolds him for being away from the hospital, where he was being treated for malaria, and, as she starts to take his pulse, she notices that his watch is missing. He shows her the pieces and tells her "a lady who wanted to be my mother-in-law" smashed it. After Nellie tells him that, while in the delirium of his fever, he had been talking to a girl, she asks if it had been his "girl back home." Cable repeats that line "with reminiscent and ironic amusement," and begins "My Girl Back Home," a somewhat wistful thirty-two-measure song with two choruses.[49] While the lyrics for the first chorus are nostalgic—Cable recalls his blue-eyed girl and his inevitable partnership in the family law firm—those for the second begin, "How far away!" and subsequently note the distance of Philadelphia "from coconut palms / And banyan trees / And coral sands / And Tonkinese!"[50]

After the song, he confides to Nellie that the "girl" he had talking to in his fever was Tonkinese, not the girl back home, and Nellie reacts with shock. Cable confronts her about her reaction, noting that Nellie's look is like one his mother would give him if she knew about Liat. He then becomes angrier, asking Nellie, "What's the difference if her hair is blonde and curly or black and straight? If I want her to be my wife, why can't I have her?"[51] Nellie's response is nervous and hesitant. "You can! It's just that—people—I mean— they say it never works. Don't they?" Cable's response is bitter. Acknowledging that people do indeed say "It doesn't work," he adds, "And then everyone does their damnedest to prove it." He continues, angrily noting that he and Liat would have no chance of social acceptance in Philadelphia's Main Line. He suggests that, if they sent out invitations for a housewarming, nobody would come. It is a powerful moment.

Nellie's response reveals her discomfort when confronted with her own prejudice and preconceived ideas. The "they say it never works" line is not an original thought—Nellie is repeating what she has learned. But she is also repeating this to convince herself and to prepare for her confrontation with de Becque, which immediately follows. The loss of this scene and the loss of Nellie's disapproval of Cable removes another aspect of Nellie's prejudice and, like the cut in 1.1, somewhat simplifies her character. In the final version, instead of seeing Nellie as generally prejudiced—that is, as a bigot—the audience sees only one particular instance of prejudice. Nellie's racism is far less blatant, and she is once again sympathetic. The 2008 Broadway revival, however, has reinstated this scene, and its effect, like Nellie's use of the word "colored," is jolting.

"My Girl Back Home" works well within the scene and brings forth Cable's conflict. It remains in the final score as evocative underscoring, played when de Becque relates word of Cable's death via radio. While the song was cut to help shorten a lengthy show, perhaps part of the reason was also to keep Nellie sympathetic. To have a doomed character confront his own racism and blame it on his society was one thing. To have a heroine (and a likable star) repeatedly express racial bigotry—as Nellie does in the sketches and drafts, even though she eventually realizes the error of her beliefs—was perhaps too much for an audience in 1949. Nellie's expression of racism was left general, therefore; it remained for Cable to make it specific. "My Girl Back Home," like the scene that introduces it in the rehearsal script, has been reinstated into the Broadway revival of *South Pacific*. However, the song has been moved to act 1, where it is less effective, in part because Cable has not yet met Liat when he and Nellie sing it.

Even in its final incarnation, its edges blunted and its heroine less blatantly tainted with the prejudices of her culture, 2.4 remains a powerful indictment of racial intolerance, and "You've Got to Be Carefully Taught" is still a jolt for audiences unfamiliar with the musical. Nonetheless, the scene is considerably less aggressive in the delivery of its sociopolitical message than it was in its earlier versions. In the end, the message is still made, but it is softened by the addition of romantic and reflective elements and by the excision of the harder-hitting confrontations originally intended.

Distilled or not, the scene—and especially the song "You've Got to Be Carefully Taught"—evoked varied responses from audience members, some of whom wrote to Hammerstein about it. The letters that are among his papers indicate that the response was mixed. For instance, Martin Wolfson wrote, "What can I say to a man who writes, 'You've got to be taught to hate and fear'? I had been told of your great heart long before I met you. Now that I know you, I feel that my informants didn't praise you enough."[52] Several other positive letters are among Hammerstein's papers, including several requests for permission to use the lyrics to "You've Got to Be Carefully Taught" in sermons and one for permission to use the song to teach schoolchildren about tolerance.

Not all the letters were positive, however. One from Barbara R. Messner, which is critical of the song, also seems to miss its point:

> To me, it is unfortunate that the song "You've Got to Be Taught" is included in the album of songs from *South Pacific*, for without benefit of seeing the show (and even within it, the fact that the song is sarcastic if obtuse) one gets the idea that it is necessary to be taught to hate. I know that was far from your intention, and I know that the beginning lines are quoted in the current appeal of the National Conference of Christians and Jews, but for the public in general, I feel the inclusion of the song particularly in the album and to some extent in the show itself is not helpful to the cause of brotherhood, your intent to the contrary notwithstanding.[53]

These letters, which are just a few of those found among Hammerstein's papers, reveal the power of 2.4 and, more generally, of the show's message. Further, the varied responses indicate the controversy that the show stirred up, and they also suggest why the distillation of the scene was necessary. If the toned-down presentation of the musical's central message raised as many eyebrows as it did, the original criticisms of intolerance would have been intolerable for many. Rodgers and Hammerstein wanted a hit; their creation of one that still packed a thematic punch indicates that they knew exactly what they were doing.

OTHER PROBLEMS

As the WWB became more involved with various aspects of the war effort, it formed subcommittees for specialized interests. A subcommittee in which Hammerstein was active was, unsurprisingly, the Committee to Combat Race Hatred. This group, in its own words, "came to the conclusion that the writers of the United States because of their habitual employment of 'stock characters' were unconsciously fostering and encouraging group prejudice."[54] The committee commissioned a study by Columbia University to research the validity of this conclusion. The study investigated cases of negative racial stereotyping and found that various media ranged from good to poor in "presenting minority characters sympathetically and honestly." The stage was found "the most liberal of all the media" in such representations; advertising copy, which "is openly and self-admittedly addicted to the Anglo-Saxon [superiority] myth," and short stories were found to use the most stereotypes.[55]

Despite the high ranking of the stage in regard to ethnic and racial stereotypes, another letter to Hammerstein indicates that, notwithstanding his plea for racial tolerance, the librettist and lyricist and/or his director were not completely free from racially biased practices, even if they were inadvertent. This letter, from Mrs. Paul Robeson, raises an issue pertaining to representation that also applies to at least one other problematic racial element of the show. In a letter dated March 9, 1949, almost a month before the Broadway opening, Mrs. Robeson wrote:

> And please, may I make one small suggestion, very respectfully? In thinking back over the play, it troubled me a little that the Negro soldier was ALWAYS jitterbugging. It is very possible that I am unduly sensitive, racially, but so are a lot of us, and it would help enormously that if just once, he appeared with his comrades NOT cutting up. . . . Now don't misunderstand me. The jitterbugging is marvelous, and belongs there, but I'd like to see him once NOT do it.[56]

To his credit, Hammerstein immediately responded. "Thank you very much for your letter," he wrote, "and the gratifying comment therein. Since you have seen the play, and before I received your letter, we have inserted an episode in which [the African American actor] Archie Savage is *not* jitterbugging."[57] The most telling phrase of Hammerstein's response is "inserted an episode," which indicates that the stereotyped behavior was retained for most of Savage's other appearances.[58]

Moreover, this representation of a racial stereotype is not an isolated event in the show. *South Pacific* also reinforces the particularly racist language used by the media to depict and demonize the Japanese enemy during the war. John W. Dower argued that the Allies thought of the Japanese enemy in blatantly racist terms, and the musical supports this. Dower observed:

> The racist code words and imagery that accompanied the war in Asia were often exceedingly graphic and contemptuous. The Western allies, for example, persisted in their notion of the "subhuman" nature of the Japanese, routinely turning to images of apes and vermin to convey this. With more tempered disdain, they portrayed the Japanese as inherently inferior men and women who had to be understood in terms of primitivism, childishness, and collective mental and emotional deficiency.[59]

Dower further noted that, while the German enemy is most often referred to as "Nazi" or "Nazi Germany," thus perhaps implying that not all Germans are Nazis, references to the Japanese enemy are more inclusive. Words like "Jap," "the Japs," and "Nips" refer collectively to the whole of the Japanese people, as if the Japanese are homogeneous.[60]

The word "Jap" is used either as a noun or adjective throughout the second act of *South Pacific*, always in a scene pertaining to Cable and de Becque's mission, and this use reflects wartime usage. Its repeated presence also adds an irony to the show's theme of racial intolerance, an irony that clearly reflects Wendell Willkie's observation quoted earlier. Was Hammerstein aware of this irony? Or was he simply making use of popular wartime vocabulary that was still in use? (The word "Jap" became offensive to Americans only when Japan became our postwar ally.) Whether intended or not, these pejorative, and ironic, uses of a racial epithet in the work are jarring to many contemporary audiences. Yet, with the exception of Mrs. Robeson's letter, neither the problematic representation of the Japanese or of an African American evoked any response from audiences in 1949. Only the criticism of intolerance did.[61]

Restricted by the political climate of the postwar times in which they were working, Rodgers and Hammerstein found the most appropriate way to express their convictions in a gripping story. The softening of the means did not weaken the end result, however, and *South Pacific* is still remembered as a challenge to the American status quo of racial intolerance, despite the presence of problematic stereotypes that betray the time of its creation. Perhaps that softening of the thematic content encouraged the work's immense commercial success, in which case the message reached many people the authors thought needed to hear it.

Hammerstein's early work on the script for *South Pacific* demonstrates his fervent commitment to racial equality and tolerance. Yet although *South Pacific* was daring in its strong criticism of racial intolerance, its creators delicately sidestepped the primary racial conflict of 1949: the institutionalized inequality of black Americans and white Americans. And although Hammerstein denounced this specific inequality in writings before and after *South Pacific*, the musical is noticeably silent about the issue beyond Cable's fleeting reference to "people whose skin is a different shade."[62] Despite, or perhaps in addition to, Hammerstein's heated passion for the cause of tolerance, however, his and Rodgers's goal was to create a commercial hit, and that goal necessitated a softening of his rhetoric. This in turn resulted in a work less explicit in its assault on American racism than originally intended. Placed in a distant paradise, the racial conflict and its consequences are always cushioned by romance, beautiful music, and the conviction that cockeyed optimists can overcome their more ominous instincts. Those who cannot simply disappear.

6

NELLIE AND THE BOYS

• • •

Situating Gender in *South Pacific*

When *South Pacific* opened in 1949, constructs of gender in the United States were in a state of flux. Wartime configurations, themselves reconfigurations of earlier Depression-era gender characteristics, changed to fit cold war standards. Popular culture, and government propaganda, was integral to the success of this relatively fluid transformation: it provided images and words that suggested ideals for the postwar American woman and man. Women were encouraged to return to a home- and husband-centered lifestyle after the non-domestic employment of the war years, employment that had provided many women with their first sense of economic and personal autonomy. And for many men, the changes in gender expectations after the war meant continuing, or at least trying, to live up to hyper-masculinized wartime ideals that persisted into the postwar era. These ideals were increasingly used as standards for affirming men's heterosexuality and their patriotism. Men who fell short of these standards often faced outsider status, and, in the cold war era, that frequently resulted in professional and personal ruin. *South Pacific* reflects the changing and increasingly conservative constructions of postwar gender, and it suggests that Hammerstein in particular embraced, or at least accepted, many of those changes. As Stacy Wolf observed, even as the show appears "intent on its progressive racial politics," it also "constantly, inadvertently produces conservative messages."[1] The most conservative of these messages, which perhaps were less inadvertent than Wolf perceived, concern gender, and they are partly the result of Hammerstein's deemphasizing the potentially controversial aspect of the characters as he found them in Michener's novel.

Hammerstein's treatment of Nellie, for instance, demonstrates many women's path from wartime autonomy to postwar domestic confinement. Indeed, in describing the musical's final image of a reunited family, Hammerstein refers to de Becque as "the boss."[2] Hammerstein further ensures Nellie's successful passage to wife and mother by removing some of the complexities

6.1. *From a stock production circa 1960. From left, Odette Myrtil, Louis MacMillan (director), William F. Dwyer, and James Michener. Courtesy of Photofest.*

Michener gives her in the novel. Through the elimination of her romantic past and the muting of her sexuality, for instance, Hammerstein makes Nellie far less controversial than she otherwise might have been. Although she still demonstrates emotional and especially musical depth throughout—the examination of Nellie's music that follows indicates a fundamental connection with de Becque and his children that in turn gives strong emotional resonance to her choice to stay with them—this is nonetheless a simplified Nellie who exemplifies an important contemporaneous trend in postwar gender construction. Michener may have been writing about Nellie as she was between 1941 and 1943, but Hammerstein's Nellie is pure 1949.[3]

Hammerstein's alterations of de Becque and Cable are also revealing. He removes any possible controversy from de Becque's past by eliminating much of his sexual history and, initially, his viability as a warrior. Hammerstein later restores that viability by sending de Becque on a dangerous mission from which he alone returns safe and victorious. De Becque's presence on the

6.2. *Myron McCormick, the original Luther Billis. Courtesy of Photofest.*

mission is Hammerstein's invention; his success on it expedites his acceptance by Americans, within the play and in the audience, and indicates his worthiness of Nellie. Joe Cable gets exactly the opposite treatment. Michener's sensitive warrior is feminized, resulting in an example of suspect postwar masculinity.

Luther Billis, the show's third principal male character, falls somewhere between these two constructs of masculinity. His heterosexuality never seems in question. He is often outspoken about his desire to get to Bali Ha'i and encounter the young women there; he has the cue line into the testosterone-filled song "There Is Nothin' Like a Dame"; and he demonstrates a protective fondness for Nellie throughout the play. Nonetheless, his appearance in drag in the second act's Thanksgiving Follies and his laundry skills—Nellie praises his work, especially noting how well he presses pleats[4]—might suggest a dent in his masculine armor. A closer examination, however, argues otherwise. First, Billis's presence in the Follies is probably due to Nellie: she is credited with staging the "Honey Bun" number in which Billis appears in drag, and his willingness to please Nellie easily explains his awkward presence in the number, the comedy of which is in direct relationship to Billis's discomfort. Indeed, if his performance is self-consciously camp or if Billis seems to enjoy the performance and is at all effeminate in it, the number's humor is dissipated. Second, Billis's laundry business is but one of several activities in the show that demonstrate his entrepreneurial drive. His ongoing competition with Bloody Mary for the island's souvenir business provides one of the show's funniest ongoing subplots, and Billis's for-profit "Bath Club" provides the setting for "I'm Gonna Wash That Man Right Out-a My Hair," one of the show's most memorable musical numbers.

Billis is more defined by class than by gender. His actions and his dialogue suggest that he is from a working-class background. During his first scene with Nellie, for instance, which comes in the middle of "There Is Nothin' Like a Dame," Hammerstein notes that Billis "is unassured and has lost all of his brashness. For him, Nellie Forbush has 'class.'"[5] Later in the same scene, when Cable mentions having gone to college in New Jersey, Billis asks if he went to Rutgers. When Cable hesitantly admits to having attended Princeton, Billis comments, "Oh. Folks got money, eh, Lieutenant? Don't be ashamed of it. We understand."[6] And as noted earlier, in act 2, after learning that one of his escapades cost the navy six hundred thousand dollars, Billis notes with pride, "[My uncle] used to tell my old man I'd never be worth a dime!"[7] Further, while he bosses around those of lesser rank, he is usually deferential to those "above" him. Because Billis is more defined by class than by gender, therefore, he remains outside the scope of this discussion.

Postwar concepts of gender and their presence in *South Pacific* are at the heart of what follows, which also addresses the excision of potentially problematic related material from Michener's novel. A discussion of Nellie precedes an examination of the musical's two principal men.

NELLIE

Nellie Forbush represents a change from the female characters in Rodgers and Hammerstein's three previous musicals. She also provides a model for some of the principal female characters that follow. Meryle Secrest noted in her biography of Richard Rodgers that *South Pacific* "marks a great dividing line in the Rodgers and Hammerstein oeuvre between heroes and heroines who are more or less evenly matched in age and stories about powerful older men and the younger women who are attracted to them."[8] However, of the six musicals written after *South Pacific*, only two—*The King and I* (1951) and *The Sound of Music* (1959)—actually demonstrate a continuation of this model.

6.3. *Mary Martin in a promotional shot of "Honey Bun." Courtesy of Photofest.*

In *The King and I*, Anna shares with Nellie the experience of being in a foreign environment. She, too, becomes involved with, and probably falls in love with, an older and more powerful man who already has a family.[9] (The relationship of Anna and the King never fully blossoms into a romance, but the attraction between the two is apparent, especially in the "Shall We Dance" scene.) In *The Sound of Music*, Maria falls in love with Captain von Trapp after serving as governess to his many children. Nellie is an older sister to them both.[10] This change also suggests another difference between the team's work before and after 1949; after *South Pacific*, the principal female characters must accept and become part of the principal male characters' worlds in order to attain self-fulfillment.[11] This second development is found more consistently than the first in musicals after *South Pacific*, and it is indicative of a growing postwar attitude that relegated women to lives defined by their husbands' careers and needs. A brief review of the three works that preceded *South Pacific* will facilitate fuller understanding of this change in Rodgers and Hammerstein's musicals.

The earliest Rodgers and Hammerstein heroine, Laurey in *Oklahoma!* (1943), is a landowner who, in the show's second act, demonstrates her ability to hire and fire employees by firing the threatening farmhand Jud Fry.[12] She is a figure of power and economic stability, even if, after firing Jud and chasing him off her property, she becomes "a frightened little girl again" who tells Curly, the show's hero, "I'm afraid, 'fraid of my life!"[13] Curly eventually realizes that, in order to marry Laurey, he must give up his life as a cowboy and adopt the life of a farmer.[14] "Oh, I got to learn to be a farmer, I can see that!" Curly exclaims. He continues, "Oh, things is changin' right and left! Buy mowin' machines, cut down the prairies! . . . Country changin', got to change with it!"[15] In other words, Curly must come to Laurey's world—he does not carry her away to his. And Laurey's world is centered on the cultivation of the land—in particular, her farm—that is about to become a state in the Union. The title number of the show expresses the powerful relationship between the people and their land, most famously in the lyrics "We know we belong to the land, / And the land we belong to is grand!"[16] Curly's exuberant acceptance of the new world on the horizon suggests that his transition to Laurey's world will be successful, as will the transition of the Oklahoma Territory into a state.

In *Carousel* (1945), Rodgers and Hammerstein's next work, Billy Bigelow's transition to his wife's world is not so successful. Further, his inability to adapt eventually brings about his self-destruction. Julie, the work's principal female character, is a working-class woman of limited means but tremendous resilience. Unlike Curly, Billy, a former barker for a carousel, does not move into his wife's world eagerly, and, once he is there, he is unsure of how to exist within it. Julie explains to her friend Carrie, "Billy don't know any trade. He's only good at what he used to do. So now he jest don't do anythin'."[17] When he learns that he is to be a father, Billy is at a complete loss as to how he will support his wife and child; the musical's famous "Soliloquy" is his musing on this dilemma, and by the song's end, he vows that he'll "go out and make it [money] / Or steal it or take it / Or die!"[18] Because he has no skills, he agrees to participate in a robbery and, when caught, he commits suicide, leaving Julie and an as-yet unborn daughter to survive without him. The musical's supernatural ending, in which the specter of Billy communicates his love to his widow before entering heaven, ensures Billy's redemption and, more generally, the transformative power of love.[19] Julie, a single mother who repeatedly demonstrates both great strength of character and unconditional love for Billy, is an independent woman who, like Laurey, learns to meet the world on its own terms and becomes even stronger for having done so.

Allegro, Rodgers and Hammerstein's third musical, is unique among all their other works, and their treatment of the principal female character is especially notable. One of only two works by the team not based on a preexistent source—*Me and Juliet* is the other—*Allegro* tells the story of Joseph Taylor Jr., a Midwesterner who becomes a doctor, moves to the big city and becomes immensely successful as a physician to Chicago society, grows disillusioned, and returns to practice medicine in his hometown, as he originally intended. The prime motivator for his move to the city is his wife, Jenny, who was his high school sweetheart but who becomes increasingly ambitious, materialistic, and emotionally cold as the story develops. Although she is the primary woman in the story, Jenny is also its villain. Before marrying Joe, for instance, she has a confrontation with his mother that ends with Jenny commenting, "You know, I feel better now that war's declared." Mrs. Taylor coolly responds, "So do I, Jenny."[20] Mrs. Taylor dies immediately after the confrontation. Jenny pushes and manipulates her husband and his career and has an affair with his boss, and Joe eventually leaves her and his practice in the city and returns to his roots.

Jenny is unprecedented in Hammerstein's earlier scripts, and no one like her exists in any of his later work. Her ambition to rise above her middle-class background and values, betraying her husband in the process, is antithetical to what Ethan Mordden called Hammerstein's "vision of a loving, protective, person-scaled community."[21] Her marriage to Joe having run its course, Jenny remains in Chicago when Joe returns to his hometown. Emily, Joe's observant and sometimes caustic nurse who is also in love with him, leaves the city with him. But Emily, who does not appear until well into the second act, is not the typical Hammerstein heroine, either. Although she sees through Jenny and loves Joe, she is brassier and more self-confident than the romantic female women in Hammerstein's other plays; indeed, if further developed, she would seem more like a candidate for the traditionally comic secondary female role. However, her insight and her loyalty to Joe, who embodies all the values that Hammerstein cherished, indicate that she is the only woman in the play who could wind up with him. Both women are atypical Hammerstein female leads, but then *Allegro* is an unusual and often challenging musical.[22]

Laurey, Julie, Jenny, and Emily fall in love with men their own age, have a strong sense of self from the beginning of each play, and begin new lives with their men (Laurey's indecision about Curly is largely a cat-and-mouse game that she plays with him before inevitably winding up with him). Jenny convinces Joe to pursue the life that *she* wants, so in a sense he, like Curly and Billy, accepts her world; unlike Curly and Billy, however, he doesn't believe in her world and eventually rejects it. Emily is the first Hammerstein woman to follow a man into his world, which in part anticipates Nellie Forbush.

Unlike earlier Rodgers and Hammerstein female characters, Nellie is approximately thirty years younger than the man she falls in love with. She is from an unsophisticated middle-class southern American background, and he is a seemingly erudite French plantation owner in the South Pacific. He has a family that she must accept if she is to have a life with him. Acceptance of his family, however, hinges on her ability to overcome her racism and accept de Becque's previous marriage to a Polynesian—a woman of color. To many southerners at that time, Nellie included, such a marriage constituted miscegenation, which was morally repugnant, not to mention illegal. In other words, Nellie must join de Becque's world, and give up her own and its biases, in order to find happiness. While Laurey and Curly find happiness in the promise of starting together in her world, and while Julie survives with her daughter in the world she brought her husband into, little Nellie Forbush from Arkansas ends up in a tropical paradise, far from her previous world, with a husband, a servant, and two children who speak a language she does not understand. And while Nellie influences and assists in de Becque's assimilation of U.S. values and culture, *South Pacific* nonetheless represents a notable change in Rodgers and Hammerstein's works, and it warrants comparison to similar changes in other contemporaneous literary works and in postwar cultural trends.

In her influential book *The Feminine Mystique* (1963), the feminist author Betty Friedan described a change in the short stories that appeared in a sampling of women's magazines around 1949. Friedan demonstrated that, whereas in the 1930s and 1940s these periodicals inspired women to move into the professional world, they began to suggest in 1949 that women should cultivate lives as little more than appendages to their professional husbands, and that they should find satisfaction in that domestic role. These magazines painted increasingly unrealistic portraits of cheerful suburban female consumers with no identities outside the home and, as Friedan observed, women found that living up to this ideal—the "mystique" of her title—was stressful and, in the end, impossible.[23]

For instance, Friedan reported that, just ten years before *South Pacific*, the heroines of stories in women's magazines shared many characteristics with the heroes of men's stories. She described this as follows:

> They were New Women, creating with a gay determined spirit a new identity for women—a life of their own. . . . There was a definite aura that their individuality was something to be admired . . . that men were drawn to them as much for their spirit and character as for their looks.[24]

The last example of this "New Woman" Friedan finds is in a story called "Sarah and the Seaplane," which appeared in the February 1949 *Ladies' Home Journal*, approximately two months before the opening of *South Pacific*. In this story, Sarah decides to learn to fly, and the story's climax is her solo flight. Friedan quoted the following from the story:

> She had to adjust herself to being alone, entirely alone in the familiar cabin. Then she drew a deep breath and suddenly a wonderful sense of competence made her sit erect and smiling. She was alone! She was answerable to herself alone, and she was sufficient.
> "I can do it!" she told herself aloud.[25]

"And then," wrote Friedan, "suddenly the image blurs. The New Woman, soaring free, hesitates in mid-flight, shivers in all that blue sunlight and rushes back to the cozy walls of home." Friedan went on to note that the same year Sarah took her solo flight, "the *Ladies Home Journal* printed the prototype of the innumerable paeans to 'Occupation Housewife' that started to appear in the women's magazines, paeans that resounded throughout the fifties."[26] They resounded elsewhere throughout popular entertainment, too. The rags-to-riches heroines who made it to the top through their own devices, such as those personified by Joan Crawford, or the ambitious independent women such as those played by Katherine Hepburn in the 1930s and 1940s, gave way to television's domestic blueprints of *I Love Lucy* and *Father Knows Best*, among others.[27] These suggested that the woman's domain was the home and that she would find only frustration and lack of fulfillment outside that domain; they also refrained from acknowledging these women's sexualities. Friedan summarized this condition as follows:

> Fulfillment as a woman had only one definition for American women after 1949—the housewife–mother. As swiftly as in a dream, the image of the American woman as a changing, growing individual in a changing world was shattered.[28]

Nellie Forbush stands at the cusp of this change. A young woman who grew up in the 1920s and 1930s (Michener gives her age as twenty-two, and, as noted earlier, his book is set in 1941–43), she combines her calling as a nurse with a desire to see the world. Nellie left a 4-F fiancé in Arkansas, promising with little conviction to return at war's end and marry him. Nellie's spirit of adventure and careerism, combined with her buoyant spirits, is key to her character.

A twenty-two-year-old navy nurse would have had at least three years' training before gaining a commission, suggesting that Nellie began her training two or three years before the beginning of the war. Nellie's choice of nursing as a career was an "acceptable" prewar career for a woman, like school teaching. Nursing was also a career in great demand during the war years, both at home and near the fronts. In a 1943 guide to women's wartime vocational options, Evelyn Steele writes, "If this is the time when you are choosing a career—then nursing may be the ideal profession for you. It is a good vocation, and one which, the moment you choose it, makes you part and parcel of the war effort."[29] Steele's discussion of nursing covers two chapters of her book, and the concluding paragraph of the second chapter stresses the long-term importance of a nursing career:

> Nursing is war work with a future. It will not only be meeting an immediate, desperate need. But later, when the war and the peace has [sic] been won and the emergency is over, the tens of thousands of newly trained nurses will have a new job—to build the health and strength of our people to levels never before envisioned. So when you consider nursing as a profession, think of it in terms of such a future.[30]

Recruiting women for wartime nursing was highly successful. Susan Hartmann described this success, noting, "Once the nation was at war nurses volunteered for military service at a rate surpassing that of any other profession. More than 100,000 volunteered, and the 76,000 who served, represented 31.3 percent of all active professional nurses. They saw duty in every theater, often right behind the front lines. . . . In return, they finally won equal pay and allowances and full military rank."[31]

While nursing was traditionally a career for women, however, Steele's wartime occupational guide ventures far from traditional career trajectories. Further, she stressed the long-term possibilities for nontraditional careers, and she did so with an emphasis that recalled Friedan's observations about the prewar and wartime choices for women that pointed them toward personal discovery and independence. For instance, in suggesting a career as a doctor, Steele wrote, "Women doctors, as do women in any other profession, still have to fight the mid-Victorian theory that a woman's place is in the home. But the women are standing firm and are commanding the honor, credit, and respect that is due them. And they deserve it!"[32] Some of the other careers suggested, many of them decidedly nontraditional, include truck driving, aviation, engineering, machine operation, welding, and science. All these areas, moreover, are discussed as careers that, like nursing, could be carried on after the war. While Steele acknowledged the possibility that some women might not want to continue a career when it was no longer necessary, she encouraged those who might be empowered by the wartime opportunities. She noted in her foreword, for instance, "Not all women will want to remain in the occupation which they enter during this wartime period. Some work will come to a stop with the end of the war. But many careers begun during the war will provide even greater futures during peace time."[33]

Following her text, Steele included an appendix from the Women's Advisory Committee of the War Manpower Commission, a subsidiary of the Office of War Information, which contained some surprising information. For instance, "The National War Labor Board established as a policy in three cases which came before it the principle of equal pay for equal work for women in war industry. This was hailed by the Federal Women's Bureau as a victory for women workers and for advocates of fair wage policies." This brief essay also suggests the need for daycare for the children of working women and a plan for pregnancy leave that would not negatively affect a woman's job security.[34] In short, women seem not only to be welcome in previously nontraditional occupations; they seem to be put on equal footing with the men who previously held their jobs.

If the war provided such empowering work and career possibilities, and if women were as valued in the workplace as the men then serving their country, what is to be made of Friedan's and other authors' observations that postwar American women were almost completely relegated to the domestic sphere from whence they came? One clue to this dilemma can be found in the very essay in Steele's appendix that promises equal pay and other benefits: paying women less than men had been paid for equivalent work would devalue the work previously done by men and, in turn, would result in a hesitancy to rehire the men at their previous wages.[35] In other words, wage levels had to be maintained in order to secure work for men after the war. "Equality" had little to do with it. This view supports the feminist historian Leila Rupp's observation:

> Historians and others have wondered at the legendary total domesticity of the 1950s following on the heels of the supposedly "liberating" war. In *The Feminine Mystique*, Betty Friedan explained the 1950s as a reaction to "emancipation," a reaction dominated by the postwar creation of the "mystique." But if one looks beneath the surface of wartime imagery, the 1950s make more sense. The feminine mystique was no new creation, but simply the 1950s version of the traditional wife and mother.[36]

Rupp argued that fundamental concepts of gender roles are very slow to change, but that "public images are subject to sudden and temporary changes imposed by economical need."[37] In keeping with this observation, Rupp further posited that the increased female workforce during the war "had no permanent impact on the trend in the size of the female labor force," and that the sudden and temporary changes in the images of women workers mentioned above were never thought by women, or by the government, to be permanent.[38] Finally, Rupp maintained that the experience in the workplace had little effect on subsequent feminist self-realization. To demonstrate this last point, she quoted from an article found in the *Ladies' Home Journal* in 1944: "If the American woman can find a man she wants to marry, who can support her, a job fades in significance beside the vital business of staying at home and raising a family."[39] The historian Maureen Honey agreed, noting, "While there is considerable disagreement over the war's liberating effect on women in the postwar world, it is generally conceded that various forces worked against the retention of most progressive changes to encourage women's entry into non-traditional fields."[40]

As Honey's observation suggests, several writers on the issue have challenged Rupp's thesis. Susan Hartmann is one. In part, she agreed with Rupp: "After the war, women's services continued to be recognized as important to the nation as a whole. But social stability had replaced military victory as the national goal; and women were needed as wives and mothers rather than as workers."[41] But she also argued that by the end of 1947, the number of women working started to increase after having fallen off at war's end, and that by the end of the decade the size of the female workforce was greater than that during the war.[42] And Maria Diedrich and Dorothea Fischer-Hornung placed the roots of later feminist movements within the wartime mobilization of women into the workforce, noting that "the changes in employment patterns, which begin during the war and which afforded women a new sense of self-reliance and power, formed a basis from which the feminist protest of the following decades could spring."[43]

How, then, does Nellie Forbush fit into these conflicting views of wartime and postwar women? When introduced to the audience in *South Pacific*, Nellie is more than a little naïve, and, in her words, "a hick"; she is not one of the "preservers of peacetime virtues and family life, which came to be equated with security, stability, and prosperity," as Maureen Honey described stateside women.[44] Not yet, at any rate. Because the war is only about one year old when the story begins, Nellie's decision to become a nurse was made well before the outbreak of the war. Further, she was motivated to join the navy and "see the world," as the recruitment posters offered, by her dissatisfaction with life in Arkansas. She is single, immensely likable, self-deprecating, and in the thick of the Pacific theater. Andrea Most observed, "Nellie establishes herself as the embodiment of American youth, optimism, energy and power, the life force of the island. . . . Nellie is straightforward, anti-intellectual, and, ironically, anti-theatrical. She refuses to put on an act."[45] This is Nellie as she came from Arkansas, free and undomesticated, and she expresses and defines herself through a vernacular U.S. vocabulary that suggests a somewhat light-weight, if irrepressible, individual.

Nothing so far suggests any difference between Nellie in Michener's book and Nellie in Hammerstein's. Michener's heroine, however, has several qualities that Hammerstein felt compelled to leave unaddressed. The result is that Hammerstein's Nellie is more in keeping with Friedan's post-1949 prototype than with the more independent woman of wartime U.S. culture. For example, Michener's Nellie has a romantic past: much is made of her boyfriend in Arkansas, and her experiences with Bill Harbison imply her readiness to enter into a romantic relationship. Hammerstein's Nellie has no known previous romantic experience.[46] In addition, Michener's Nellie is a sexually vibrant woman. She excites Harbison when he first sees her in a swimsuit, and she is completely willing to have sex with him. Even their first kiss suggests sexual passion: "It was a long helpless kiss, and both officers found it thrilling and delicious."[47] Hammerstein's Nellie is devoid of any such explicit sexuality. Her most passionate moment is expressed wholly by the orchestra: Hammerstein describes the *music* as reaching the "ecstatic heights . . . of two people falling in love," and he refers to the "turbulent thoughts and feelings" in the couple's "hearts and brains." The emphasis is on emotional and intellectual love, not physical attraction. Indeed, at the end of "Some Enchanting Evening," which follows this moment and which ends with the lyric, "Never let her go," de Becque and Nellie stand looking at each other in silence. Not only do they not kiss: they do not even touch.[48]

Excising Nellie's overt sexuality also left the star Mary Martin's tomboy and somewhat androgynous persona intact. (She was playing Annie Oakley in *Annie Get Your Gun* when Rodgers and Hammerstein thought of her as Nellie.) This persona was skillfully developed throughout her career. Edith Head observed the following about what she called Martin's "audience appeal":

> First, she doesn't antagonize women. They regard her as wholesome, friendly, warm. Any housewife can vicariously live the role Mary enacts. Second, men like her because she is peppy and stimulating without making them feel inferior. When Mary worked here [in Hollywood], every man on the lot wanted to be near her.[49]

Safely appealing to housewives and attracting men with her pep, Martin was not an actress who exuded sexual attraction. She was "safe," as the postwar woman was supposed to be, and Hammerstein was careful to craft Nellie as a reflection of this persona.

6.4. *The iconic final tableau. Courtesy of Photofest.*

Trimmed of her sexuality, Hammerstein's Nellie is a clear example of the post-1949 woman whose fictional representation Friedan wrote about. Before the play begins, she has begun to fall in love with an older man; during the course of the play, she overcomes her personal prejudices and accepts him, his children, and his world, although it is a world altered by her, and other Americans', presence in it. At the end of the musical, Nellie is at home with the children, hoping for de Becque's return from a dangerous spying mission. (She does not yet know that he has survived.) At this point, she is also presented as somewhat helpless; she cannot quite identify all the ships and planes ("The big ones are battle ships and the little ones are destroyers—or cruisers—I never can tell the difference. . . . And what on earth are those?"[50]) and she cannot speak French with the children beyond a few fractured words. The final stage directions are telling. After de Becque returns, announcing himself by joining in the singing of "*Dites-moi*," which Nellie and the children have begun, the script tells us, "The music continues. The children drink their soup. Nellie comes back to consciousness enough to realize that Emile must be hungry. She leans over and hands him the large bowl of soup with an air of 'nothing's too good for the boss!'"[51]

Hammerstein's use of "the boss," noted earlier, describes Nellie's response to de Becque and suggests the postwar reestablishment of a male-dominated household, which in turn recalls a similar transformation in postwar society noted by Maureen Honey. "The central role of the family in wartime propaganda," she wrote, "with the vulnerable homemaker as its figurehead, led easily into the idealization of the male breadwinner/female hearthkeeper at the end of the war."[52] Indeed, as Most commented, from the moment of de Becque's return, he, Nellie, and the children become a "nuclear family," the unit of supreme importance in the postwar era. Honey described the roles played by each member in this unit, and the importance of it to postwar American society, as follows:

> The nuclear family came to represent the values of all Americans and was used as a symbol of unity. It also stood for the survival of decency and humanity in a world rent by suffering. The nostalgic view of the family that gained such strength during the war years reflected widespread yearning for familiar rituals, childhood innocence, and physical comfort, but within a context that attempted to stir the passions of civilians.[53]

This passage almost perfectly describes the final scene: the familiar family ritual of singing the children's song "*Dites-moi*," which began the musical; the presence of de Becque's two young children that recalls the innocence of the play's opening moments; and the physical comfort of de Becque's plantation, which is the home that Nellie has already adopted as her own. Honey continued:

> As the war drew to a close, this view grew stronger, and women became the chief heralders of peace just as they had been the militant home-front fighters in battle. The desire for rest, tranquility, comfort fed easily into the depiction of women in a traditional helping role, and they were idealized as healers who would salve men's wounds while nurturing the generation that would harvest the rich fruit of postwar prosperity.[54]

The musical's end could not be described any better.

Although the final scene of *South Pacific* has been interpreted in several ways, any consideration must come to terms with Nellie outwardly accepting women's traditional postwar situation. Stacy Wolf declared that it "privileges the nuclear family over heterosexual romance," and Most found the final scene rings false because Nellie stops singing before the others and "the family that does not sing together cannot stay together."[55] Wolf commented that the final song is not a love song, and Most observed that "the European has not learned the American songs and the American has

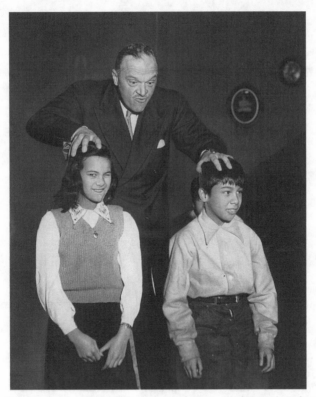

6.5. *The director Joshua Logan rehearses Barbara Luna (Ngana) and Michael De Leon (Jerome) for the final scene. Courtesy of Photofest.*

stopped singing altogether. Meanwhile, the Eurasian children simply repeat the same French song they sang at the opening of the show."[56] Neither found the final scene satisfying, and neither found it romantic or musically convincing.

Earlier in her discussion of the music in *South Pacific*, Most emphasized that Ezio Pinza, the original de Becque, was an opera singer and that Mary Martin was a musical-theater singer. Indeed, when Martin expressed concern about singing with a booming basso, Rodgers reassured her: "[She asked] how could we possibly expect her to sing on the same stage with Ezio Pinza? Because there was some logic in what she said, I assured her that we'd write the score without a single duet for her."[57] Arguing that this vocal separation indicates a "distance between Emile and Nellie," Most suggested that, "despite the fact that they share the stage, Martin stars in one musical—the *South Pacific* of 'Cockeyed Optimist,' 'Honey Bun,' 'I'm Gonna Wash That Man Right Out of [sic] My Hair'—and Pinza in another: the *South Pacific* of 'Some

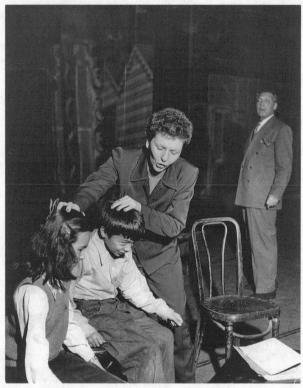

6.6. *Mary Martin rehearses the same scene with the children, just before de Becque makes himself known. Courtesy of Photofest.*

Enchanted Evening' and 'This Nearly Was Mine.' "[58] And it is with this observation that Most missed the musical point.

Because Rodgers could not have his two principal romantic characters sing together—a fairly unusual occurrence in a romantic musical, especially one that, like much of *South Pacific*, has deep roots in operetta—he came up with another, far more subtle, way to unite them musically. This musical connection between Nellie and de Becque not only dispels Most's notion of "distance" between the two characters; it also reveals their similarity, closeness, and equality on a deep, and often unspoken—or sung—level, despite the outward differences in their musical and personal styles. In act 2, Nellie says to de Becque, "We have something very important in common. . . . We're—we're the same kind of people fundamentally—you and me."[59] Most comments, "This is scarcely an argument for marriage. The connection between Emile and Nellie is hard to render in romantic terms because it is neither sexual nor financial—it is dramaturgical."[60] But a strong argument can be made that the connection between the two—their fundamental "alikeness"—is indeed romantic, if not sexual, and that it is rendered in the most romantic terms of all: it is rendered in the score. Further, the score suggests that Nellie perhaps does not slip into as completely a subservient role as Hammerstein's book implies; instead, it suggests from the first scene that her interior musical vocabulary and de Becque's are of equal emotional and stylistic depth, indicating a connection not immediately apparent in the book. In short, Rodgers musically expresses the internal similarities of his two principal characters and similarly indicates the emotional strength of his principal female character.

Rodgers accomplishes the musical connection between Nellie and de Becque through the subtle and ingenious use of a short motive that is heard, if briefly, before either character appears onstage. In the very opening moments of the show, after a six-measure orchestral introduction that establishes the intimate mood, the orchestra plays a two-measure introduction to the children's song "*Dites-moi*," after which it plays a chorus to underscore the children's pantomimed business. The children sing the second chorus. The first measure of the introduction, which also occurs under the first sung measure, exploits a descending tetrachord, or four-note figure, that later transfers to much of Nellie's music and to music she shares with de Becque. Admittedly, the use of the motive is subtle, and some might think its presence serendipitous at best. After all, the motive's intervallic content, that is, the relation between whole steps and half steps, occasionally changes. And descending tetrachords are not unusual in much Western music or, for that matter, in much music by Richard Rodgers, Still, the consistency of the motive throughout the score, in addition to the occasions of its use, suggests that it might be there for reasons that are not accidental.

The tetrachord in question consists of a descending half step followed by two descending whole steps. Its first manifestation in the opening jumps from the first note (C) in the bass on beat one to a B followed by an A in the treble, one beats two and three, after which the tetrachord is completed by a G in the bass on beat four. If the pitches are treated as pitch classes, that is, as pitches without categorization by octave or register (C is C no matter where it lies on the staff, for instance), the tetrachord is simply C-B-A-G (see Example 6.1). In the next measure of the opening, the gesture is suggested but not replicated exactly: only three pitches occur, and the interval between the first and second pitches is altered. While the initial statement of the tetrachord is fleeting and part of a longer musical idea, it is nonetheless audible and clearly recognizable when it reoccurs later in the scene.

Example 6.1a. Opening of "Dites Moi."

Example 6.1b. The tetrachord.

The initial importance of this motive is that it is heard in relation to the children. The eventual connection of de Becque and Nellie through the children begins without either of them knowing it—Nellie does not meet them until the end of act 1—but it is one of the earliest and strongest indicators that, as Nellie says, the two of them are "the same kind of people." The short motive that links them all ultimately gives voice to Nellie's emotional strength and her ability to overcome her prejudice, and its use in the first scene between Nellie and de Becque begins that process.

The children exit after the brief opening song, and Rodgers and Hammerstein introduce their leading characters unobtrusively, perhaps trying to subvert the stars' customary entrance applause by having them talk through the entrance. The scene's quiet intimacy continues undisturbed. After extolling the beauty of the scenery, which she says encourages her to think that perhaps the world is not a completely hopeless mess, Nellie tells de Becque that the other nurses call her "Knucklehead Nellie" because of her perennially positive attitude. She then sings "A Cockeyed Optimist," which ends with the lyrics, "But I'm stuck / (Like a dope!) / With a thing called hope, / And I can't get it out of my heart . . . Not this heart!"[61] The song, which was initially titled "Not This Heart," is integral to introducing Nellie; the lyrics are straightforward, unadorned, and completely in the vocabulary of the unaffected nurse from Arkansas, and Rodgers's diatonic and largely conjunct melody perfectly matches them. They represent what we might call the "Nellie style," a popular song–informed musical expression with lyrics rich in American slang that suggests a naïve American expressing herself in a comfortable stylistic vocabulary. In short, not a note or word is false in Nellie's song, and the result is a subtle musical characterization.

After the song, a short dialogue scene ensues in which we learn that de Becque fled to the South Pacific after he killed a man in France. We also learn

6.7. *Rossano Brazzi and Mitzi Gaynor in the 1958 film version of "Twin Soliloquies." Courtesy of Photofest.*

that Nellie thinks she arrived in the South Pacific as a result of running *to* something—to a discovery of the world: "I wanted to meet different kinds of people and find out if I like them better [than people in Little Rock]."[62] De Becque then offers Nellie some cognac, and as he pours it, Rodgers and Hammerstein create a memorable effect by having the two characters sing alternating soliloquies.

Rodgers and Hammerstein established the stylistic convention of soliloquies for principal characters in each of their earlier shows. Jud's "Lonely Room" in *Oklahoma!* is the first example in a Rodgers and Hammerstein show of how powerful a contemplative solo can be. After his humiliation by Curly in the preceding scene and song ("Pore Jud Is Daid"), Jud pours out his venomous sexual desire for Laurey in an intense and disturbing soliloquy, eventually making up his mind to pursue Laurey at any cost. It is one of the best moments in the show—indeed, in all of Rodgers and Hammerstein's work—and in a good performance its power remains undiminished after more than sixty years. In *Carousel*, the lengthy (eight-minute) soliloquy for Billy Bigelow is a turning point in the show, as noted earlier: learning that his wife is pregnant, Billy contemplates several scenarios before arriving at the conclusion that he must join his friend in a hold-up in order to get money for his unborn child; this action ultimately results in his suicide. And in *Allegro*, Emily sings "The Gentleman Is a Dope," a consideration of her feelings for Joe Taylor, while unsuccessfully trying to hail a cab. In other words, the use of a soliloquy was already a common Rodgers and Hammerstein technique.

"Twin Soliloquies," as the duo called their alternating soliloquies for two characters, was without precedent, however.[63] The source of the number is in Michener's story "Our Heroine." Sitting in a pavilion on de Becque's plantation, Nellie says to herself, "I shall marry this man. This shall be my life from now on. This hillside shall be my home."[64] Compare this with Nellie's first lyrics in "Twin Soliloquies": "Wonder how I'd feel, / Living on a hillside, / Looking on an ocean, / Beautiful and still."[65] Nellie's matter-of-fact statements become questions in the score, but the focus of those questions is the same as that of the statements in the story—the hillside, the beauty, the possibility, or even the probability, of a life there. Michener's de Becque then muses, "This is what I've been waiting for. . . . Who ever thought a fresh, smiling girl like this would climb up my hill?"[66] This is quite close to Hammerstein's lyric: "This is what I need, / This is what I've longed for, / Someone young and smiling / Climbing up my hill."[67] The two characters continue to sing alternately, both thinking of the obstacles in the way of their relationship but at the same time trying to look past them.

The two-measure introduction to the number immediately establishes a relatively calm mood not without a subtle element of tension. It also exploits the descending tetrachord, which hereafter is present in music for Nellie and music Nellie shares with de Becque. The motive provides a fluid musical connection between the two that demonstrates their status as emotional equals and strengthens the argument that Nellie does not defer musically to de Becque. Instead, this aspect of Nellie's musical character, interior in the soliloquies and exterior in the rest of her music, informs and is at home in de Becque's more expansive musical vocabulary. Nellie does not take on de Becque's music: it is already a part of her, even if she may not know it, and they both share it with the children who will eventually bring them together.

The first measure of "Twin Soliloquies" consists of a sustained tonic D-major chord in the lower strings on beat one followed by a descending three-note group (C#, B, A), beginning on the upper leading tone, on beats two, three, and four (see Example 6.2a). The major-seventh relation between the sustained tonic and the leading tone (C#) is not unrelated to the initial melodic gesture of the song "Bali Ha'i," which consists of an octave leap and a

Example 6.2a. Opening of "Twin Soliloquies."

Example 6.2b. The tetrachord.

descending minor second. The initial instability of this accompanying motive provides a wonderful setting for the vocal melody of "Twin Soliloquies," which is completely diatonic.[68] However, as in its initial appearance, this presence of the tetrachord can also be analyzed using octave equivalence: on beat one, for example, the D in the lower strings can be heard as the first note of the tetrachord, which is continued in the higher strings. The measure can be read as a single motivic statement: D, C#, B, A (see Example 6.2b). The opening one-measure motive is repeated continuously throughout the first twenty-two measures of the number, although the tonal center shifts several times.

Another especially noteworthy observation about the opening of "Twin Soliloquies" is that Nellie sings first. Of equal importance is that although the harmony under Nellie's melody moves from the tonic (D-major) to the major mediant (F#-major), when de Becque first expresses himself in the next phrase, he returns to D-major. In other words, he returns to Nellie's tonality to express himself, and he sings the same melody for the first three measures, after which the tonality shifts to C-major (the motive continues, now in C). De Becque and Nellie's fundamental similarities, as Nellie calls them, are musically, and unambiguously, demonstrated.[69] But at this point they are still interior. These similarities are further observed in the twenty-third measure, when Rodgers matches the change of mood in Hammerstein's lyrics. Previously contemplative, the lyrics here become nervous and are again initiated by Nellie, who sings, "Wonder why I feel / Jittery and jumpy! / I am like a schoolgirl, / Waiting for a dance."[70] De Becque again assumes Nellie's music, comparing himself to a nervous schoolboy and wondering if he has a chance with Nellie. Under this, the orchestra, in addition to the "jumpy" accompaniment, plays a chromatically altered version of the motive: C#-C-natural-B-A. (The C# is enharmonic with D-flat, and the intervallic content of the motive is altered by the two consecutive half steps: C#-C-natural and C-natural-B. If begun on D-flat, the tetrachord would read D-flat, C-natural, B-flat, A-flat.)

Originally, "Twin Soliloquies" came to a rather abrupt end after this section. Dialogue resumed after de Becque's last lyric and eventually led into "Some Enchanted Evening," de Becque's first big solo. The director Joshua Logan, however, wrote that he was not satisfied with the transition and worked with the arranger–pianist Trude Rittman during rehearsals to find an alternative transition. Logan later wrote the following about the problem and its solution: "This ["Twin Soliloquies"] was the moment for me the show became great. But the song stopped too quickly; the music had to continue to strengthen the passionate, almost sexual feeling. Trude provided the thrilling continuation later."[71] (Note Logan's use of the phrase "*almost* sexual" regarding the feeling between the two characters.) What the German-born Rittman provided was the one truly operatic moment of the score. The passage, mentioned earlier, is titled "Unspoken Thoughts," and it provides the subtext for the action. After his final sung thoughts in "Twin Soliloquies," de Becque, who has been pouring brandy into two glasses, hands one to Nellie. Unaccustomed to the large snifter, Nellie watches de Becque as he lifts the glass to his lips and drinks from it; she does the same. The melody that Rittman uses to express this interior moment is the one first sung by Nellie, and for the first three measures it is accompanied by the descending tetrachord, after which Rittman alters the tetrachord while maintaining its effect.

"Unspoken Thoughts" consists of three repetitions of the first three measures of that melody in a harmonically unstable setting, followed by a six-measure coda. The music expresses exactly what the passage's title suggests and the stage directions describe: complex and wordless thoughts that grow out of the preceding (sung) musical number and then transcend it. The combination of a slow crescendo, the insistent repetition of the melodic motive, and the changing harmonic background perfectly reflect the "thoughts and feelings" mentioned in the script.

This use of the orchestra to express subtext is Rittman's invention, of course, and care should be taken not to ascribe to Rodgers the creative role of Wagnerian music dramatist. Logan describes his personal desire for orchestral subtext as part of his overall concept for the production, calling it "the use of music under the dramatic pantomime for changes of thought."[72] To achieve this, Logan recalls, he worked with Rittman, who had arranged dance and incidental music for the earlier Rodgers and Hammerstein shows. Rittman, noted Logan, "would create passages based on Dick's themes, to illuminate thoughts and feelings."[73] As he thought out where he wanted these passages to occur, Logan remembered, he imagined he was creating an "operatic form" for the musical.[74] "Unspoken Thoughts" stands out as the most successful (and operatic) of Rittman's attempts at psychological underscoring—the "operatic form" of *South Pacific* is largely in Logan's imagination—and its power creates one of the most memorable musical moments in the show, a moment inspired, but not created, by Rodgers and his melody for Nellie.[75] And it indicates, through the use of this melody as the fundamental building block of the passage, that Nellie not only is of equal musical, and therefore emotional, stature as de Becque, but that, fundamentally, they are musically and emotionally close, not distanced. This memorable passage demonstrates Scott McMillin's observation that "the unseen, omniscient orchestra knows what is in the minds of the characters even before the characters do."[76] It also knows what is in their hearts, as this exquisite music reveals.

After this dramatic moment, the dialogue is subdued. Referring to their earlier chance encounter at the Officers' Club, de Becque then sings the famous "Some Enchanted Evening," an extended lyrical moment. While this song will be considered in more detail later in this chapter, one observation belongs here because it suggests Nellie's musical presence in de Becque's song. At the bridge of the song—"Who can explain it / Who can tell you why?"—the melody, sung over a pedal-like G in the orchestra (the G is sounded on beats two and four for three measures), consists of the familiar descending tetrachord: F, E, D, C (see Example 6.3). The intervallic integrity of the original motive is retained, and we find Nellie's musical and emotional presence in de Becque's solo music. Indeed, at the end of the song, where the motive is used as a coda, the lyrics specifically refer to Nellie: "Once you have found her, / Never let her go."[77] Further, Nellie's musical presence in "Some Enchanted Evening" supports its use at the end of the show, when the orchestra has the last musical utterance: because the song represents both Nellie and de Becque, it brings them together as emotional equals.

The next place Nellie informs and adds to de Becque's musical voice is 1.7. The development of this scene has been discussed elsewhere; here, the principal concern is the central and pivotal use of "Some Enchanted Evening" as a duet within the scene.[78] In its final form, as in an earlier draft, 1.7 is tripartite: "Some Enchanted Evening" is surrounded by two solos for Nellie, the first of which—"I'm Gonna Wash That Man Right Out-A My Hair"—reveals her

Example 6.3. The tetrachord in the bridge of "Some Enchanted Evening."

The **PLAYBILL** *for the Majestic Theatre*

•   **SOUTH   PACIFIC**   •

6.8. "Playbill" cover featuring Mary Martin and Ezio Pinza at the end of act 1. Courtesy of Photofest.

somewhat unconvincing eagerness to end the relationship with de Becque. This first solo is also representative of what was earlier called the "Nellie style."

Following Nellie's first solo is a mid-scene encounter with de Becque and the reprise of "Some Enchanted Evening." The inclusion of Nellie in "Some Enchanted Evening"—she sings an introduction and several lines of the song—is an integral moment in the show that has been interpreted in several ways. Andrea Most, for instance, saw Nellie's joining in de Becque's music as the establishment of a "musical dynamic." "From the moment Emile asks Nellie to marry him [in 1.7]," Most observed, "Emile's musical style will dominate. And, after this moment, whenever they share the stage, Nellie will defer to Emile musically."[79] As has been demonstrated, however, Emile's music is much more closely related to Nellie's than Most recognized.

After the reprise of "Some Enchanted Evening," Nellie's second song— "I'm in Love with a Wonderful Guy"—expresses her exuberance and exhibits many characteristics of the "Nellie style," especially in the unpretentious vernacular lyrics. But the grand waltz setting, with its long phrases and extended structure, suggests a further connection between de Becque's stylistic sensibility and Nellie's music, not a domination of the latter by the former. To understand this connection, and to further situate Nellie's presence in de Becque's music, a reexamination of the scene is in order.

"I'm Gonna Wash That Man Right Out-a My Hair" is one of two songs in the show—"Honey Bun" is the other—that purposely imitates U.S. popular songs and represents the "Nellie style." Nonetheless, Nellie and her popular-song styling do not contradict what we already know to be her emotional core: the opening phrase of her playful plan to send de Becque "on his way" is the familiar tetrachord in retrograde (see Example 6.4). Further, the song actually exploits several song styles, each popular during the war and each with a distinct form. The first section of "I'm Gonna Wash That Man Right Out-a My Hair," as noted earlier, is in lyric binary form (AABA); it also exhibits extended limbs—the first two A sections are extended by one measure of orchestral fill, while the bridge and final A section are each eight measures, resulting in a thirty-four-bar song instead of the customary thirty-two bars. All three A sections feature an opening musical and lyrical phrase that is repeated three times and that is then followed by the phrase "and send him on his way."[80] The opening phrase swings, the dotted rhythms of the pick-up ("I'm gonna") and the phrase "out-a my hair" creating a tension with the ascending quarter-note walking-bass line played beneath them; the quarter notes of the melody following the pick-up ("wash that man right") anticipate the second set of dotted rhythms and push the vocal line forward. At the eighth bar, the trumpets and winds play a two-bar syncopated figure that further emphasizes the rhythmic contrast (see Example 6.5). This tension, combined with the three repetitions of the opening phrase, suggests a big-band arrangement of the 1930s or 1940s. The bridge ("Don't try to patch it up," etc.) sounds straighter—the walking-bass line is replaced by a repeated

I'm gon - na wash that man

Example 6.4a. The tetrachord, retrograde, in "I'm Gonna Wash That Man Right Out-a My Hair."

Example 6.4b. The tetrachord.

Nellie and the Boys | 133

Example 6.5. *"I'm Gonna Wash That Man Right Out-a My Hair,"* syncopated figure in orchestra, mm. 12–13.

Example 6.6. *"I'm Gonna Wash That Man Right Out-a My Hair,"* violin part, mm. 31–32.

Example 6.7. *"Blues"* section from *"I'm Gonna Wash That Man Right Out-a My Hair,"* mm. 39–42.

tonic-dominant pattern (in the dominant key, as is customary in the bridge), although the melody retains the dotted-eighth-, sixteenth-note pattern. The final eight bars, which repeat the lyrics of the opening eight bars, recall the suggestion of swing. This is further reinforced in the last eight measures of the chorus by the addition of a riff for the strings consisting of dotted eights and sixteenths (see Example 6.6).

At the end of the first chorus, Rodgers brings forth another style. Changing the meter to six-eight, the half note of the previous cut time equaling the dotted quarter of the new meter, he suggests a slow blues. The vocal line moves in quarter notes and eighth notes, emphasizing a lowered leading tone, as is often found in blues. The lyrics also suggest a blues, or torch song ("If the man don't understand you, / If you fly on sep'rate beams," etc.) (see Example 6.7). The harmony of this section is a variant of the tonic–subdominant–dominant harmony characteristic of the blues, and the twelve-bar structure of the section further indicates blues form, although Rodgers adds a two-bar tag ("oh ho!") at the end of the blues section before repeating it. The blues reference is evident, if not literal. This inferred blues style—the torch-song aspect of this section— would be known to Nellie from popular music of the time. Being from Arkansas, she might also have heard some rural blues. But Nellie's "blues vocabulary" is decidedly in the popular-music vein.

Example 6.8. Syncopated dance section, "I'm Gonna Wash That Man Right Out-a My Hair."

After a repeat of the blues section ("If you laugh at diff'rent comics," etc.), this time without the two-bar tag, Rodgers retains the principal melodic material but switches to a quick two-four meter ("You can't light a fire . . .," etc.). This section is sixteen bars long, and at its end Nellie sings an eight-bar recitative-like passage ("You can't put back a petal . . .") that is followed by a six-bar transition in six-eight meter ("Oh, no! / Oh no!").

At this point, the orchestra plays a dance arrangement that again is very evocative of big-band swing. (The score supports this by giving the instructions "ride it," a term connected with swing-era performance.[81]) The ninth through the twelfth bars of this dance music emphasize a repeated syncopated riff figure that makes the swing feeling unmistakable (see Example 6.8). The freedom and energy of this orchestral passage is another perfect example of Nellie's connection to popular music, and the dance continues for twenty-four more bars (thirty-six bars total), at which time Rodgers returns to the six-eight blues style for the vocal reentrance ("If his eyes get dull and fishy," etc.). Finally, after Nellie has completed washing and rinsing her hair, she again sings the opening chorus, this time to the more conclusive lyrics, "I went and washed that man right out-a my hair," and the number reaches a big finish, after which de Becque enters.

The ensuing dialogue acknowledges Nellie's use of then-popular song styles. De Becque asks if the song was "a new American song." Nellie responds, "It's an American *type* song. We were kind of putting in our own words." De Becque comments that he finds American songs strange: "In all of them one is either desirous to get rid of one's lover, or one weeps for a man one cannot have."[82] This dialogue also emphasizes the diegetic aspect of the number. "I'm Gonna Wash That Man Right Out-a My Hair" is not an interior monologue or soliloquy. It is Nellie's spontaneous and improvisatory expression of her feelings through the vocabulary of popular song, a vocabulary that, as we learned in the previous scene, is familiar to her. (In 1.6, seeking advice from Cable about her growing attachment to de Becque, Nellie asks, "Do you agree with [my] Mother about people having things in common? For instance, if the man likes symphony music and the girl likes Dinah Shore—and he reads Marcel Proust and she doesn't read anything. . . . Well, what do *you* think?"[83]) This spontaneous popular-song reference also indicates that perhaps Nellie is not serious about what she is saying. In 1.1, Rodgers and Hammerstein (and Rittman) have already musically demonstrated Nellie's complex emotions, especially those that connect her with de Becque, and the bouncy carefree nature of this song is antithetical to what is already known about Nellie's deeper feelings. Moreover, the retrograde tetrachord, which is used as the first melodic gesture of the song and is much repeated, suggests the presence of de Becque, and Nellie's connection with him, even as Nellie sings about getting rid of him: the song only superficially *seems* furthest from her actual feelings. The audience, and probably Nellie, knows that the song is only pretend, made up at the moment; while it is a wonderful production number, it is unconvincing on an emotional level, and the repeated retrograde tetrachord tells us why.

When de Becque then invites Nellie to dinner the following night, she declines; but when he explains his reason for inviting her—"I want you to know more about me . . . how I live and think . . ."—Nellie remembers her earlier promise to Captain Brackett, made in 1.5, to find out more about de Becque. Begun as an amusing "interrogation" scene—Hammerstein suggests that "Nellie pace like a cross-examiner"—the ensuing conversation suggests, as Andrea Most observed, a House Un-American Activities Committee hearing. Most insightfully referred to it as "a sort of anxious parody."[84] But after Nellie gathers her information, her return with it to Captain Brackett insinuates that, at least inadvertently, she is also an informer. Nellie, and, later, Captain Brackett decide that de Becque is squarely on the "right" side, but their machinations to find that out are presented, if lightheartedly, with subtle criticism. The political is never too far below the surface here or elsewhere in *South Pacific*.

Following the interrogation scene, and with "Some Enchanted Evening" played as underscoring, de Becque asks Nellie to marry him. Recalling his request in 1.1, de Becque asks Nellie if she has been thinking about his earlier proposal. She says yes, and begins her introduction to the reprise of "Some Enchanted Evening." This is the first and only appearance of this music in the score, and its intimate yet uncomplicated diatonic character is deceiving: this short passage is full of musical information, and it again connects Nellie and de Becque on a fundamental level.

Geoffrey Block made the astute observation that Nellie's introduction to this reprise of "Some Enchanted Evening" is related harmonically and melodically to "*Dites-moi*."[85] The reference to "*Dites-moi*" in Nellie's music connects

Example 6.9. Vocal introduction to reprise of "Some Enchanted Evening," mm. 11–16, with melody of chorus superimposed in parentheses.

her with de Becque through his children, who are still unknown to her. Nonetheless, suggestions of their presence in Nellie's music reinforce their importance. This short introduction has even more information packed into it. For example, the harmony of the first eight measures is also that of "Some Enchanted Evening" if the melody is augmented (sung in longer note values, in this case one note of the melody per beat); a conjunct descending line in the orchestra—D-C-B-A—recalls the bridge of "Some Enchanted Evening," which has already been related to the introductory material of "Twin Soliloquies" (see Example 6.9). And the dialogue that precedes the introduction refers to Nellie's interior thoughts: de Becque asks her if she has been thinking about what he mentioned in 1.1—that is, marrying him—and Nellie replies that she has. Her thoughts, this time spoken–sung, constitute the lyrics.

The introduction segues directly into the reprise of "Some Enchanted Evening," which de Becque begins. In this reprise, Nellie begins the bridge, which, as noted earlier, is built on the descending tetrachord—"Who can explain it? / Who can tell you why?"—and de Becque completes the rest of the phrase; Nellie sings the phrase again in the coda, "Once you have found him, / Never let him go." After that phrase, de Becque repeats, "Once you have found her, / Never let her go." Nellie's singing the introduction and then joining the chorus of this expansive song indicates that she is ready to externalize the feelings that, until now, have remained internal. Having contributed musical elements to de Becque's song, she is now ready to join it. This is the moment in the musical when Nellie reveals that she is much more than the "hick" from Arkansas she has suggested; this is the moment in the work when Nellie becomes its emotional core. Yet the brevity and diatonicism of the phrases she sings, and their relationship to her earlier music, also reveal her straightforward character and the lack of guile in the way she expresses her feelings, which are as deep as they are simply expressed. This is not, as Most suggested, the moment of Nellie's capitulation to de Becque and his elevated musical style. This is the moment that their emotions are revealed as equal in stature because they are musically equal. Most got it half right when she granted that de Becque has "the final triumphant notes." He has the final notes, but they are not "triumphant," as they were the first time de Becque sang the number; here, they are soft and intimate. Nellie's vocal presence changes the song. She does not capitulate; she changes de Becque's musical voice. The scene, in other words, is not about Nellie deferring to de Becque. It is about her increased recognition of her deepening emotions, which are finally articulated in song. In the reprise of "Some Enchanted Evening," the couple is again on equal emotional standing, singing music rooted in the earlier music they shared. Rodgers and Hammerstein found the perfect musical voice to trace Nellie's emotional growth in relation to de Becque's. "Some Enchanted Evening" is no longer "his" song. It is now "their" song, and Nellie's lack of sophistication should not be mistaken for a lack of intelligence or sensitivity.

After the reprise, de Becque kisses Nellie and asks if she will come to dinner on Friday. Transfixed, she agrees, as underscoring begins. Her response—a distant "Uh-huh"—breaks the serious romantic mood with a gently comic gesture. As de Becque exits, Rodgers and Hammerstein continue the change in mood by having a girl giggle offstage; another nurse comments, "Well, she sure washed him out of her hair!" and the mood shift is complete. The music segues into a brisk waltz vamp in C minor, and the third section of the scene, and with it the third musical number, has begun.

The third section of 1.7 consists solely of the musical number "I'm in Love with a Wonderful Guy." This number exploits Nellie's characteristic ebullience and straightforward self-expression, and it is, like the introduction to the reprise of "Some Enchanted Evening," the perfect musical voice for Nellie at this point in the plot. And it is a voice that again connects her to de Becque. For example, while the accompaniment to the verse suggests the tetrachord, the first phrases of the accompaniment to the chorus present an unaltered version in half notes (the first note is a quarter note)—C-B-A-G (see Example 6.10). If the preceding section of the scene demonstrates that Nellie is not

Example 6.10. The tetrachord in the opening chorus of "I'm in Love with a Wonderful Guy."

always "cock-eyed," as she suggested in 1.1, this number stresses that she is nonetheless an optimist and, at least at this moment, without emotional complication. This does not imply that she is without emotional depth, however.

To demonstrate the ebullience of Nellie's character at this point, and to relate it further to de Becque, Rodgers and Hammerstein create for her an irrepressible waltz, one of three important waltzes in the score ("You've Got to Be Carefully Taught" and "This Nearly Was Mine" are the other two). A waltz is the perfect dance type to express Nellie's spontaneous exuberance, and its old-world connotation also suggests the presence of de Becque. The song, Most observed, "celebrates the powerful theatrical possibilities latent in a union of the older European and younger American lovers (and musical styles)."[86] But it certainly does not suggest, as Most did several sentences later, that this relationship is based on de Becque always having the last word. The song suggests elements of both characters, but it is unequivocally Nellie's and provides her with the scene's last word.

At the end of the first act, Rodgers demonstrates another musical transference: in part to tease Nellie, de Becque assumes her musical style and demonstrates a more playful side of his love for her. Here, de Becque reveals a relaxed informality and an increased comfort with Nellie's vernacular musical style. Again, she has influenced his musical voice. The two of them harmonize on a bit of "Cockeyed Optimist"—this is the only time they actually sing together in the show, and it is to Nellie's music—and de Becque offers an amusing version of "I'm Gonna Wash That Man Right Out-a My Hair," imitating Nellie at the point in the song when he earlier interrupted her. De Becque is not mocking Nellie, and he is not offering a critique of Nellie's music. He is embracing it, as is she, and demonstrating again that he has assimilated her musical voice. This playful and slightly inebriated stylistic bonding between the two also sets up the dramatic confrontation that ends the act: when

Nellie learns of de Becque's earlier marriage to a Polynesian woman, her preju-dice overwhelms her and she abruptly departs. When he is left alone, de Becque returns to "their" song and again sings the end of "Some Enchanted Evening," beginning with the bridge (the tetrachord). The number brings down the first-act curtain. The end of the act would be far less powerful if the audience had not experienced the growing stylistic closeness of the two characters.

In act 2, Nellie also recalls "their" song after she learns that de Becque has gone on the mission and that Cable has died. Speaking to de Becque, although he is not present, she begs him to return so that she can tell him she realizes the error of her thinking; she then sings the final part of "Some Enchanted Evening," stopping before "Once you have found him" to entreat, "Don't die, Emile." Stopping the song at this point means that the last lyrics Nellie sings—"Then fly to his side, / And make him your own, / Or all through your life you may dream all alone"—suggest what she fears most: that because she put her prejudices before her true feelings, she will lose de Becque forever. Andrea Most suggested that by not finishing the phrase, Nellie indicates that "she understands her new subservient position in the relationship."[87] This seems a misreading of, or an overlooking of, the many subtle exchanges of music between Nellie and de Becque that have preceded, and led up to, this moment. It also overlooks the dramatic appropriateness of ending with the lyrics that the reprise ends with. And it overlooks the practical need for the remaining phrases of the song to cover the rest of the scene in which Bloody Mary and Liat enter and tell Nellie that Liat will marry no one but Cable, who she does not yet know is dead. The moment has nothing to do with Nellie's "subservience."

Nellie, then, demonstrates two oddly complementary character traits, one rooted in Hammerstein's book and the other revealed by Rodgers's score. In the book, she makes the common postwar transition from career-oriented independent woman to young wife and mother. Rather flighty and an intellectual lightweight, she appears to give over her identity to a cultured Frenchman—an older and wiser man—who is capable of providing her the comfortable dependent life as a wife and mother that she really craves. Hammerstein indicates the future of this relationship when he defines de Becque as "the boss" in the final stage directions. And in order to make Nellie's transition to postwar woman unassailable, Hammerstein exorcises all controversial attributes from Michener's character.

On the other hand, Rodgers's score suggests that although Nellie accepts de Becque's world and assumes the role of wife and mother, she does not relinquish her identity as wholly as might at first seem apparent. This Nellie is the self-confident woman who sets out to learn about other people and in

Example 6.11. The tetrachord in the "Finale Ultimo."

turn learns about herself, finding an emotional strength and maturity that, although a part of her all along, nonetheless surprise and perhaps frightens her when she discovers them. She reaches this maturity through her ability to love unconditionally, an ability that comes only after she understands her prejudice and overcomes it. Throughout this, she maintains a musical identity that connects her to de Becque on a fundamental level and reveals essential similarities between them. Her musical identity anticipates and then reflects her emotional transformation as she eventually incorporates de Becque's musical style into hers, just as he incorporates hers. In the score, Nellie and de Becque learn from each other and grow together. Although she chooses to assume her role in the nuclear family, Nellie does not at all defer to de Becque musically; although she accepts de Becque and becomes a part of his world, like many postwar women did with their husbands, she also informs him and his world, and he, hers.

As if to drive home his musical point, Rodgers, at the very end of his score, adds one final statement of the tetrachord. After a complete chorus of "*Dites-moi*," the orchestra plays a four-measure tag of "Some Enchanted Evening," and in the bass line leading into the final chord, the tetrachord is as present as it was in the musical's opening moments (see Example 6.11).

MODELS OF MASCULINITY

In his consideration of masculinity in wartime, David H. J. Morgan wrote, "Of all the sites where masculinities are constructed, reproduced, and deployed, those associated with war and the military are some of the most direct. Despite far-reaching political, social, and technological changes, the warrior still seems to be the key symbol of masculinity."[88] Further, since the end of World War II, the warrior has often been cast in the image of the soldier from that war. Christina S. Jarvis observed that although some aspects of American masculinity have altered since 1945, the "models and images of manhood" from World War II have the strongest staying power. Jarvis subsequently

6.9. *Billis (Ray Walston, center) and the boys in the 1958 film. Courtesy of Photofest.*

notes that "the popular resurgence of the war film during the late 1940s was especially vital in perpetuating World War II's almost mythical status in the American imagination. . . . At the forefront of this wave of new World War II films was [the] 1949 film *Sands of Iwo Jima*."[89] In the same year, *South Pacific* brought the war to the musical stage and, with it, some reflections of postwar constructs of masculinity.

How the men in Michener's novel live up to the expectations of warriorlike behavior often defines them: Harbison's cowardice, for example, or Cable's heroic self-affirming last stand. Hammerstein changes the novel's heroics, however, and the resulting reconstructions of masculinity deserve attention. For instance, although de Becque has no standing as a warrior in the novel, he achieves warrior status in the musical through his participation in Cable's dangerous spying mission in act 2; he makes his final entrance "in dirt-stained uniform, helmet, paratroop boots and musette bag."[90] In short, he is a returning warrior. This change was in part to ensure de Becque's credentials as a hero worthy of the all-American Nellie Forbush's hand. Cable, on the other hand, who dies a combat hero in the novel, is de-masculinized in the musical; while he establishes that he previously has been in combat, and while he briefly demonstrates leadership of the mission that he and de Becque set out on, he dies anonymously offstage, unable to resolve or act on his insights about his own racism. In death, he is the tragic romantic figure from the effete upper classes, not an action hero. "Poor little Joe Cable," as Nellie reflects.[91]

The conflicts of de Becque's and Cable's masculinities, and Hammerstein's resolution of them, are even better understood when viewed through the lens of the postwar period in which the musical was created. "The return from World War II plunged American men into a confusion about identities," Suzanne Clark noted, and that confusion is clearly reflected in these two characters.[92] The postwar challenge to men was to maintain wartime ideals of masculinity during the cold war era, which restricted their control and power. De Becque and Cable demonstrate how that challenge is or is not met. These two characters also exhibit gendered aspects of the postwar era's anticommunist fervor, a subject that must be dealt with in order to fully understand contemporaneous constructs of masculinity.

The historian Robert D. Dean offered an excellent introduction to the specifically gendered character of this period:

> Previous scholarship has stressed anticommunism as the central ideology of the Red Scare. But this focus has neglected the extent to which "McCarthyism" was also driven by related and equally deep-rooted concerns about sexual and gender order. In this conservative vision of politics and society, effective resistance to communism or other threats to "100 percent Americanism" demanded that citizens adhere to a traditional, patriarchal sexual order. The public performance of "respectable" masculinity became increasingly crucial as a test of political legitimacy.[93]

What Dean called "respectable" masculinity was in part defined by its difference from the "elite" masculinity of those in the government who had been responsible for the New Deal and, after the war, for foreign relations—what Dean called the foreign policy "establishment." Dean continued, noting,

> As biographers of "establishment" figures have indicated . . . the actions and attitudes of foreign policy decision makers were grounded in prescriptive lessons learned in a series of exclusive male-only institutions—boarding schools, Ivy League fraternities and secret societies, elite military service, metropolitan men's clubs—where imperial traditions of "service" and "sacrifice" were invented and bequeathed to those that followed. . . . [These] institutions served to imbue men with a particular kind of "manhood," [and] one of the crucial experiences of individuals in such institutions is . . . the ritual creation of a fictive brotherhood of privilege and power.[94]

This brotherhood, which Dean called "imperial," was the target of postwar conservative politicians who longed for "a means to regain power after the long years of the New Deal, wartime 'internationalism,' and Democratic rule."[95] And one of the targets of these politicians was what they regarded as the suspicious masculinity—or, perhaps, the suspicious *lack* of masculinity, as they saw it—in Dean's "imperial brotherhood." While his treatment of de Becque recalls the suspicions of the conservative movement—de Becque is held in suspicion by the American military until he volunteers for the mission, for instance—Hammerstein quells those suspicions by creating the redemptive call to arms noted above, after which de Becque is a welcomed, assimilated, and demonstratively useful member of (American) society, even if he lives on an island in the middle of the South Pacific. Hammerstein's treatment of Cable in turn suggests the possibly unhappy consequences of insufficient or inappropriate masculinity.

DE BECQUE

In Michener's novel, de Becque comes to the South Pacific after killing a man in France. The man was a bully, de Becque tells Nellie, and the town "was glad to see him die." De Becque admits, still "showing some satisfaction," that he killed the man with a knife in a purposeful, swift, and violent gesture. Once in the South Pacific, Michener's character further demonstrates that he is a man of action. "When the Japanese threatened," another character reveals, "M. De Becque and a young sea captain went to all the islands and arrested all suspicious persons. If the Japs had landed, he would have been our resistance leader." But the Japanese never invade, so de Becque's leadership in combat goes untested. De Becque is also described as "a powerful man" having "strong features" who acts "from conviction" and is a fighter. These characteristics are assumed throughout "Our Heroine," and they are never questioned. De Becque's masculinity, in other words, confirmed early by the aggressive homicide, is assumed unassailable.[96]

Hammerstein's de Becque is not immediately on such steady masculine footing, however. To begin with, Hammerstein changes de Becque's narrative about what happened in France. In an early draft of the story, the man burns down de Becque's father's house and barn, and de Becque seeks him out. They fight, and de Becque kills the man by choking him with his bare hands. De Becque still directly kills the man in this version, as in Michener, but Hammerstein adds a more personal motivation. (The house and barn burnings, in fact, hearken back to an incident described in *Oklahoma!*[97]) When de Becque notices Nellie's fear after he tells her about the incident, he reassures her that he is no longer violent and that she should not fear him.[98] No such reassurance is necessary in the final version, however, since de Becque's actions have been divested of any violent intent. The man threatens to kill de Becque; they fight; de Becque knocks the man to the ground, the man hits his head on a stone and dies.[99] In other words, De Becque's heroics are accidental, even if the result saves the town. A swift premeditated act of violence in the original story has been transformed, first into an understandable act of revenge and finally into an accident. De Becque still must prove his masculinity in an arena of action.

De Becque must also assimilate into the mainstream American culture that seems comfortably situated within the island's wartime environment. Unsurprisingly, this culture also suggests postwar American culture, its interrogations, informants, and suspicions of "outsiders" demonstrated by Nellie's grilling of de Becque about his politics. A further quote from Suzanne Clark provides an explicit context for de Becque within this social structure:

> The Cold War in its early years . . . propped an illusory coherent subject–of national and individual identity—upon gendered identities that were, in fact, on trial. The nuclear bomb exploded any possibility of maintaining the old heroic manliness of the frontier. But the initial response to the fragmentation of a masculinized society reasserted warrior culture.

De Becque's transformation from highbrow European outsider into an all-American action figure suggests this reasserted behavior model and also the more general change from a foreigner into an American, an assimilation that earns him the respect of the navy—Brackett refers to him as a "wonderful guy" when de Becque is in the midst of the mission—and the acceptance of the audience.[100] This recalls William S. Graebner's observation that, during the 1940s, "Americans paid lip service to tolerance but generally remained committed to assimilationist ideas."[101] Hammerstein sets this up early on, and de Becque's journey to socially sanctioned masculinity (through action in war) and subsequent assimilation is a sometimes subtle but always integral aspect of his character.

Before he compels de Becque to action, however, Hammerstein develops his character in several other ways. First, as a cultivated European in a predominantly American environment, de Becque's masculinity is in question from his first appearance.[102] The audience is informed early of de Becque's elevated musical and literary taste.[103] These tastes leave de Becque vulnerable to certain criticisms made against postwar intellectuals. According to James Gilbert, "Their isolation from mainstream American culture, their European orientation, their occasional radical politics, and their sometimes complex artistic creations raised serious questions about their gender identity. . . . As in other areas of American culture, 'womanly' or 'feminine' were sometimes code words for submissive, soft, flighty, emotional, and consumerist, while 'masculine' implied productive, inventive, creative, action-oriented, and tough-minded."[104] At the end of the first act, de Becque is shown "learning" American popular culture—he is assimilating, in other words—but, until then, his musical style is more reminiscent of operetta than popular song (although the song that demonstrates this—"Some Enchanted Evening"— became a very popular song). Nonetheless, as already noted, Nellie's music informs de Becque's in an intimate way, insinuating a fundamental quality both share. The outer differences in de Becque's style require closer examination, however, because that style reflects the construction of his masculinity.

Andrea Most's comments on the outward characteristics of Nellie's and de Becque's music are correct: "Nellie's style" and de Becque's indeed are structurally different, even if sometimes motivically related. After the shared "Twin Soliloquies" and the unsung "Unspoken Thoughts," de Becque's first solo is an expansive and deeply romantic utterance. While the song demonstrates what Graham Wood called lyric binary form, it also demonstrates what he called a "macro chorus," meaning a larger-than-usual chorus exploiting small-part forms within its larger sections. This cross-pollination of forms creates an extended fifty-six bar chorus (plus seven-bar coda); but while "Some Enchanted Evening" is, overall, an AABA lyric binary form, the first two A sections of the song demonstrate parallel period form. They do this in two ways. First, the initial sixteen-bar section (the first A, ending with "That somewhere you'll see her again and again"[105]) is the antecedent phrase, and the second sixteen-bar section (the second A, ending with "The sound of her laughter will sing in your dreams") is the consequent: this creates a thirty-two measure parallel period chorus. Second, what Wood termed the "textual/emotional contour" of the parallel period chorus is present. This contour can be demonstrated as follows:

(a) 1st idea	(b) 2nd idea	(a) 3rd idea	(b) 4th idea
presentation	building/expansion	restatement of 1st idea, or new perspective on 1st idea	resolution, confirmation, summary & climax, or recall of opening idea[106]

"Some Enchanted Evening" demonstrates this plan. The first eight measures—the first quatrain of the lyric—expresses the primary idea of the song, which is that "Some enchanted evening / You may see a stranger." The second eight measures build on this idea, noting, "you know ... somewhere you'll see her again and again." The third section—the antecedent phrase of the second A section—offers a new perspective of the moment ("You may hear her laughing / Across a crowded room") to the same music as the first eight measures, and the fourth section confirms that the stranger is not going away, at least figuratively—"The sound of her laughter will sing in your dreams."

This thirty-two bar section is followed by the bridge, or B section, which is only eight measures long but is important in that it musically connects de Becque and Nellie. (How curious that this musical connection occurs after de Becque sings of Nellie's "sound" and how it exists in his dreams.) The lyrics contemplate the situation, asking if there is any possible explanation for it. Then the song repeats the A section, using the image of "some enchanted evening" and the "crowded room," but concluding with the urgent advice to "fly to her side / And make her your own." The song ends with a coda, which is a repeat of the bridge material sung to the words, "Once you have found her, never let her go," which is the familiar tetrachord.

The extended structure of "Some Enchanted Evening" is appropriate because it is natural for de Becque. This is a believable way for an erudite Frenchman to express his emotions. The song informs the audience that de Becque is romantic, passionate, and tenacious; but for many postwar Americans, those qualities were suspect unless found in a man of action for whom they were secondary characteristics. And nothing is forthcoming about de Becque's capacity for action in "Some Enchanted Evening." Only his desire not to let go of something is apparent.

In act 2, when de Becque expresses his desolation over Nellie's refusal to marry him, he again evokes European musical traditions by singing "This Nearly Was Mine," a song Geoffrey Block called "a pessimistic romantic waltz ballad."[107] Like "Some Enchanted Evening," "This Nearly Was Mine" is expansive: while it is in lyric binary form, each section is sixteen measures long, or double the standard length, and the trio section is thirty-two measures long. In it, de Becque realizes he is alone on his island—the final A section begins with the line, "Now, now I'm alone," and the stage directions following the song indicate that de Becque is "a lonely and disconsolate figure."[108] While the song is beautiful and provided Ezio Pinza with a big second-act moment, it presents de Becque as the antithesis of a "100 percent American" postwar man, and de Becque must overcome his emotionally dependent state to be worthy of the woman he loves, even if she rejects him. And yet, as Ethan Mordden suggested, the song is the musical climax of the show. Mordden went on to note that the song "calls up quotations of earlier songs in the orchestra parts—of 'Bali Ha'i' (in the brass) during the introduction, then of 'Some Enchanted Evening' and 'I'm in Love with a Wonderful Guy' (in the woodwinds) during the refrain."[109] The last two references are especially interesting, given that both songs, as demonstrated earlier, contain motivic connections between de Becque and Nellie.

"This Nearly Was Mine" is also the dramatic climax of the show in that it is the last exquisite gasp of de Becque's European, or outsider, sensibility before he becomes a man of action and, therefore, a warrior. De Becque's status as a European outside American culture (and musical styles) is established early, as is his status as a civilian who has never served in the military; the two are not unrelated. Isolated on his island plantation, he accepts the U.S. presence on the island but is not really a part of it beyond his sympathies as a de Gaullist; when he is first asked in act 1 to participate in the spying mission with Cable, he refuses, stating that he will do nothing to endanger his future with Nellie. In addition to the grandeur of his music, this civilian identity in the midst of a theater of war and his refusal to become involved in the war mark de Becque as suspicious: as Dean observed, not serving in the military during the war "could be read as evidence of questionable 'manliness'."[110] De Becque's outsider status to the war effort and to society is not resolved until he decides to accompany Cable on the mission, an act prompted in part by the disconsolation of "This Nearly Was Mine." As Michael Kimmel noted, "Violence [in this case, war] is often the single most evident marker of manhood. . . . [It] is the willingness to fight, the desire to fight" that reveals masculinity.[111] De Becque's climactic decision to accompany Cable is his defining moment, and it is a moment that recalls Kathy Ferguson's observation that "identity is something one *does*, an active corralling of practices, events, contingencies, a regulatory semiotic and material operation."[112]

Once de Becque leaves with Cable, once he puts his life on the line for the cause of the war, he demonstrates the one quality he has thus far lacked: bravery in a military maneuver. And this action earns his place at the head of the nuclear family that has begun to develop in his absence and that awaits his requisite manly presence. The "cultured Frenchman," as Nellie refers to him in "Twin Soliloquies," is now also a returning hero whose masculinity is no longer in doubt to anyone. Only after de Becque lives up to those masculine ideals can he and Nellie, along with de Becque's children, be united as a postwar family.

6.10. *William Tabbert, the original Joe Cable. Courtesy of Photofest.*

CABLE

To understand the impact of Hammerstein's changes to the character of Joe Cable, Michener again must be recalled. Like de Becque's, Cable's masculinity is never in question in the novel. Indeed, the first thought Bloody Mary has when she sees him, according to the author, is, "Here was a man." Later, the author adds his own reaction to Cable, which is not unlike Mary's: "He was a powerfully competent man. I thought then that he would probably give a good account of himself in a fight. . . . His face, although not handsome, was masculine. . . . To this quiet assurance he added a little of the Marine's inevitable cockiness." Michener establishes, as does Hammerstein, that Cable has seen battle; in the novel, Cable has done a "tour of battle on Guadalcanal." In the book's last chapter, Cable's story is concluded: he rejects Liat, and he has a series of fights with enlisted men and with officers because they give him a hard time about his relationship with a Tonkinese girl. Once he is again in combat, however, Cable's fighting energy is solely focused on the enemy. The African American custodian of a cemetery on Hoga Point, where many of the characters from the earlier stories are buried, notes in the final story (in a problematic representation of African American speech), "Well, come de beachhead . . . [and] dis yere Marine, he about de bes' we got on our side. He go after them Japs plenty tough."[113] As Michener's narrator observed, Cable "gave a good account of himself."

In the musical, Cable appears directly after the hyper-masculine musical number, "There Is Nothin' Like a Dame," in which sailors and soldiers sing about having "every kind of feelin' / But the feelin' of relief."[114] They list the desirable attributes of the women they don't have, and they do so in a sexually charged staging that Joshua Logan later noted as "one of the things most remembered about my work."[115] After the number, Cable enters and is immediately greeted by Bloody Mary; after the two say hello, the music of "Bali Ha'i" is heard in the background. Cable is therefore immediately connected with the chromatic, "exotic," and feminine music of Mary and the islands. After Cable establishes that he has seen combat, Mary begins telling him that he is sexy, or "saxy," in her Pidgin English, and she repeatedly mentions his attractiveness. After referring to Bali Ha'i, she almost mystically tells Cable that the island is his special island and that it is calling to him. Mary does not yet reveal that, in addition to finding Cable attractive, she also sees him as a potential marriage partner for her young daughter, who she keeps on Bali Ha'i. To convince Cable that she knows something of his fate, or that she might have a hand in it, she sings "Bali Ha'i," the song that famously bears the name of the island. Because the song is directly connected to Cable, and because it is gendered, it requires further examination.

Rodgers's use of chromaticism in this song—tritones and passages exploiting movement by half step in the melody; diminished chords and chromatic countermelodies in the accompaniment—recalls Hollywood's popular musical expression of the South Pacific and its peoples in the 1930s and 1940s.[116] The song stands out from the others in the score because of its implicit evocation of otherness, of the mysterious, and, therefore, of the feminine. The use of chromaticism also embodies desire—Mary's for Cable; her need to entice Cable to the exotic island and, subsequently, to her still-virgin but sexually alluring daughter; Cable's desire for something outside his world of experience with which, as will soon be apparent, he is less than comfortable.

The use of chromaticism to suggest feminine sexuality in "Bali Ha'i" is not unprecedented. Susan McClary's insightful comments on Carmen, the

6.11. *Juanita Hall, the original Bloody Mary, sings "Bali Ha'i." Courtesy of Photofest.*

character in Bizet's *opéra comique* of the same name, offer assessments also appropriate to this discussion. In what could be a description of "Bali Ha'i", McClary wrote of a particularly chromatic vocal line that it "reveals her [Carmen] as a 'master' of seductive rhetoric." McClary expounded, "She knows how to hook and manipulate desire. In her musical discourse she is slippery, unpredictable, maddening: hers is the music we remember from the opera."[117] Likewise, Bloody Mary's song also provides a memorable musical "theme song" for *South Pacific*; it is the first music heard in the overture, and it is repeated at key moments to indicate Cable's awakening sexuality and the relationship of that sexuality to the island. Its status as a representation of otherness is confirmed in 1.9 when, after Cable's arrival on the island, it is sung in French. Cable is seduced and manipulated by Mary's music, to use McClary's vocabulary, and it pulls him away from the masculine arena of combat and into the darker areas of feminine desire and sex, his response to which contributes to his destruction. In this context, Rodgers's comments on the composition of "Bali Ha'i" are especially interesting:

> For months Oscar and I had been talking about a song for Bloody Mary which would evoke the exotic, mystical powers of a South Seas island. I knew that the melody would have to possess an Oriental, languorous quality, that it would have to be suitable for a contralto voice, and even that the title was going to be "Bali Ha'i."[118]

"Exotic," "mystical," and "languorous" all suggest a "South Seas" stereotype common in 1949, but they also serve as indicators of gendered characteristics other than masculine. However, while Rodgers's musical representation of the enticing island can be read as seductively feminine—Mary's voice repeatedly envoices the island as she sings, "Here am I, / Your own special island! / Come to me, come to me!"—Hammerstein's lyrics are gender-neutral.[119] The musical implication is persuasive, but it is never verbally explicit. By the scene's end, the music possesses Cable and he sings the final twelve bars of the song as the lights fade.

Between Mary's version of the song and Cable's, Cable's masculinity is further contrasted with that of the other sailors and Marines on the beach. The exchange between Cable and Billis regarding Cable's pedigree reflects not only Cable's patrician background but also his discomfort with it and the response of the enlisted men to it. Although Hammerstein omits the details that Michener provides about Cable's socioeconomic status—Hammerstein's Cable is more generically upper crust—an upper-class background and an Ivy League education were postwar indicators of an elite status that were anathema to increasingly working- and middle-class standards of masculinity. (In both the book and the musical, Cable's upper-class roots become increasingly problematic as his involvement in the plot continues.) Cable also reveals that, although he has come to the island to organize a spying mission on a Japanese-held island, he was "elected" to do so. While the success of the mission would make him a hero, he is not necessarily anxious to achieve that status. In short, by the end of the scene in which he is introduced, the audience knows that although Cable has established his masculinity in combat, he is about to have that masculinity challenged.[120]

Later, in 1.9 and 1.10, Cable goes to Bali Ha'i when his mission is temporarily postponed. Here he is introduced to Liat, Mary's daughter, and further gender conflicts are quickly discernible. For instance, after meeting the young—Hammerstein suggests that she is "perhaps seventeen"—and beautiful Liat, Cable asks her if she is afraid. She replies no, but when he approaches her she says yes. Hammerstein notes that "he stops and looks at her, worried and hurt. This sign of gentleness wins her."[121] His behavior with her is as far from that of the edgy, relief-seeking sailors of "There Is Nothin' Like a Dame" as we could imagine, and it also is less masculine: Cable's sensitivity with Liat is romantic, but it is not butch.[122]

After a few more sentences, as Cable takes Liat in his arms, "the music builds in a rapturous upsurge" and the lights fade as Cable begins to undress Liat.[123] Such blatant eroticism was unprecedented in any musical by Rodgers and Hammerstein, and probably by anyone else. When the lights come up after an interlude in which "the music mounts ecstatically," Cable is standing shirtless and Liat sits, her hair now loose and hanging down her back.[124] This display of Cable's body, like the display of the men's bodies in earlier scenes (1.2 and 1.3), was both a recollection of wartime depictions of the male body and a postwar statement by a director whose onstage depictions of homoeroticism were already well established.[125]

Joshua Logan wrote in his memoirs that "*South Pacific* had added to my reputation of the nudity king of Broadway." As Logan told it, Leland Hayward, the producer of Logan's war-era play *Mister Roberts*, worried that Logan hadn't done anything "to interest the women" in the audience for that play. Logan continued, "In thinking about it, it struck me that what would appeal

6.12. *The original Broadway cast in "There Is Nothin' Like a Dame." Courtesy of Photofest.*

to women was the thought of the physical love they missed during the war, so when the crew takes its shirts off, a privilege given them by Roberts, I decided that women might prefer to see handsome, sculptured male torsos instead of the usual comic, flabby bodies in the corny service films." However, several paragraphs later, Logan made a telling observation: "And again, I discovered how much more stage nudity is noticed by the same sex than by the opposite sex. One of the toughest woman-chasing guys I know saw *South Pacific* on opening night and then saw it a year later. I expected him to complain about the loss of Pinza or a sloppier performance, but instead he said, 'You ought to have those guys go to the gym and shape up—you know, the ones without any shirts on.' I said, ' . . . Is that what you were looking at?' He said, 'No, but they used to look so great.'"[126] Logan's subsequent work—the film of *South Pacific*, the musical *Wish You Were Here*, the stage and film versions of *Picnic*, and the film *Ensign Pulver*, among others—is notable for its display of attractive men in semi-dress. Indeed, in the film version of *South Pacific*, Bloody Mary is constantly framed by stunning men, most shirtless, throughout her performance of the song "Bali Ha'i"; they have nothing to do with the song, but they are nonetheless in almost every shot. While this indicates a sexual objectification of the male body, which certainly does not fit into the postwar notion of "respectable" masculinity, it also reflects wartime images of men's bodies, many of which were, and still are, homoerotic.

Christina S. Jarvis has written at length about the changing representations of male bodies from the Depression era through World War II. Uncle Sam himself underwent a remarkable change, from scrawny old man to a steel-muscled leader, and Jarvis observed, "With images of a newly hardened Uncle Sam, World War II ushered in a distinctly masculine national symbol, as the U.S. began to imagine itself more thoroughly within masculine terms."[127] These hard bodies were aggressive soldiers, however, not romantic lovers; muscular male bodies were nearly always shown loading ammunition into massive artillery (images that were often highly phallic) or otherwise engaged in combat-related activities. These contexts legitimized the voyeurism encouraged by the display of men's bodies. Jarvis noted the more general effect of these images as follows:

It was not until World War II that American men, the media, and the government began to imagine the United States in explicitly masculine terms. . . . Integral to this shift in perception were the widespread wartime representations of powerful, youthful male bodies in posters, advertisements, and other public images. With their comic book physiques and implied steel-like force, these images communicated messages of national strength as American mobilized for war.[128]

The revealing of Cable's body after sex with an underage girl, unlike the display of the horny soldiers' and sailors' bodies earlier in the act, is private and nonaggressive. In other words, it serves no propagandistic goal. If not, effeminate—he has, after all, just had what was probably his first sexual encounter with a woman—the display, from a postwar perspective, is nonetheless suspect. By 1949, the manliness of the solider in World War II had transformed into what K. A. Cuordileone called "anxieties about sexuality, manhood, and the self [that] surfaced in cold war political rhetoric and intersected with anxieties about Communism and national security," and the gratuitous display of the male body fueled those gendered anxieties. After the war, "conservative ideals that exalted the nuclear family, traditional gender roles, and sexual restraint were promoted after decades of social disruption brought on by depression and war," and sexuality, including representations of the body, was to be "contained within heterosexual marriage and the nuclear family."[129] Standing shirtless in a jungle hut after having sex with a seventeen-year-old girl, Cable represents neither marriage nor family, and his body, like the sexual act he has just experienced, suggests a transgression of postwar ideals.

Until this encounter, Cable has come off as a young, rigid, somewhat self-deprecating, and by-the-book military man. But when the lights come up after sex with Liat, he is changed. When he hears the bell on his boat signaling the return trip, he comments, "Aw, let them wait," and begins the song "Younger Than Springtime." Any song in this position would have to convey his passion and his innocence, his amazement and his concern for the young woman to whom he has just made love. Cable's musical voice at this moment must demonstrate more than just the voice of the young romantic lead; it needs to soar with his realization that he is capable of this kind of passion, an insight that is new to him. In short, finding the right musical voice for the character at this moment presented the creators with a challenge. It was not a challenge that they immediately met, but the song they eventually settled on is also, perhaps unsurprisingly, gendered.

Joshua Logan reported that the show went into rehearsals without a song for this spot. According to him, the first attempt was a song called "My Friend." Logan quoted the first two lines—"My friend, my friend, / Is coming around the bend"—and then stated that he hated the song.[130] Apart from the lines that Logan offered, only the lyrics for an interlude to the number are in either Rodgers's or Hammerstein's collection at the Library of Congress. Found in the Rodgers Collection, the interlude to "My Friend" reads, "Funny little thing, / You stand there silently blinking, / Funny little girl— / I'd like to hear what you're thinking. / *Je t'aime*."[131] Musically, only a melody with some fundamental Roman numeral chords beneath it exists; this melody is appropriately lyrical and rather charming.[132] Rodgers was thinking of an expansive musical number, however, because he has provided music for a verse and chorus in addition to an interlude. However, Logan's disappointment with the number must have been matched by Rodgers and Hammerstein's, for the song was cut before it was even written out in more than a rough sketch.

The next attempt at a song for Cable is well known. The literature is confused about the facts, however, and wants clarification. Logan wrote that Rodgers and Hammerstein came to him the next day with their new attempt. "It was a lilting schottische," wrote Logan, "the words of which began like this: 'Suddenly lucky, / Suddenly our arms are lucky.'"[133] Recent scholarship has suggested that Logan's memory is incorrect, and that the next draft for this spot was titled "Suddenly Lovely."[134] But Logan did not mistitle the song: it was "Suddenly Lucky." "Suddenly Lucky" appears on two typewritten pages for 1.12, the original number of the scene that eventually became 1.10; further, it contains both a complete introduction and the completed chorus. The introduction, for which no music exists, begins, "We've had a break, / A very good break," and the chorus indeed begins exactly as Logan says it did. However, "Suddenly Lucky" might have postdated "Suddenly Lovely": the lyrics on the two pages of the sketch for 1.12 have a line drawn through them, and Hammerstein has written in the right margin, "All of Younger Than verse." On the second page, directions for the interlude after the first chorus of "Younger Than Springtime," the ship's bell, and Cable's vocal reprise are also written in pencil.[135] At the top of the first page, in pencil, is written "2-18," suggesting the date in rehearsals that "Younger Than Springtime" was added to the score. The melody to the discarded "Suddenly Lucky / Lovely," as is widely known, gained prominence two years later in *The King and I*, where it had new lyrics that began, "Getting to know you . . ."

Logan liked the song but thought it "a bit lightweight for a hot, lusty boy to sing right after making love to a girl who will change his life."[136] So Rodgers and Hammerstein came up with "Younger Than Springtime," the melody of which already existed.[137] What makes the lyric to "Younger Than Springtime" especially interesting in regard to gender and Cable is the transference of images from Liat to himself, which results in his defining himself with the same terms he used to define her: he gives himself *her* characteristics. The verse starts this process immediately—"I touch your hand and my arms grow strong"—and the chorus makes it explicit. The form of the song, which is an example of thirty-two-bar lyric binary structure with a one-bar extension in the final A section, also lends itself to this transference. The initial A sections are about Liat: "Younger than springtime are you, / Softer than starlight are you," sings Cable, the "are you[s]" set off from the images by a quarter-note rest. The last image that he uses—"Angel and lover, heaven and earth are you to me"—reveals that his experience with Liat has implications more profound than just his physical awakening with her. "Angel" and "heaven" suggest transcendence.

The bridge describes the infusion of Liat's qualities into Cable, or, perhaps, the transformation of Cable through Liat, in two succinct lines plus one transitional word. "And when your youth and joy invade my arms / And fill my heart as now they do . . . / Then . . ." Following this, in the final A section, Cable reveals himself in terms that he has probably never before used. They describe qualities that we certainly have not seen in him, although his response to Bloody Mary's mystical description of Bali Ha'i suggested their latency. And, importantly, they are the same images with which he described Liat: "Younger than springtime am I, / Gayer than laughter am I, / Angel and lover, heaven and earth am I with you."[138]

The repetition of the combined images ("angel and lover, heaven and earth") in the last line is particularly inspired. At this point, Cable is able to see in himself, and in Liat, spiritual and physical qualities that are beyond time and place. This is a moment of revelation for him. Later, his inability to reunite these qualities contributes to his downfall; the "heaven" is rent from the "earth," and Cable is destroyed by his inability, or unwillingness, to reunite them and by his inability to again join the masculine and feminine (the "you" and "I" of the lyric). In short, these lyrics, which have lost much of their amazing freshness and insight after years of often mediocre performances, contain within them the explanation of Cable's eventual tragedy. Infusing himself with the feminine characteristics of his lover, Cable betrays his previously won masculine status. Nowhere in the show is a character's musical voice more perfectly captured than in "Younger Than Springtime." Its thirty-three bars are virtually a well-made drama unto themselves.

The next time Cable appears, in 2.2, he has slipped out of the hospital where he was undergoing treatment for a mild case of malaria and encounters Mary and Liat. After a short scene and the musical number "Happy Talk," Cable gives Liat a gold watch that belonged to his grandfather and father: "It's kind of a lucky piece, too. My dad carried it all through the last war."[139] At this point, Mary asserts that Cable and Liat should get married, but Cable, looking "tortured," tells Mary that he cannot marry Liat. Mary explodes in a rage, tears the watch out of Liat's hands and smashes it on the ground. The destruction of Cable's "lucky piece" seals his fate. When Mary and Liat exit, Cable sings the end of "Younger Than Springtime," this time in the past tense.

Unable to break down the barriers of gender and class, Cable, through his inability to accept and change his situation, is inactive. And inaction is not masculine. By calling into question what Robert Dean labeled "traditional, patriarchal" gender constructs, which were powerful and constricting models for postwar performances of gender, but not being able to alter them, Cable is in an inordinately difficult spot: if he marries Liat, he must give up living in mainstream U.S. society; if he gives up Liat and returns to his mainstream American life, he is emotionally destroyed. Thus, after realizing the root of his intolerance and his emotional devastation, and after realizing de Becque's similarly desperate emotional state, he finally becomes motivated for action. He decides that, if he survives, he will stay on the island and marry Liat.

At one point, Hammerstein decided to let Cable live. In a draft for 2.11, Cable returns from Marie Louise.[140] The first person he meets is Billis, who he immediately tells to get a boat so he can go to Bali Ha'i and marry Liat. Cable succinctly explains how he and de Becque survived, after which Cable and Billis exit in search of a boat. Hammerstein, however, soon realized that Cable could not survive and marry Liat; while he is willing to say that Nellie's and Cable's racism is wrong, and that people can overcome having been taught racist behavior and thoughts in their youth, Hammerstein is not brave (or commercially daring) enough to allow Cable and Liat to marry. By letting Cable die, Hammerstein equivocates.[141] Cable can realize that his and, subsequently, Nellie's, racism is learned, not essential, and the audience can realize the same lesson. But asking the audience to accept Cable marrying a seventeen-year-old Tonkinese girl is too much.

Two other factors are also important to Cable's eventual fate. First, when he decides not to go back to the United States after the war, Cable is rejecting (American) society and declaring his own outsider status. The minute he does this in a Rodgers and Hammerstein musical, he is doomed. From Jud Fry to Billy Bigelow to Jenny Taylor, those who stand outside the mainstream and/ or who challenge community values in Rodgers and Hammerstein's earlier shows must be assimilated or eradicated. Joe Taylor also finds himself outside the community he grew up in and wants to be a part of, but he is allowed the opportunity to redeem himself. He sees the errors of his, and his wife's, ways and returns to his, and Hammerstein's, core values.

Second, a marriage to Liat would suggest that Cable rejects the American masculine ideal. When she suggests that Cable marry her daughter, for instance, Mary tells him that she would do all the work: "Give all de money to you an' Liat. You no have to work. I work for you."[142] This is a transgression of every American ideal imaginable, from gender to work ethic. While it would provide a "happy" ending, something Rodgers and Hammerstein obviously considered, it ultimately would have been far more problematic, for the audience if not for the creators, than Cable's death. In 1949 most U.S. audiences simply were not ready to see a successful mixed-race relationship—the creators' plea for general racial tolerance was disruptive enough. In short, "poor little Joe Cable" does not stand a chance.

GENDER AND 1949

The more closely *South Pacific* is read in terms of its gender constructs, the more it seems reflective of its time. Like the postwar–cold war era in which it was created, the musical is more complicated than it might at first seem. Hammerstein's book alone recalls Betty Friedan's image of women in post-1949 women's magazine stories: Nellie becomes an extension of de Becque's world. Younger and less experienced than de Becque, she is not unlike a child bride (she is only five years older than Liat) whose future growth and experience is directed by her mentor–husband. Once Nellie's racism, the most complex and interesting element of her character, is "fixed," she is free to move into de Becque's sphere of existence and lose herself in it.

Yet the score provides a more complex portrait of Nellie, one that reveals her equal emotional and cultural standing with de Becque. Outwardly worried about her banal taste in music as a reflection of her being a "hick," Nellie is inwardly connected to de Becque in ways that reveal how the two are "fundamentally alike," as she observes in the play. The sophisticated motivic connections between Nellie and de Becque in the score suggest that, upon careful investigation, there is more to Nellie than first meets the ear.

Likewise, de Becque and Cable demonstrate postwar constructs of masculinity. De Becque is moved to action and heroism, and his achievement in those areas indicates that he is ready to be a "good American," even if he never technically becomes one. De Becque's trajectory is toward the ideal, and when he shows that he is more than an effete European isolationist, he is ready to be a part of the extended American community. On the other hand, Cable rejects the extended community just before reentering the sphere of action, and that rejection dooms him. As de Becque's masculinity factor increases, Cable's decreases, and the further he moves from the postwar masculine ideal, the surer is his fate. Cable has already demonstrated his masculinity when he is first encountered, but he spends the rest of the play chipping away at it as he becomes increasingly inner-focused.

South Pacific is a text that reflects the challenges and changes indicated by postwar American gender constructs. As its layers of information are

6.13. Martin Wolfson, the original Brackett. Courtesy of Photofest.

uncovered and analyzed, the musical recalls Bruce Kirle's observation: "If musicals reflect the material conditions in which they were originally produced and received, popular musicals, through their wide and broad range of appeal, become markers that document American attitudes toward identity during the past half-century. It seems logical that particularly successful musicals typically unite the world of the author with the concerns of the audience."[143] *South Pacific* is just such a marker, and it provides stimulating insight into postwar American gender constructs. As Kirle's comments suggest, *South Pacific* provided its early audiences with a musical and dramatic mirror in which they could view their own complex identities. The show's greatness is, at least in part, its continuing ability to encourage similar reflection among contemporary audiences.

7

CULTURE CLASH

• • •

Colonialism and *South Pacific*

Two sets of stage directions exist for the beginning of 1.1. Both reveal the outside of an island plantation home, and both introduce Jerome and Ngana, two children described as "Eurasian." These are de Becque's children, although the audience does not know this yet, and they perform "*Dites-moi,*" the show's first song. The young boy is Hammerstein's invention; in Michener's book, de Becque has eight daughters, all by different mothers and four of whom live with him on his plantation. Hammerstein found the children's names in the story "The Cave," in which Jerome and Ngana are a husband-and-wife team working with the so-called Remittance Man. Beyond the script's use of the word "Eurasian," which the audience probably would not be aware of, the children's mixed ethnic heritage is suggested by their names, found in the program; their appearance; and the French lyrics to their folklike song, which is marked "*À l'antique*" in the score.

Both versions of the opening scene also present two aspects of the show that remain important throughout. First, the scene indicates that the story, at least for the time being, is not going to be about the conflict of battle. Indeed, although the drama is set on an island inhabited by hundreds or even thousands of sailors, Marines, Seabees, and nurses, and while the background is a global war being fought in the Pacific, the actual plot is intimate and personal. Like much of the book they adapted, Rodgers and Hammerstein's musical is only incidentally about the war that provides its setting. Second, each version also presents initial images of contrasting and/or conflicting cultures, thus introducing the problematic issue of colonial presences in the South Pacific before, during, and, by 1949, after the war.

The first stage directions for the scene, which are unmentioned in the literature about *South Pacific*, are found in the Richard Rodgers collection at the Library of Congress and describe the accompanied pantomime that leads into the song. "They [the children] advance timidly towards the house. They stop and whisper and giggle, childishly exaggerating some secret joke." Jerome peeks in a window and runs back to Ngana. They sing. After their song, "they strike a pose of two lovers in a mock embrace and burst out laughing."[1] The song is both a children's song and a commentary on what Jerome and Ngana see going on in the house. The children are spectators, mimicking the actions of someone inside, and their pose at the song's end suggests more mimicry. Their words declare that life is beautiful because the singer's love for the sung-to is returned. Unbeknownst to the audience, the children also are fore-shadowing the scene that follows.

The stage directions in the published script provide an interesting com-parison. "[The children] are, with humorous dignity, dancing an impromptu minuet. A birdcall is heard in the tree above. Jerome looks up and imitates the sound. The eyes of both children follow the flight of the bird. Ngana runs over to the pagoda and poses on it as if it were a stage. Jerome lifts his hands and solemnly conducts as she sings."[2] (While the score calls for both children to sing, as does the first set of stage directions, the pub-lished script calls for only Ngana to sing, and she sings alone on the orig-inal cast recording. In the 2008 Broadway revival, however, both children sing the song.) In this opening, the children seem oblivious to what is going on in the house. Their mixed heritage, as in the first version, is sug-gested by the juxtaposition of the European song and dance (which, because it is in duple time, is not a minuet); it is emphasized further by their response to the call of the wild bird. Jerome's imitation of the bird-call indicates he is familiar with the island locale, just as his mastery of the dance steps and knowledge of conducting indicate a European sensibility. Ngana is also drawn to the bird, but when it is out of sight, she, too, returns to European-influenced behavior, mounting a "stage" and allowing herself to be led by a "conductor." In this mock concert hall, her French words, while unexpected, are not totally surprising. Indeed, in 1949 many in the audience may have been cognizant of the longstanding French presence in the Pacific islands. Nonetheless, although these children appear decidedly Westernized by the end of the song, the audience still does not know who they are.

In both versions of the opening, the pronounced presence of Western culture in the children's behavior suggests that some kind of colonialism is on display. The published stage directions reinforce this by contrasting the chil-dren's imitation of the tropical bird's call with their singing a presumably Western song. Further, the "performance" of the song works on two levels. First, the young actors are obviously performing the song for the audience. Second, the characters are acting out a performance ritual that they may or, more probably, may not have experienced. The language and the song also suggest that Western culture is dominant, and that the children are well schooled in its ways. The entrance of Henry, an indigenous servant who speaks only French, once again suggests a Western cultural influence. After some playful banter with the children, Henry herds them into the house. The importance of these opening minutes is in large part due to the presentation of indigenous people as children and/or servants who speak a European language. Only as these three exit do we hear dialogue in English, which is also a language imported to this setting.

Later versions of *South Pacific* have begun otherwise. The 1958 movie version, for instance, opens as if it were a wide-screen Hollywood war adventure. After the opening titles, the first scene is in the cockpit of a transport plane bringing Joe Cable to the island, after which the camera pans to the beach and the sailors sing "Bloody Mary." Subsequent stage productions have borrowed this idea and opened the show with the soldiers and sailors. This is a subversion of the plot's focus. The personal stories should not be overshadowed by the war. Instead, the influence of the war should appear within, and be reflected by, the personal stories, which are the show's principal concerns. Changing the beginning of *South Pacific* distorts the emphases of its theme and plot. It also dissipates the power of opening the show with images of multiple and contrasting cultures, images that inform all of what follows.

The effect of the opening scene and its suggestion of the children's mixed ethnicities were not lost on audiences during the original Broadway run. In September 1949, for example, five months after the show's opening, Everett R. Clinchy, the president of the National Conference for Christians and Jews, Inc., wrote in a letter to Hammerstein, "I was especially appreciative of the race relations problem which runs through the play from the first sight of the planter's children. . . . You have [shown] what Shakespeare said the theatre should be, a mirror held up to nature, and the way in which you dramatized an important human problem makes darned good theatre."[3]

When the children return at the end of the scene, after Nellie's exit, they join their father, who "conducts" a reprise of the opening number. As they finish, the beginning of the second scene overlaps the ending of the first and the audience is startled by a boisterous group of Seabees, sailors, and Marines singing the praises of Bloody Mary in the number named for her. And Mary, who first speaks between verses of the song, is one of two non-Western characters who are integral to the musical. The other is Liat, Mary's daughter. Both are from Tonkin, approximately the area that is now North Vietnam.

7.1. *Juanita Hall as Bloody Mary in selling mode. Courtesy of Photofest.*

BLOODY MARY: DRAGON LADY OR ANTICOLONIALIST?

In his autobiography, Michener recalled Bloody Mary when he wrote about the strained relationship he encountered in the South Pacific between the French colonialists and the indentured Tonkinese, who worked on the French plantations. The original agreement between the planters and the workers was somewhat satisfactory to both parties. The Tonkinese signed on to work for three to five years at a fair wage, most of which was profit, after which they returned to Tonkin. However, since the onset of the war made it impossible for the Tonkinese to return home, the plantation owners continued to work them at the wages negotiated before the war, even as the workers became more skilled and, thus, more valuable. Unsurprisingly, many of the Tonkinese were unhappy with the situation, although their options were few. Hammerstein originally had Cable explain this situation to Nellie in 2.4, following "My Girl Back Home," but the brief speech, dated January 22, 1949, was eliminated.[4]

Michener recalled how he learned about this problem from a Tonkinese woman whose speech regarding the indentured workers' rights was unusually bold and confrontational. Further, he noted that it was her strong resistance to colonialist exploitation, a resistance seen by the French as leftist or even pro-Communist, that earned her the nickname "Bloody" Mary. Local workers mirrored her resistance throughout the New Hebrides and New Caledonia, which she implied would also lose their indentured workers after the war: "We all go home. Plantation all finish." Michener went on to note his intuition that when Mary finally returned home, she probably worked to subvert the French colonialists' power there, too. In later years, during the U.S. presence in Vietnam, Michener again thought of Mary and wondered if U.S. leaders understood that the enemy "consisted of millions of determined people like Bloody Mary." But Michener admitted that at the time he wrote *Tales of the South Pacific*, he did not quite understand Mary, adding, "I depicted her not as a potential revolutionary but as a Tonkinese woman with a pretty daughter to care for."[5] Indeed, he even changed the source of her name from her leftist political motivations to the color of the betel juice that ran down the corners of her mouth. Yet the story "Fo' Dolla'" and the musical *South Pacific* suggest that both Michener and Hammerstein were more expressive of Mary's anticolonialism than either has gotten credit for.

Mary's immediate threat to colonialist economics in "Fo' Dolla'" and *South Pacific*, however, derives not from her anti-French politics but from her savvy and practical approach to entrepreneurial capitalism. When the U.S. forces arrive on the island to await deployment, they have cash and a desire for souvenirs, grass skirts in particular. Mary organizes her fellow Tonkinese into a labor force to meet this demand, and before long the workers are making more money from Mary than the French plantation owners can, or will, pay them. Michener's narrator learns of this from a sailor, whose summary of the situation is succinct: "The economy out here went to hell." The French, unable to stop Mary, pass a law stating that the grass skirts can be sold only to them; they, in turn, can sell them to the Americans. When this fails to solve the problem—the U.S. soldiers are no fonder of the French island government controlling the souvenir market than are the newly solvent Tonkinese—the French turn to the U.S. military, which is even less successful than the French in solving the problem. Moreover, when the demand for grass skirts becomes greater than the Tonkinese workers' ability to provide them, Marines and Seabees go to work for Mary. She is, Michener's narrator comments, "the only woman who dared defy both the civil and military governments." Mary's daring, he notes further, was appreciated by the young soldiers, who viewed it as "a symbol of age-old defiance of unjust laws."[6]

In the musical, Mary's first appearance is as a vendor. Between the second and third choruses of the song "Bloody Mary," she looks out at the audience as if it were a G.I. and, speaking in an approximation of Pidgin English, makes a brassy attempt to sell a grass skirt. When the "customer" appears uninterested, she responds with a barrage of insulting, if tame, terms. A Marine then encourages her to "tell 'em good," and Mary asks, "What is good?" The Marine tells her to call the G.I. a "stingy bastard," which she does. She then comments that she is learning the language fast, and that soon she will speak as well "as any crummy G.I."[7] This passage recalls a more poignant description of the same phenomenon in Michener's story. After noting that the "old, tough Marines" provided lessons in off-color language to the "old, tough Tonk," Michener further observed that "the old miracle of the subdued races took place again." While Mary learned countless words from the Marines, they learned not one Tonkinese word from her. Nonetheless, when Mary mastered the worst language the Marines had to offer, "they made her an honorary Marine, emblem and all."[8]

The Marines' recognition of Mary's linguistic accomplishments indicates that an even further-reaching cultural transference is occurring. Mary's adoption of the Marines' English, and its direct relationship to her entrepreneurial ambitions, suggests a reaching for power from within what might at first appear to be a situation of powerlessness. Of course, Mary and many other Tonkinese have already learned French for similar reasons. The historian Bill Ashcroft observed, "Whereas many theories of (or at least assumptions about) imperial power tend to see the position of the 'powerless' colonial subject as one of almost passive victimage, it is clear that individuals are almost always able to operate within the framework of the dominant discourse to their own advantage. They do this by acquiring the cultural capital the colonizing power presents to them as dominant." For Mary, the "dominant discourse" is the language of the prospective consumer, and the "cultural capital" she acquires through learning English is the ability to sell, an ability recognized as desirable in the vocabulary of U.S. capitalism. Indeed, as Ashcroft argued, "The interpolation of imperial culture, and the appropriation and transformation of dominant forms of representation for the purposes of self-determination, focus with greatest intensity in the functions of language."[9] Mary's English, therefore, works in two stages. First, because her linguistic skill is not yet fully developed, it underscores her status as an outsider who must earn entrance into the dominant culture. Second, as her English skills develop, they increasingly enable her to communicate within the dominant culture of the Americans and, subsequently, to manipulate that culture's economic system to empower herself.

The Marines' acceptance and appreciation of Mary due to her growing language skills and her defiance of French authority demonstrate an affectionate relationship despite the imperialist implications of their one-way language exchange. As the postwar U.S. presence in the South Pacific and Southeast Asia increasingly assumed a role similar to that previously played by the French, however, and as the Tonkinese returned home to fight for the demise of Western dominance, the kind of affection the servicemen felt for Mary became all but impossible.

The song "Bloody Mary" jubilantly introduces Mary and the servicemen, and it depicts their relationship as playful, although the men are somewhat patronizing. While they sing of her as the girl they "love," her age and appearance suggest that this is a rude, if affectionate, joke. The third chorus of the song, following Mary's attempt to sell a grass skirt, covers the quick scene change into act 1, scene 3, which follows without pause. As part of her continuing sales pitch in the ensuing scene, Mary begins to dance, and the sailors and soldiers join her in a comical jitterbug performed to a swing-like version of "Bloody Mary." Early sketches for the lyrics also suggest dancing, referring to Mary as "a dancin' fool" who "learned to dance from a Chinese mule" and who "dances fast and loose" while not wearing a girdle "'cause it ain't no use!" As in the final version of the song, each chorus ends, "Now ain't that too damn bad."[10] The unused lyrics do not scan to the final version of the song, however, and no music seems to have been written for them. Moreover, seeing Mary dance seems to have eliminated the need to sing about her doing so.

The initial depiction of Mary in 1.3, as in the short scene that precedes it, is that of a sharp-tongued but comical vendor of souvenirs, an image reinforced by her comic dance. Immediately after the dance, the scene continues with comic business between Mary and Luther Billis, who attempts to undercut Mary's control of the market for grass skirts. Try as he may, Billis cannot get the upper hand when dealing with Mary, and while the interchange between the two is amusing, Billis's verbal treatment of Mary is almost abusive. He refers to her as "Sweaty Pie" and "Dragon Lady," insults that Mary ignores because of her sustained ability to outsmart him. Although his otherwise-successful entrepreneurialism is clearly indicated by the presence of a beachfront laundry bearing his name and, in a later scene, a primitive "bath club" consisting of an onstage shower, his first scene with Mary clearly indicates that she is more than a match for his desire to control the souvenir market.

The exchange between Mary and Billis is followed by the number "There Is Nothin' Like a Dame," after which Cable enters. He and Mary immediately acknowledge each other, at which point, according to the script, the orchestra quietly plays the opening figure of "Bali Ha'i" as underscoring. (The score indicates a somewhat later and less effective cue for this music.) This was the first music heard in the overture, but it has not been played since. The tone of the scene and, indeed, of the entire musical, is altered when it is played at this point. The transformative quality of the song was an early decision on the part of Rodgers and Hammerstein, but while Rodgers sought an evocation of the South Seas, he did not seek a literal representation of indigenous music. James A. Michener recalled one of the few conversations he had with Rodgers about the score. "Jim," Rodgers asked, "do I have to use wailing guitars and ukuleles?" Michener answered, "Only musical instrument I ever heard the natives play was two clubs beating hell out of a gasoline drum." Rodgers response indicated a sense of relief. "'Thanks,' he said with a deep breath, 'I hate guitars.'"[11]

Despite the mood change that the underscoring suggests, however, Mary does not immediately lose her earthiness when she meets Cable—a few lines later she tells Cable that he is a "damn saxy [sic] man," and Hammerstein indicates that she "has been looking adoringly" at him. She even offers to give Cable a shrunken head, which infuriates Billis. "You never give *me* anything free," he complains. "You no saxy like Lotellan," she retorts.[12] When Cable asks Mary where the head came from, she tells him Bali Ha'i, at which point she becomes somewhat mysterious and suggests to Cable that the island is calling to him. The song "Bali Ha'i" follows.

"Bali Ha'i" can be read either as a mystical moment in which Mary and the island "speak" to Cable or as a manipulative con job, the purpose of which is to entice Cable to the island and, subsequently, to Liat. The use of the song to begin and end the overture, however, and its use throughout the show and as the final tune in the exit music, suggest its intent was probably more the former than the latter. Ethan Mordden supported this idea, noting, "From the first moment of the overture . . . the audience [feels] itself, like Nellie and Cable, and the other Americans, drawn into an alien and beautiful and perilous world."[13] Mary is the character who gives voice to this world. And the song she sings continues to resonate with audiences who still imagine "special hopes" and "special dreams," as the response to Loretta Ables Sayre's performance in the 2008 Broadway revival demonstrates.

After Mary finishes the song, Billis comically sings phrases of "Bali Ha'i" to Cable to convince Cable to requisition a launch for a trip to the island, where Billis hopes to acquire expensive souvenirs. He reinforces the implied feminine character of the song, telling Cable between phrases that Bali Ha'i is full of young French women kept there by the protective planters and that the islanders use the location for a ceremony that involves women dancing in nothing but skirts. Indeed, in 1.9, when Mary, Cable, and Billis go to Bali Ha'i, the song is reprised in French by groups of young French women and "native

7.2. *The Boar's Tooth Ceremony in the 1958 film. Courtesy of Photofest.*

girls," as they are called in the script. (The score mentions only the French women.) The translation of the lyrics, the timbre of the women's voices singing in unison and in a higher key than Mary's, and the ambience of the setting all reinforce the exotic quality of "Bali Ha'i." Its sensuality is reflected by Cable's interest in the young women, which is mentioned in the stage directions. In the scene that follows, Cable and Liat meet and make love, after which Cable sings "Younger Than Springtime." Soon thereafter, Cable must leave, and "Bali Ha'i" is again sung by the women's chorus as he departs. The song frames the fragile yet passionate encounter with precisely the "mystical powers" that Rodgers sought to evoke.[14]

Billis's impromptu and suggestive travelogue in 1.3 is interrupted by the arrival of Captain Brackett, the chief naval officer of the base, and, through Brackett, the focus returns to Mary as an economic force. "You," Brackett forcefully barks at Mary, "are causing an economic revolution on this island." This recalls the comment made to Michener's narrator, although Brackett's use of the word "revolution" is even more powerful than the observation that the economy is "going to hell." When Brackett reminds Mary that the planters are short of laborers because she pays them more, she demonstrates her new vocabulary from the previous scene with a terse reply: "French planters stingy bastards!"[15] Brackett has no immediate response.

Billis fills the lull by suggesting that the Seabees could make the grass skirts, which further infuriates Brackett. He returns his attention to Mary and tells her to get all her merchandise off navy property. She stands defiant until Cable pulls down her kiosk and tells her to move, which she does. Cable is the only person capable of dissuading Mary from her profit-making endeavors, and she even thanks him as she exits. Far from the harridan she seems with Billis and Bracket, Mary is, for the time being, gentle and adoring in her dealings with Cable. By the end of the musical's third scene, Mary has demonstrated her anticolonialist economic prowess, her craftiness, her humor, and her seductiveness. Mary's anticolonialist stance reappears in the play, but only in connection with her daughter's and Cable's future; her shrewish—and her maternal—qualities remain central to her characterization, however.

After a short scene in which he tells Brackett about the mission he is on, Cable is left alone. At this point, the orchestra again plays the music of "Bali Ha'i," and this time Cable hears the island's call. Staring at Bali Ha'i's volcanic peaks that rise above clouds in the distance, he softly sings part of the song, and the lights fade. The island's, and Mary's, powers have begun to determine the young Marine's fate.

MARY AND THE "SELLING" OF LIAT

As the preceding discussion demonstrates, Bloody Mary is more than the representation of "World War II stereotypes of grinning Chinese peasants" that Andrea Most suggested. She may be a "Dragon Lady" to Billis, but she is an emotionally rich and multidimensional woman when played by a capable actress–singer. However, as Most also maintained, the musical's depiction of Mary's daughter Liat is indeed "plagued by . . . problems of stereotype."[16] Rodgers and Hammerstein's simplification and almost complete silencing of Michener's Liat is a fascinating and problematic aspect of the musical, in part because their characterization of Liat and her relationships with Mary and Cable demonstrate what Christina Klein called "the infantilization of racialized Others." Klein's comment is supported by the script and its source. The stage directions describe Liat as "perhaps seventeen" years old, Mary refers to her as a girl, and Cable comments that she is "just a kid."[17] And although she is integral to the show's principal thematic conflict, she speaks only five short lines, most of which consist of one to three words.

Liat's speechlessness is especially surprising in light of Michener's character, who speaks fluent French and who is regarded by Sister Marie Clément, her teacher, as the best student on the island. Her conversations with Cable, who also speaks French, are extended and often touching. For example, midway through the story she seems to anticipate its outcome when she asks Cable, "If I were a French girl, it would be alright, wouldn't it?"[18] In the musical, Cable and Liat immediately reveal to each other that they know only a little French—Liat speaks no English—and their verbal communication swiftly gives way to physical passion. Their conversation before the first sexual encounter is minimal in the story, too, but afterward and throughout their subsequent encounters, they converse at length. Late in Michener's story, Liat, who is promised to a French planter when Cable refuses to marry her, reveals a touching understanding of her situation. Noting that her mother had told her something great would happen for her, and acknowledging that Cable is that something, she quietly adds, "You love me. You will go away somewhere. I will marry somebody else."[19] Liat is not granted the opportunity to express such insightful and touching thoughts in the musical. Indeed, she is not given the opportunity to express much of anything. She is the delicate Oriental girl–woman, betrayed by the Westerner she loves, and she is as sad as she is exquisite. From Puccini's *Madama Butterfly*, which Rodgers and Hammerstein were afraid of imitating, to *Miss Saigon*, which retells Butterfly's story, the prototype is ample.

The scene between Cable and Liat, which occurs late in the first act, is the only time Liat appears in that act. Mary and Liat reappear in act 2, scene 2, and Mary's vocabulary regarding her daughter's obvious love for Cable betrays her economic sensibility. This is a quality completely absent from Michener's Mary when she addresses Cable concerning his future with Liat. In both works, Mary suggests that Cable and Liat can remain on Bali Ha'i and live off Mary's considerable money, thus avoiding Cable's fear of taking Liat back to Philadelphia's upper-crust society. But this is the only connection Michener makes between Mary the businesswoman and Mary the loving mother, and it is simply a means of convincing Cable to stay with Liat. Hammerstein adds something further, however, and it gives a slightly different flavor to Mary's desire for the two young people's future. Whereas in the story she often asks Cable, "You like?" in regard to Liat, Hammerstein adds, "You buy?" after the first question. These are the same questions she uses in act 1 to peddle grass skirts and shrunken heads; here, she uses the pitch to "sell" Cable on marrying Liat and a subsequently idyllic life, and the result is somewhat unsettling. Further, when Mary asks these sequential questions in 2.2, they act as the cue for the song "Happy Talk," which is her further attempt to "sell" Cable on her proposition of marriage and a good life.

7.3. *Mary, Liat (Betta St. John), and Cable in "Happy Talk," original Broadway production. Courtesy of Photofest.*

While the lines in the song recall Mary's sales tactics from the first act, they also reveal her maternal nature. She may be an entrepreneur who thinks she knows a good match for her daughter when she sees one, but she is also a caring mother. In addition, the song allows Liat interaction with both her mother and Cable, who is as troubled by Mary's implications for his future as he is attentive to the playful song. Indeed, "Happy Talk," which is the first song in act 2, sets up Cable's refusal to marry Liat and the tragedy that subsequently ensues. The simplicity of Mary's vision is complicated by Cable's inability to accept it, and the song provides a transition between the lighter aspects of the act's opening and the darker elements that later combust in 2.4.

Like "Bali Ha'i," "Happy Talk" is verse–chorus number. While the verse is a somewhat standard sixteen measures, the brevity of the chorus—eighteen measures—is rare in this and other scores by Rodgers. The abbreviated structure of the chorus, like that of "*Dites-moi*," suggests a child's song or a folk song, as does the overall character of the song, and it subtly reflects the supposed simplicity of the life Mary suggests. (Rodgers and Hammerstein successfully achieved a similar effect with "Oh, What a Beautiful Mornin'," the opening number of *Oklahoma!*) The simple chorus also strengthens Mary's appeal to Cable through the frequent repetition of the song's primary message—"You got to have a dream." This idea of a dream returns in act 2, scene 4, both in Cable's dialogue and in de Becque's subsequent dramatic solo, "This Nearly Was Mine." The reference to a dream also recalls "Bali Ha'i," in which Mary tells Cable to imagine his "own special dream."

Rodgers begins this simple song with delightfully mixed rhythmic messages. The two-measure accompaniment pattern, essentially a rhythmic ostinato, divides two measures of common time, or eight beats, into two consecutive sets of three beats and one of two beats, with accents on beats one and four of the first measure and beat three of the second measure. The straightforward melody of the verse is sung over this syncopated accompaniment, and the rhythmic conflict between the melody and the accompaniment adds to the overall playful nature of the song. This syncopated pattern also occurs regularly under the chorus. These contrasting rhythms between the orchestra and the melody are the most complex element of the number.

The first verse is played as orchestral underscoring to Mary's speech about the joys of the life she proposes, after which she sings the first chorus. The subsequent two verses and choruses are followed by a dance, which the published script describes as "gentle" and "childish" and which consists of an additional orchestral verse and chorus. Following the dance, Mary sings a more reflective verse at a slower tempo, after which she sings a final chorus at the original tempo; this is followed by a twelve-bar coda in which she reminds Cable that if you never have a dream, "den you'll never have a dream come true."[20]

If the description of Liat's dance as "childish" is also meant to imply "childlike," it is an appropriate word for the entire song. The uncomplicated diatonic melodies of the verse and chorus, and the syncopation and dotted rhythms of the chorus, create a strong contrast to the extensive chromaticism of "Bali Ha'i," Mary's first musical utterance. Liat's performance of what the script says "seem to be traditional hand gestures" during Mary's singing also suggests a child's folk song with ritualized physical accompaniment. The combined performances of Mary and Liat demonstrate, too, the closeness of the mother–daughter relationship and the desire of both to please Cable. When Cable kisses Liat at the end of Mary's slow verse, after the words, "You and me is lucky to be us," Mary's singing "becomes triumphant." She seems confident that her plans for the young couple's future have taken root, and she comments, as a tag to the number, "Is good idea . . . you like?"[21] This time she omits, "You buy?"

The initial draft for "Happy Talk" suggests that its final design did not spring fully formed from Hammerstein's imagination. Instead, it implies the far more typical structure of a verse followed by a rather lengthy refrain in AABA form. The original four-line verse did not survive the rewrite, and it is not missed. Primarily an entreaty to Cable, referred to as "a fella" asking why he would want to talk about unhappy things, it is followed by the refrain, which refers to happier topics. The lyrics to the three A sections of the refrain are the same as those of the three verses in the final version of the song: "Talk about a moon . . . bird . . . star," etc. The first two A sections are followed by a four-line bridge, the lyrics for which—"Talk about breafus['], coffee an' toast / Opposite de one you love de most, / Dinner an' supper, plen'y to eat, / Gravy and potatoes on your meat!"—do not appear in the final version of the song.[22] The bridge is followed by the final A section. The song is followed by what Hammerstein designates as a coda. The first six lines of lyrics for this section became the refrain of the final version of the song; the final three lines are what became the coda ("If you don't talk happy," etc.).

Hammerstein's markings on the draft indicate how he rearranged the lyrics to create a completely different form. The initial quatrain, marked "verse" in the draft, is crossed out in pencil. (The word "verse" is also crossed out.) Following this, the word "refrain," which designates the next four sections of lyrics, is also scratched out in pencil and the word "verse" is written next to it, marking the first formal change. The bridge of the song is entirely crossed out in pencil, thus eliminating another formal element and further simplifying the structure. Finally, the word "coda" is scratched out in pencil. In addition to these generally changed formal indications, specific numbers appear in the margins in red pencil. In the left-hand margin, for instance, next to what was originally indicated as the coda, are the numbers one, three, and five. Those same lines, plus the final three that serve as the coda for the final version, are bracketed in the right-hand margin and marked "seven." What were formally the three A sections of the refrain have the numbers two, four, and six written next to them in the left margin. This reordering matches the final version of the number, minus the orchestral verse and chorus added for the dance. The cutting of a few redundant lines and the reassembling of the lyrics that were left create a more direct and effective song, and it is in this final form that audiences enjoy the number. "Happy Talk" is, in its simple repetitiveness, a perfect expression of Mary's misplaced confidence in the future of her daughter with the young Marine. It is also not without a tinge of melancholy, indicated by the stage directions at the song's end: "Cable is deeply disturbed."[23]

Cable's state of mind is explained immediately after "Happy Talk" when he tells Mary that he cannot marry Liat. Her rage is immediate and direct. Telling Cable that this was his last chance—although in fact it has been his only chance, since marriage has not been mentioned before—Mary smashes a watch Cable has given Liat and drags her daughter offstage. Her final words to Cable, just before she smashes the watch, are revealing. They constitute the worst language she has learned thus far from the Marines, and are therefore the most insulting in her vocabulary. And, perhaps more importantly, they are the words that equal "no sale" in her economic parlance: "Stingy bastard!"[24]

Liat, torn from her beloved and physically removed from the stage, does not speak. Later, in act 2, scene 10, Mary and Liat discover Nellie on the beach. Nellie has just addressed the missing de Becque—she has learned of his participation in the mission and of Cable's death—and sung a reprise of "Some Enchanted Evening." Nellie does not know who the two women are at first, but Mary identifies herself as the mother of Liat and says that the girl will marry no one but Cable. Nellie is overcome and embraces Liat as the lights fade. Even here, her will having overcome even the formidable force of her mother's, Liat is silent. Whether brokered by her capitalist mother, loved but rejected by the blueblood Cable, or embraced by the most sympathetic American on the island, Liat remains voiceless and dominated by the cultural and economic forces surrounding her.

THE PLANTATION AND BEYOND

As demonstrated in the 2008 Broadway revival of South Pacific, audiences are still moved by the musical's final scene. The director Bartlett Sher retains the original final pose, which is almost iconic: Nellie and de Becque grasp hands under the table as his, now their, "Eurasian" children look on in well-fed satisfaction. This finale is among the most powerful in musical theater, and audiences are unable to resist its ennobling message, which ensures Nellie's (and America's) triumph over racism and secures a bright future for Nellie and her new family. However, this memorable tableau also suggests that Nellie, in addition to becoming part of a loving family, is poised to become a part of a colonialist lifestyle not completely alien to her earlier prejudice and racial insensitivity. As such, it is a lifestyle that might seem out of step with American values. For while de Becque's masculinity has been proven and his adherence to American warrior ideals established, the problem of French colonialism in the South Pacific and, specifically, de Becque's part in it, appears to be unresolved. However, French colonialism, as the history of the postwar Pacific suggests, was soon replaced by U.S. dominance, and Nellie represents that moment of shifting political and cultural power. The musical provides a fascinating and subtle presentation of this shift, never more clearly than in its final image.

Early in Michener's story "Our Heroine," which provided Rodgers and Hammerstein with the de Becque–Nellie romance, Nellie attends a dinner at a French plantation. Michener notes that Tonkinese men serve the food. A bit later in the story, de Becque hosts a lavish dinner attended by other French plantation owners, their wives, and American doctors and nurses. At one point, an American nurse asks, "How did you train the natives so well? . . . They actually seem to enjoy it." De Becque responds, "I am patient with them."[25] Hammerstein's character makes no such patronizing comments about, or to, his servants. Indeed, only two servants are ever seen: Henry, already mentioned, in 1.1 and 1.12, and an additional, nameless, servant in the latter scene. While the dialogue makes it clear that de Becque owns and runs a plantation, no other indication of servants or labor is ever made. While this aids in the "Americanization" of de Becque, he and his plantation are nonetheless part of the economic system of French planters that Bloody Mary is successfully undermining. Indeed, he might even be one of those planters assailed by Mary as "stingy bastards," although the more romantic the actor who plays de Becque, the less likely that the audience will make that connection.

Despite the near invisibility of de Becque's relationship with the indigenous people who are his servants, however, the French colonialist presence is apparent throughout the musical, as it is in Michener's book. The opening scene establishes French as a predominant language of the island, for instance. And later, at the beginning of act 1, scene 12, the audience hears the offstage guests at de Becque's party offering their thanks and farewells in French. When Nellie says goodnight in English, a guest emphasizes that she must speak French. Her labored attempts to do so provide some comic moments here and later, before the finale, when the children want her to join them in "*Dites-moi*." But despite the humorous aspects of her elementary language skills, her need to learn French seems apparent. The script also indicates the presence of French nuns on Bali Ha'i when Cable follows Mary there in act 1, scene 9. (While Hammerstein does not explain their presence, he modestly decided after the Boston dress rehearsal to eliminate them from the post-coital choral reprise of "Bali Ha'i."[26]) Michener's story indicates that the nuns teach both the daughters of the French plantation owners and the indigenous and Tonkinese young women. Michener describes Liat as "a good mission Tonkinese . . . who was a Christian instead of a Buddhist."[27] In the musical, Mary informs Cable that Liat's name is French, which emphasizes Liat's puzzling inability to speak more than a few phrases of French.

The predominance of the French language within the island's plantation system reveals a principal element of French colonialism. As D. K. Fieldhouse noted, the assimilation of native peoples, to the French, was less political than cultural, "combining the eighteenth-century concept of the universality of man with the nineteenth-century belief in both the civilizing mission of Europe and the special value of French culture." "Insofar as one can measure such things," Fieldhouse continued, "the French seem to have believed more passionately in this than in any other purpose of colonialism."[28] The nine-teenth-century ideals of French colonialism probably would have been well known to de Becque, who arrived on the island during the second decade of the twentieth century, probably just before or just after World War I. (Michener, whose work is set in 1942, gives de Becque's age as "middle forties," and later de Becque says that it took him twenty-six years to build up the plantation.[29]) De Becque's behavior seems far more enlightened than that espoused in 1910 by Jules Harmand, a supporter of French colonialism and a writer whose work de Becque might have been familiar with. "The basic legit-imation [sic] of conquest over native peoples," Harmand maintained, "is the conviction of our superiority, not merely our mechanical, economic, and mil-itary superiority, but our moral superiority. Our dignity rests on that quality, and it underlies our right to direct the rest of humanity."[30] While both Ham-merstein's and Michener's Frenchman suggests a man steeped in high cul-ture, and thus one who might well believe in the "civilizing" nature of that culture, whether or not de Becque actually believes in the French prerogative to "direct" humanity—his words and actions suggest otherwise—becomes irrelevant after the war. Further, Michener's de Becque seems presciently aware that the French control of its Pacific and Southeast Asian colonies will ultimately give way to an increased U.S. dominance in the region. When he mentions that he will probably die before Nellie, for instance, he states, "By that time there will be an American base here. Your little girls will have fine American young men to choose as husbands."[31]

Although the United States began its imperial reach into the Pacific during the nineteenth century, it took over as the primary outside presence in the area when the British and French colonialist powers waned in the postwar era. Although nineteenth-century U.S. expansionism added Hawaii, Wake, Guam, and Samoa to the list of American-controlled territories, which they remained during and after the war, the postwar United States also retained most of the wartime military bases on islands throughout the Pacific and formalized its presence in many other areas in the Pacific and in Asia. Christina Klein observed, "As this expansion unfolded, U.S. policy-makers and journalists resurrected the nineteenth-century imperial idea of the Pacific as an 'American lake.'"[32] And to keep its lake placid, the postwar United States made rules and enforced them on the occupied cultures. Edward Said explained that this American path to globalism "had the effect of depoliticizing, reducing, and sometimes even eliminating the integrity of overseas societies that seemed in need of modernizing." He also noted that postwar U.S. expansionism, while primarily economic, "is still highly dependent on and moves together with, and upon, cultural ideals and ideologies about America itself, ceaselessly reiterated in public."[33]

Klein was especially concerned with how so-called middlebrow American cultural texts, the musicals of Rodgers and Hammerstein in particular, reinforced postwar expansionism and demonstrated an increasing acceptance of U.S. global power. She argued that these texts were created by artists who "saw themselves as educating Americans about their changing relationship to the world at large."[34] Of course, Rodgers and Hammerstein were deigned middlebrow or, to use Dwight Macdonald's term, "midcult," long before Klein's work. Writing in 1962, Macdonald referred to "the folk-fakery of *Oklahoma!* and the orotund sentimentalities of *South Pacific*" in his criticism of "watered-down" highbrow culture for middle-class, middlebrow American audiences.[35] Nonetheless, Klein's argument is persuasive, in particular when she suggested that, in the 1940s and 1950s, "middlebrow intellectuals, texts, and institutions tried to educate Americans about their evolving relationships with Asia, and how they created opportunities—real and symbolic—for their audience in the forging of these relationships."[36] Rodgers and Hammerstein demonstrate this "education" in subtle but unmistakable ways.

Klein's interpretation of the final scene demonstrated her reading of the show as political pedagogy. She situated the scene outside the specific problem of Nellie's acceptance of French colonialism and within the more general realm of U.S. dominance in the postwar Pacific. As opposed to seeing a sentimental finale exemplifying an American ability to overcome racial intolerance, Klein interpreted the final tableau as follows: "Like Washington's aid programs in Indochina, this family invigorates an aging and weary France, gives provincial America access to the colonial sources of French wealth and prestige, and maintains the childlike Asians in a condition of security and dependence. . . . It visualizes and narrativizes America's emerging role in Southeast Asia."[37] This image, or Klein's reading of it, encourages American audiences to accept American cultural values as bonding and capable of bringing people together in the postwar era. If the French had "civilized" the islanders through the imposition of a colonialist social order, in other words, the Americans would make everyone a happy family. Klein argued further that the show's final image supported, and perhaps promoted, the postwar movement for trans-racial adoption launched by the author Pearl Buck and supported by Michener and Hammerstein, among others. She wrote, "The figure of the white parent to the non-white child has long worked as a trope for representing the ostensibly 'natural' relations of hierarchy, . . . [and] has been a standard rhetorical means of legitimating unequal power relations."[38]

From this postwar perspective, Nellie's need to learn French seems increasingly less important than the growing need for the French on the island to learn English. Bloody Mary's move in this linguistic direction is prescient of what others on the island can expect to experience in the near future. Michener was aware of this when he wrote *Tales of the South Pacific*, although the story most integral to suggesting a greater U.S. presence in the area, "Lobeck, the Asiatic," was cut from the collection before publication. Lobeck was a professor of anthropology who "developed the idea that America's destiny would not be determined by her relations with Europe, as he had always been taken for granted, but rather Asia." By 1951 Michener had taken on Lobeck's mindset, noting, "The destiny of the United States will be determined in large part by the decisions we make regarding our relations with Asia."[39] However, as the Michener biographer John P. Hayes observed, "When a Gallup poll asked Americans where they wanted to travel after World War II, Great Britain and France received the majority of votes; Asia did not even make the list."[40] But if tourists were not yet ready to explore Asia and the South Pacific, representatives of U.S. military, commercial, and cultural interests were already on the scene.

THE CULTURAL POWER OF POPULAR SONG

Klein's reading of the show as a demonstration of transformed U.S. interests in the South Pacific also suggests that Nellie is a cultural powerbroker. The persuasiveness of Nellie's musical styles throughout the show supports this idea, and two of her songs—"I'm Gonna Wash That Man Right Out-a My Hair" and "Honey Bun"—are recognizably rooted in American popular-song traditions. And, as observed earlier, in 1.12 de Becque affectionately spoofs Nellie's "I'm Gonna Wash That Man Right Out-a My Hair," the song that earlier in the act sparked their brief discussion of American popular music. That discussion, in 1.7, is Hammerstein's idea. Michener made no mention of music in his stories, and if he had, it no doubt would have been "classical" music. In his autobiography, Michener discussed his interest in symphonic and operatic music at some length; his discussion of "nonclassical music," however, was brief. He offered that he "liked but did not respect" most popular music, in part because he found it either racist or insulting to ethnic minorities.[41] Nellie does not defend her taste in popular music, however; instead, she seems rather embarrassed by it. De Becque's playful performance of the infectious blend of swing and blues in "I'm Gonna Wash That Man Right Out-a My Hair" compliments his increasing interest in Nellie and her culture and reflects his growing comfort with her. It also suggests that de Becque's Old World sensibilities are at the very least making room for Nellie's Americanisms and that he is not adverse to this change. This will serve him well as the Americans increasingly become the dominant cultural presence in the area.

"Honey Bun," the second number in the score to consciously evoke American popular song, is a diegetic number performed in 2.3 as the finale of the Thanksgiving Follies, an amateur revue given by and for the island's military personnel. Nellie is instrumental in the creation and execution of the Follies, and her performance of the verse and first chorus of "Honey Bun" provides *South Pacific* with an image even more iconic than the final tableau. Nellie performs the song dressed as a sailor, wearing a white uniform many sizes too big and a white cap. A picture of Mary Martin in this costume became part of the advertising campaign for the show, and her rolled-up pants and long black tie became part of U.S. popular culture's visual vocabulary in the late 1940s and early 1950s. As a testament to the image's staying power, the poster for the 2008 Broadway revival uses the same image of Nellie. In addition to a cross-dressed Nellie, the number also features Luther Billis in drag; he wears one of his grass skirts, a straw wig, and a coconut-shell bra.

The placement of the song, in addition to the overall structure of the first four scenes of the second act, demonstrates Rodgers and Hammerstein's keen sense of dramaturgy: scenes 1 and 3 are comic and take place within the Follies, while scenes 2 and 4 are among the show's most serious and occur backstage during the performance. For instance, 2.3 follows Cable's reflective reprise of "Younger Than Springtime," which he sings at the end of scene 2 after Mary has called him a "stingy bastard" and dragged Liat away from him. "Honey Bun" provides a comic counterpoint to this moment and to scene 4, which contains the climactic confrontation between Nellie and de Becque and the songs "You've Got to Be Carefully Taught" and "This Nearly Was Mine." This use of a comic song in anticipation of a dramatic scene is also used to great effect in the first act, where de Becque's amusing reprise of "I'm Gonna

Wash That Man Right Out-a My Hair" immediately precedes the entrance of his children and the ensuing conflict with Nellie that ends the act.

Like "I'm Gonna Wash That Man Right Out-a My Hair," "Honey Bun" suggests a popular musical style; it is written to sound like an older tune the performers all might have known already, a musical familiarity imported to a setting "far away from home," as Nellie will say in scene 4. To this end, Rodgers wrote a vaudeville-like tune that somewhat recalls "Alexander's Ragtime Band"; both exploit the prominent use of the raised supertonic, or second-scale degree, and dotted rhythms in their opening melodic gestures, for instance. The insinuation of a familiar song is perfect for a moment that, in addition to providing comic relief, provides a fun tune to which the onstage audience of homesick military personnel might sing along.

Later in the second act, however, "Honey Bun" is used to create a rather chilling effect. This reprise is rooted in the soldiers' familiarity with the tune, and it demonstrates the exploitation of popular song in the context of war. At the end of 2.11, a scene that depicts "members of all forces, ready to embark" for battle, an officer orders all the men and women to "move out" to their designated modes of transportation. They are on their way to a major battle in which the U.S. forces, acting on information gained by de Becque and Cable on their mission, anticipate victory. "The whole picture of the South Pacific has changed," notes Harbison. "We're going the other way."[42] As the men and women fall into formation, the martial underscoring crescendos and segues to a chorus of "Honey Bun," which the soldiers sing while dispersing to their assigned areas. In the score, this reprise is accompanied by the orchestra. In the 2008 Broadway revival, however, this moment is further intensified. The underscoring, instead of continuing throughout the scene, drops out. At the order "move out," the men and women, in formation and facing the audience, begin marching in place while singing the chorus of "Honey Bun" without accompaniment. They turn in precision and exit, still in formation, as the song fades along with the lights. The Americans, having brought their popular culture to the island, are now taking it to battle. The power of the moment is stunning.

The essential conflicts in *South Pacific* are racial. Hammerstein's long-held views of racial equality motivated him to write a book and lyrics that, while criticized by some authors viewing his work from a late-twentieth-, early-twenty-first-century perspective, were daring at the time they were written. Always aware of the narrow ledge he walked by trying to create a popular commercial success that also contained a potentially controversial message, he created a work that, in addition to criticizing racial intolerance, reflected the varied and changing cultural conflicts in which his discussion of race is situated. His handling of colonialism and the growing U.S. economic, cultural, and military powers in the South Pacific is deft and sure-handed, and his final scene is as effectively evocative and rich with meaning as his first. Viewed through the exuberance of the immediate postwar era, his optimism about the future of such cultural interaction is understandable.

8
STILL DREAMING OF PARADISE
• • •

On Sunday, January 18, 2009, the composer, lyricist, and Hammerstein protégé Stephen Sondheim and the former *New York Times* theater critic Frank Rich sat down to a public conversation on the stage of Lincoln Center's Avery Fisher Hall. Titled *Stephen Sondheim, A Life in the Theater: An Onstage Conversation with Frank Rich,* the evening promised to be a recollection of Sondheim's career in postwar American musical theater, and much of the conversation was indeed centered on Sondheim's oeuvre and his collaborators. But throughout the evening, Sondheim also offered ideas and frank opinions about many works by others for the musical theater. He described *My Fair Lady*, for example, as "the most unnecessary musical ever written." (This comment provided a bit of autobiographical context for a lyric in "Opening Doors," a number from Sondheim's *Merrily We Roll Along* score, in which the aspiring composer Franklin Shepard commented that he had seen *My Fair Lady* and "sort of enjoyed it."[1]) Among the other shows that Sondheim assessed was *South Pacific*, a musical he does not particularly care for. After observing that he liked the Nellie–de Becque plot, he quickly turned to the lyrics of "There Is Nothing Like a Dame," suggesting they offered a picture of a "happy" war that he could not accept. "I don't write 'Happy Talk,'" he subsequently commented.[2]

The producers of the 2001 television version of *South Pacific* seem to have agreed with Sondheim: they excised "Happy Talk" from the score.[3] The 1958 film version, however, which was directed by Joshua Logan, made relatively minor cuts to the score and, overall, stayed close to the original stage production.[4] The opening was changed in order to introduce the military before the romantic characters, as mentioned earlier, and "Happy Talk," while maintaining its place in the order of numbers, was moved to a setting on Bali Ha'i and occurs before the Thanksgiving Follies instead of during it. Further, as Geoffrey Block has pointed out, the transition from stage to film involved some maneuvering of language and sexual innuendo, and although the audience still gets the point, it sometimes loses some of its effect. Nonetheless, opening less than six months after federal troops were sent to Little Rock to enforce the integration of Central High School, the film version of the musical had as much, or perhaps even more, cultural relevance as the original production. Despite the much-maligned use of color in the film and the political and sexual caution still practiced by Hollywood studios at the time, it remains a strong reading of the original work.

Beyond occasional productions at City Center and the New York City Opera, summer stock and amateur productions, and occasional tours featuring stars in one or both of the leading roles, *South Pacific* did not again achieve national visibility after the film's release until the 2001 television production. This version, directed by Richard Pearce, demonstrates the show's resilience against tampering, which in turn shows how a well-known work can be an open text, for better or worse. From the problematic casting of Glenn Close as Nellie—Close was then in her early fifties and was also one of the producers—to a somewhat drastic reordering and, often, reconceptualization of the musical numbers, the television version made many changes to the show. Yet, among the more controversial alterations—the age of Nellie, and the restructuring of the narrative for increased and more realistic emphasis on the war—at least one change put this production more in line with Michener than any earlier version. Harry Connick Jr.'s Joe Cable is a fascinating combination of sensitive leading man and believable Leatherneck. He is seen fighting other soldiers in defense of his relationship with Liat, and his death is staged as a heroic moment at the end of the mission with de Becque instead of as an offstage event. Although "You've Got to Be Carefully Taught" is reconceived as a reflective and decidedly unrhythmic musical number—Connick's characteristic crooning style is exploited and the song is performed as a pensive interior monologue—Connick's Cable is as believable a warrior as he is a lovesick and increasingly self-aware young man. Nonetheless, the production in general was a disappointment, especially in the voice department; apart from Close, who had much musical-theater experience (featured roles in *Barnum* and *Sunset Boulevard*, for example), and Connick, the voices were not what aficionados of the score expected—de Becque, in particular, was unusually lightweight (and a tenor, no less)—and the resultant performance of the score was unfulfilling, as was the overall production.

A subsequent national tour of the show, directed by Scott Faris, unfortunately coincided with the attacks of September 11, 2001, which occurred between the beginning of rehearsals and the tour's opening. The cast, which was rehearsing within twenty blocks of ground zero, was understandably affected. In December 2001, the actress Erin Dilly noted to Sally Cragin of the *Boston Globe*, "What has been the most gratifying piece of this experience is that every night Michael Nouri [de Becque] makes a curtain speech about the September 11 Relief Fund. We sing 'God Bless America' and go out there with hats and dufflebags." Cragin further noted that, "Their impromptu USO efforts . . . helped raise $200,000, but more important is the redemption that Rodgers and Hammerstein hard-wired into their masterpiece." Dilly continued, "When I hear Lieutenant Cable [Lewis Cleale, in a memorable performance] sing 'You Have Got to Be Carefully Taught' [sic], it could be the anthem right now for understanding the Taliban . . . I think people need theater right now. We all need the catharsis and the ritual, and having the lights come down, then being told a story and ultimately feeling more hopeful when you leave." Cragin's use of the word "redemption" for *South Pacific* is astute. Through Cable and Nellie's revelations about their intolerance and Nellie's ultimate triumph over hers, the audience indeed experiences a kind of redemption from, or at least insight into, its own prejudices. Another of Dilly's comments, this one about Nellie, also speaks to the audience's experience: "She's a smart woman who comes from a very small town. So her experience pool may be shallow, but as a human she's got extraordinary depth. She says, 'I have to be bigger than where I've come from.'"[5] Facing the challenges of a post–9/11 world, U.S. audiences understood the need to be "bigger" than their individual pasts, and this well-performed production had an immediacy matched only by the Lincoln Center revival. A high-profile production between the tour and the current revival, however, was somewhat less urgent, although it was not without its insights.

Considering the fifty-four years between the studio film and the made-for-television film version, the appearance in 2005 of a semi-staged concert version of the show at Carnegie Hall and, subsequently, on PBS and commercial DVD, was timely: the impact of 9/11 was still felt and the United States was at war in Iraq and Afghanistan, yet the production seemed somewhat unconnected to what was going on in the country at the time. While the presentation suggested a deserved and continued interest in the show, it seemed under-rehearsed and much of the comedy was played in an especially broad style. Nonetheless, it featured some noteworthy casting and individual performances. Reba McEntire was a solid choice as Nellie, having demonstrated her musical-theater skills in 2001 by replacing Bernadette Peters in a Broadway revival of *Annie Get Your Gun* and getting rave reviews for it. (While McEntire was not the first replacement, she was the most successful, and her reviews were in many cases better than Peters's.) Perhaps McEntire's greatest strength as Nellie was her ability to suggest a Southern sensibility without seeming condescending or affected. Brian Stokes Mitchell, her de Becque, was a relaxed and romantic leading man, and the ovation he received for a deeply moving performance of "This Nearly Was Mine" brought the performance to a standstill. That Stokes Mitchell, Lillias White (Bloody Mary), and Renita Croney (Liat) were African American added an interesting dimension to the plot's racial tensions. Despite the unchanged dialogue references to Mary and Liat as Tonkinese, for instance, White's and Croney's presence made Hammerstein's consideration of homegrown intolerance even more blatant; early twenty-first-century audiences who might have had trouble understanding the problem with Cable's bringing home a young Asian wife could still understand the difficulties of bringing home an African American. Without ever insinuating that the characters were anything other than Tonkinese, the production clearly reinforced for its audiences the central problem of U.S. domestic intolerance. In his notes for the DVD release of the performance, Ted Chapin, president of the Rodgers and Hammerstein Organization, wrote that Rodgers and Hammerstein "fashioned a show that, despite sensibilities that seem anchored in its time, has proven timeless."[6] The casting of Stokes Mitchell, White, and Croney helped ensure that timelessness, even if the overall production seemed strangely disconnected from then-current events.

The current (as of this writing) Lincoln Center revival maintains the show's legendary status without being overwhelmed by it. By reinserting material cut from the original production, the director Bartlett Sher has pumped up the controversial aspects of the show, but only to the point where contemporary audiences can face them and still continue to enjoy the musical. In a conversation with the designer Michael Yeargan, who did the sets for the current revival, Sher observed that *South Pacific* "is one of those rare musicals that were written immediately following actual events," adding, "It's almost like a national memory, an expression of survival, and for this reason it is a profoundly resonant show." Yeargan agreed, noting, "The show still works, and because we're at war now it resonates like crazy." Sher and his collaborators have created a production that is almost completely devoid of sentimentality, which is an especially notable achievement considering the nostalgia many feel for *South Pacific* from earlier encounters with it. But Sher was aware of the multifaceted aspect of these memories, further noting that "the play summons a sort of memory of being under threat."[7] And that threat is always just beneath the surface of this production, which makes the scene of the soldiers marching off to war while singing "Honey Bun" exceptionally powerful: it is as loaded with fear as it is with bravery. Like the earlier tour, this production feels vital and relevant. It also demonstrates the work's powers of redemption, as mentioned earlier by Sally Cragin.

Each of these productions of *South Pacific* demonstrates that "paradise" continues to be rewritten to fit various and changing historical contexts. Sher's production reintroduces into the script dialogue that was far more problematic in
1949 and 1958 than it is today, and while his restorations do not change the
work's message, they put it in terms appropriate for early twenty-first-century
Americans. Sher in particular, and with the insightful blessing of the Rodgers and
Hammerstein Organization, has returned to the script with the same spirit that
the original creators had: the desire to make the show an unmistakable criticism
of racial intolerance while assuring its status as a commercial success. Yet, people
still remain surprised by the social critique embedded in *South Pacific*; exiting the
theater, audience members can regularly be heard commenting that they didn't
remember the musical being so "political," or that it was about racial intolerance.
Although the show, like its creators, has become a cultural icon representing one
of the highest achievements in the musical theater, the element of that achievement that reflects U.S. society's problematic relation to race seems to get lost
amid the luscious score and often-memorable performances. This gives the show
something that much art lacks: an ongoing ability to surprise. Even when played
exactly as written in the published script, with the score unaltered and the production "traditional," *South Pacific* still surprises or even shocks people because of
its thematic concern. Surely that is a suggestion of its greatness.

Other suggestions of that greatness endure as well. Harold Prince recalled
being grilled by his mentor George Abbott about why the opening night of
South Pacific, which both had attended, was such an important event. Abbott
explained, as Prince recalls, that "for the first time, a musical had moved
without interruption, had flowed as if it were a film." In Abbott's mind, "This
was Rodgers & Hammerstein's most integrated score. And it was as near perfect as any show could be."[8] (The production's fluidity was greatly influenced
by the staging of *Allegro*, the Rodgers and Hammerstein musical that preceded it. Perhaps Abbott missed the earlier show or forgot it.) The "integration" of the various elements of *South Pacific*—not just the book music, and
lyrics, but all its components—gives it a seamlessness that remains difficult
to achieve in musical theater: advanced technology and stagecraft do not
always prevent dramatic or musical stasis. Nonetheless, productions such as
Prince's *Cabaret* (1966) or, especially, Michael Bennett's original staging of
Dreamgirls (1982), which flowed cinematically and sustained an almost fero-
cious intensity in part through its perpetual movement, demonstrate, along
with many other subsequent productions, that the lessons of *South Pacific*
and Logan's directorial techniques have been absorbed. George Abbott knew
the importance of both the production and the show, and he also recognized
the need for his young assistant to know that importance, too.

Like the decade of the 1950s, which it anticipated in so many ways, *South Pacific* can be read with appreciative nostalgia and fondness for a sunnier and more sedate era even as it depicts the storm clouds of war. But, also like the decade, the show belies such a reading: racial tension, challenges to societal norms of gender, an uneasy U.S. presence in Southeast Asia, domestic paranoia and unease about who and what is "American" in the face of outside threats (read: Communism), and a growing awareness, and subsequent concern, about conformity in the marketplace and in society in general all lurked just beneath the eerily clean Formica counters and mass-produced suburban cottages of the 1950s, and the unrest that also lurked there exploded in the following decade. As we have observed, *South Pacific* suggests aspects of that unrest.

The American musical underwent notable change in the 1960s. Theatrically, the decade began with the death of Hammerstein, whose last show— *The Sound of Music* (1959)—was both sentimental and highly successful. It also marked the beginning of the demise, at least for a number of years, of the romantic, operetta-influenced musical play that was Rodgers and Hammerstein's signature. Five months after *The Sound of Music* opened, for instance, *Bye, Bye Birdie* both celebrated and satirized rock 'n' roll, introducing the "new" music, or a softened version of it, to the musical stage and suggesting its possibilities in the commercial musical theater. By the end of the decade, modest amplification had become "sound design," notably in *Promises, Promises* (1968), which the composer Burt Bacharach wanted to sound like a highly produced record (it did), and in *Hair* (1967 Off Broadway, 1968 Broadway), the music for which was a mixture of rock and pop and which also introduced a counterculture mindset to the Broadway stage. Moreover, each show was among the last to provide top-40 hits for the U.S. record-buying public: the Bacharach–Hal David score for *Promises, Promises* produced the title song and "I'll Never Fall in Love Again," both recorded to great success by Dionne Warwick; and the pop group the Fifth Dimension had a huge hit with a medley of "Aquarius" and "Let the Sun Shine" from *Hair*. The sound of the newer shows, and their songs, made *South Pacific* seem hopelessly dated, as did its patriotic "good war" sensibility, which was decidedly out of vogue during the growing discontent over U.S. involvement in Vietnam. Even the musical *1776* (1969), which celebrated the signing of the Declaration of Independence with unembarrassed patriotism, contained the song "Mamma, Look Sharp," a wrenching ballad about battle that only partially subdued its antiwar message behind the scrim of historicity.

Yet, as we have seen, *South Pacific* continued to be revived throughout the years, even if none of those revivals were on Broadway. Although Rodgers

8.1. *Mary Martin, Richard Rodgers, and Ezio Pinza listen intently to a playback during the recording of the original Broadway cast album. Courtesy of Photofest.*

and Hammerstein's musicals were often considered old-fashioned, they nonetheless remained an indelible part of the musical-theater landscape, and generations of amateurs often gained their first theatrical experience in a community-theater or high-school production of *Oklahoma!* or *South Pacific*. When the thematic concerns of the latter show again reached public awareness—as we have seen, race and war were very much in the American public's consciousness when the Lincoln Center revival opened—audiences were again reminded of the work's relevance and of its exquisite score. And no matter how many times *South Pacific* is rewritten, reconceived, or reconstructed, it remains, at least in musical-theater terms, paradise.

APPENDIX 1

• • •

THE STRUCTURE OF *TALES OF THE SOUTH PACIFIC*

10. "Fo' Dolla'"

9. "Dry Rot"	←	regarding letters to/ from home	→	11. "Passion"
8. "Our Heroine"	←	cultural encounters, confrontations	→	12. "A Boar's Tooth"
7. "Alligator"	←	stories that end in preparation for battle	→	13. "Wine for the Mess at Segi"
6. "The Milk Run"	←	the individual and the honor of the group	→	14. "The Airstrip at Konora"
5. "The Cave"	←	private refuge from war	→	15. "Those Who Fraternize"
4. "An Officer and a Gentleman"	←	individuals in opposition to the group	→	16. "The Strike"
3. "Mutiny"	←	preparation for battle	→	17. "Frisco"
2. "Coral Sea"	←	battle action	→	18. "The Landing on Kuralei'"
1. "The South Pacific"	←	reflections	→	19. "The Cemetery at Huga Point"

APPENDIX 2

• • •

SCENE BREAKDOWN FOR *SOUTH PACIFIC*

Note: This breakdown follows the published script found in Richard Rodgers and Oscar Hammerstein II, *Six Plays by Rodgers and Hammerstein* (New York: The Modern Library, 1953), 267–366. The action takes place on two islands in the South Pacific during World War II.

1.1. A terrace on Emile de Becque's plantation.

Characters: Ngana, Jerome, Henry, Nellie Forbush, de Becque.

Synopsis: Ngana and Jerome, two "Eurasian" children, sing and dance a folklike song and are chased off by Henry, a servant. De Becque, the French owner of the plantation, and Nellie, an American nurse, enter. The audience learns that Nellie is from Arkansas and is an incurable optimist. De Becque tells Nellie that he left France and came to the South Pacific because he killed a man. A strong attraction is apparent between the two, as are their distinctly different cultural backgrounds. De Becque expresses his interest in a future with Nellie and she leaves. The children return, and the audience learns that de Becque is their father.

Songs: "*Dites-moi*," "A Cockeyed Optimist," "Twin Soliloquies," "Some Enchanted Evening."

1.2. An unidentified setting on the island. Immediately following 1.1.

Characters: Servicemen, Bloody Mary.

Synopsis: Seabees, sailors, and Marines sing lustily of Bloody Mary, a Tonkinese woman who tries to sell souvenir items to the men. They teach her some vulgarities, which she enjoys immensely.

Song: "Bloody Mary."

1.3. Another part of the island. Billis's laundry and Mary's kiosk are visible. A short time after 1.2.

Characters: Above, plus Luther Billis, Lieutenant Cable, Captain. Brackett, Commander Harbison.

Synopsis: Luther Billis, a Seabee and entrepreneur who runs a laundry and tries to compete with Mary in the souvenir trade, is introduced. Mary tricks him into buying an expensive boar's tooth ceremonial bracelet, which he knows comes from the restricted island Bali Ha'i. Billis expresses his desire to get to Bali Ha'i and see the Boar's Tooth Ceremony, and the indigenous women who are secluded there. The men sing about the lack of women in their lives. Nellie and the nurses enter jogging during the song, and Nellie gets her laundry from Billis, who is uncharacteristically shy around her. The nurses leave, and the men finish the song. Lt. Joe Cable, a handsome young Marine from Philadelphia by way of Princeton, enters, and Mary is fascinated by him. She tells him that Bali Ha'i is his special island, one where he can realize his dreams, and she tries to persuade him to come there with her. Billis sees an opportunity for an officer who can get a boat for a trip to Bali Ha'i. Captain Brackett and Commander Harbison enter, determined to tear down Mary's kiosk and remove her from military property. Cable reveals that he has been sent to head a dangerous intelligence mission that could provide information about enemy activity in the area. The scene ends with Cable, alone, contemplating Bali Ha'i.

Songs: "There Is Nothin' Like a Dame," "Bali Ha'i."

1.4. A company street on the island. Immediately following 1.3.

Characters: Billis, Cable, Stewpot, sailors.

Synopsis: Billis informs Cable that he has signed out a boat in Cable's name for a trip to Bali Ha'i. Cable tells him to cancel it.

1.5. Inside Brackett's office. A short time after 1.4.

Characters: Brackett, Harbison, Cable, Nellie.

Synopsis: Because de Becque is familiar with the surrounding islands, the military thinks he would be helpful to Cable on the mission. Knowing that Nellie has been seeing de Becque, Brackett and Harbison interrogate her, but she reveals that she does not know much about him. They ask her to gather some information on de Becque, including why he killed a man in France and what his political views are. When Nellie and Cable leave, Brackett and Harbison discuss the mission, which involves surveillance from positions on a small island. Harbison surmises the spies might last a week before they are caught.

1.6. The company street from 1.4. Immediately following 1.5.

Characters: Nellie, Cable.

Synopsis: Nellie and Cable discuss the difficulties in a relationship between an older man and a younger woman. Cable suggests that Nellie reconsider her relationship with de Becque.

1.7. The beach, including Billis's makeshift pay shower. Immediately following 1.6.

Characters: Billis, Nellie, de Becque, nurses.

Synopsis: Again revealing his fondness for Nellie, Billis gets the shower ready for her, including extra hot water for her weekly shampoo. While she washes her hair, Nellie light-heartedly sings of terminating her relationship with de Becque. At the end of the song, de Becque enters. She at first refuses his invitation to a party, even after he tells her that he is giving it so she can meet his friends. Then, as suggested by Brackett, Nellie begins interrogating de Becque about his past and learns of his belief in democratic ideals and why he killed the man in France. De Becque again confesses his love for Nellie and she realizes, after initially stating their differences, that she feels the same way. She agrees to attend the party and de Becque leaves, after which Nellie exuberantly sings of her love for de Becque.

Songs: "I'm Gonna Wash That Man Right Out-a My Hair," reprise of "Some Enchanted Evening," "I'm in Love with a Wonderful Guy."

1.8. Brackett's office. Shortly after 1.7.

Characters: Brackett, de Becque, Cable.

Synopsis: After listening to Brackett explain the mission, de Becque refuses to join in. Cable suggests that the only reason de Becque is saying no is his love for Nellie. De Becque agrees, adding that his life with Nellie is the most important thing in the world for him. De Becque's decision scuttles the mission, and Cable asks if he should leave the island and return to his outfit. Brackett suggests that Cable take a few days off and go fishing. This reminds Cable of Bali Ha'i, and he heads out to secure a boat for the trip.

1.9. Bali Ha'i. Not long after 1.8.

Characters: young island women, Cable, Billis, Bloody Mary.

Synopsis: After Mary arranges for Billis to be taken to the Boar's Tooth Ceremony, she leads Cable off in another direction, promising him a good time.

Song: reprise of "Bali Ha'i."

1.10. The interior of Bloody Mary's hut on Bali Ha'i.

Characters: Cable, Bloody Mary, Liat.

Synopsis: Mary introduces Cable to Liat, a beautiful young woman, and then leaves the two of them alone. After a brief scene between Cable and Liat in which their mutual attraction is apparent, they embrace and the lights fade. After a musical interlude, the lights come up again, revealing both in a state of semi-undress. Cable learns that Liat is Mary's daughter. As his boat's bell beckons in the distance, Cable sings of the joy he has found with Liat. Hesitatingly, he leaves.

Song: "Younger Than Springtime."

1.11. Another part of Bali Ha'i. Immediately after 1.10.

Characters: Billis, Cable, Bloody Mary, islanders.

Synopsis: Nervously awaiting the overdue Cable, Billis apologizes to Mary for his inappropriate behavior during the Boar's Tooth Ceremony. Cable enters, still in a state of bliss. After he and Billis go off to the boat, Mary confidently announces to the islanders that Cable is going to be her son-in-law.

1.12. A terrace of de Becque's home. Several days later.

Characters: Nellie, de Becque, Ngana, Jerome, Henry.

Synopsis: After de Becque's party, Nellie is slightly tipsy and enjoying herself. Her comfort with and affection for de Becque are apparent, and the two of them playfully sing with each other. Ngana and Jerome, accompanied by Henry, enter to say goodnight. Nellie thinks they are Henry's children, but de Becque tells her that they are his. Nellie at first does not believe him, noting the children's Eurasian appearance, but de Becque tells her that their deceased mother was Polynesian. Nellie is taken aback and grows extremely uncomfortable, and she quickly begins to make excuses for a quick exit. Refusing de Becque's offer to drive her back to the barracks, Nellie nervously thanks him and says goodnight, obviously distressed by what she has learned. As she leaves, de Becque again expresses his love for her. She says that she loves him, too, but makes a hasty exit. Left alone, de Becque stares after her.

Songs: reprise of "I'm in Love with a Wonderful Guy," "This Is How It Feels," reprise of "I'm Gonna Wash That Man Right Out-a My Hair," "Finale Act 1."

2.1. Onstage during a performance of "The Thanksgiving Follies." Two weeks after act 1.
    Characters: Nellie, servicemen, and nurses.
    Synopsis: The scene consists largely of an amateur show performance for which Nellie is the M.C. After announcing the participants in a dance number that opens the scene, Nellie introduces the next act. Before it can begin, however, a power failure occurs. Over confused voices, the scene changes.

2.2. Backstage. Immediately after 2.1.
    Characters: Billis, de Becque, Cable, Bloody Mary, Liat.
    Synopsis: As Billis and his assistants deal with the power failure, de Becque enters with flowers for Nellie. Billis asks de Becque not to see Nellie, confiding that she has been very upset and has applied for a transfer to another island. When de Becque insists that he must see her, Billis asks that he wait until after the performance. De Becque agrees. Cable enters, still feverish with a malaria infection and desperately looking for Billis. Cable tells Billis that he needs a boat to go to Bali Ha'i. Mary and Liat enter, and Cable momentarily thinks he is imagining them. Mary announces that Cable must marry Liat or she will be given to a rich French plantation owner who desires her. De Becque informs Mary that Cable is ill and then expresses his concern for Cable, who responds bitterly and accuses de Becque of not caring about anyone but himself. Insulted, de Becque exits. Mary tries to convince Cable that a life with Liat would be idyllic and free from cares. After Cable gives Liat an heirloom watch—his good luck piece—Mary assumes that he has agreed to marry Liat. When he tells Mary that he has not, Mary grabs the watch and smashes it to the ground. She then drags off the helpless Liat and, as the voice of Nellie can be heard announcing the next act in the "Follies," Cable looks off after the two women.
    Songs: "Happy Talk," reprise of "Younger Than Springtime."

2.3. Onstage of the "Follies." Immediately following 2.2.
    Characters: Brackett, Harbison, Nellie, Billis, servicemen, and nurses.
    Synopsis: After some brief comments about how poorly the American fleet has been doing in the war, Brackett introduces Harbison, who announces the finale of the "Follies." Nellie, dressed as a sailor, sings a song about her "Honey Bun," who turns out to be Billis in drag. The scene concludes with a chorus of sailors and nurses reprising the chorus onstage with Nellie and Billis.
    Song: "Honey Bun."

2.4. Backstage, as in 2.2. Immediately following 2.3.
    Characters: Billis, Nellie, Cable, de Becque.
    Synopsis: Billis gives Nellie the flowers from de Becque and an accompanying card, which she reads and which obviously disturbs her. Cable sees that she is upset and light-heartedly offers sympathy, but Nellie scolds him for not being in the hospital. He tells her about Liat and wonders why he is unable to marry a woman he loves. She quietly reassures

him. De Becque enters and confronts Nellie about her request for a transfer. She explains that she cannot marry him because his first wife was Polynesian. He does not understand this, and Nellie counters with the argument that she was born with her feelings of prejudice. De Becque angrily argues that no one is born with such feelings, and when Nellie turns to Cable for support, she gets none. Nellie leaves, and de Becque asks Cable about Nellie's feelings. Cable replies that people are not born prejudiced, but such feelings are taught to them when they are young. Cable then remarks that now he understands de Becque's lack of desire to get involved with the war, and that when the war is over he will not return to the United States but instead will return to Bali Ha'i. De Becque, however, comments that now that he has lost what mattered most to him, he is no longer so unwilling to commit to an action greater than his own self-interest. He then agrees to go with Cable on the mission, and both men rush off to inform Brackett of their decision.

Songs: "You've Got to Be Carefully Taught," "This Nearly Was Mine."

2.5. A landing strip on the island. A day or two after 1.4.

Characters: several naval aircraft mechanics.

Synopsis: In a brief crossover scene, the mechanics watch the takeoff of the plane carrying Cable and de Becque to their mission.

2.6. The communications office (radio room). A day or two after 2.5.

Characters: Brackett, Harbison, Billis, Lieutenant. Buzz Adams, a radio operator.

Synopsis: Brackett and Harbison are grilling Billis and Adams about an incident that occurred as Adams was delivering Cable and de Becque to a submarine, which was in turn to deliver them to their mission. The plane, piloted by Adams, was bit by enemy fire. Billis, who had hidden on board to get to the island where he thought he might obtain souvenirs, fell out, and Adams circled once to drop a raft to him. As Adams flew on to deliver Cable and de Becque, Billis was protected from enemy fire by New Zealanders in P-40s and American Navy planes. Adams assures the irate Brackett that Billis's action served as a diversionary tactic and ensured the undetected arrival of Cable and de Becque to their destination. De Becque and Cable are then heard on the radio, reporting that they are in place and giving the first report on the movement of the Japanese fleet.

2.7. An undisclosed area with a radio. A few days later.

Characters: A group of pilots, an operations officer, voice of de Becque.

Synopsis: The pilots hear another report from de Becque and prepare to act on it.

2.8. The radio shack. A few more days later.

Characters: Brackett, Harbison, Nellie, radio operator.

Synopsis: Nellie comes to the radio shack and, although she knows it is against protocol, asks if de Becque is on the mission that everyone on the island is talking about. Just as Brackett tells her yes, de Becque's voice is heard. He tells of Cable's death from wounds received three days earlier and then relates that the Japanese are pulling out from the area in great confusion after having been repeatedly surprised by American planes. The mission has been successful. Nellie wonders if de Becque will return, and she is reassured by Brackett.

2.9. Outside the radio shack. Immediately following 2.8.

Characters: Nellie, other nurses, a lieutenant.

Synopsis: As Nellie comes out of the radio shack, stunned by the news of Cable's death and the possibility of de Becque's, a nurse and a lieutenant ask her if she is going to a dance that evening. When she doesn't answer, other nurses tease her by singing, "She's in love with a wonderful guy."

Song: reprise of "I'm in Love with a Wonderful Guy."

2.10. The beach. Immediately following 2.9.

Characters: Nellie, Bloody Mary, Liat.

Synopsis: Nellie, looking out over the ocean, speaks to de Becque, imploring him to return so she can tell him how foolish she has been and that their being together is all that matters. Mary and Liat enter, asking where they can find Cable. When Nellie asks who they are, Mary tells her that Liat will marry no one else but Cable and that they must find him. Nellie, overcome with emotion, embraces Liat.

Song: reprise of "Some Enchanted Evening."

2.11. The company street. Days later.

Characters: Billis, Brackett, Harbison, servicemen, nurses.

Synopsis: Over the sounds of truck convoys, a crowd of servicemen organizes to embark on a mission. Harbison notes that the tide of the war in the Pacific has changed due to the success of Cable and de Becque's mission. Billis, to his chagrin, learns that he has been assigned to a ship commanded by Brackett and Harbison.

Song: reprise of "Honey Bun."

2.12. De Becque's terrace. Not long after 2.11.

Characters: Nellie, Jerome, Ngana, de Becque.

Synopsis: Nellie, Ngana, and Jerome are eating lunch and watching the planes leave the island. The children get Nellie to sing with them and, when she stumbles with the words of the song, de Becque, who has quietly appeared unseen, begins singing them. As he finishes the song, the children continue their lunch as if everything is back to normal, and de Becque and Nellie stare gratefully and lovingly into each other's eyes.

Song: reprise of "*Dites-moi.*"

APPENDIX 3

• • •

"THE BRIGHT YOUNG EXECUTIVE OF TODAY"

Bill [Harbison]
When I get out of a uniform
Will I be happy again,
Working under the watchful eye
Of good old W. N.!

Joe
(Speaking)
Who dat?

Bill
(Faintly annoyed and flattened by the
interruption.)
That's my boss, Woodcock Nordlinger. We call him
W. N.

Joe
Oh.

Bill
Where was I?

Joe
Under his watchful eye.

Bill
Oh yes.
(He resumes singing.)
His hearty voice and his piercing look

I can still hear and see,
The day that he gave me extravagant praise
And followed it up with a nominal raise,
And said these unforgettable words to me:
"The hope of the world
Is the well-trained, wide-awake,
Bright, young executive of to-day.
The cream of the crop
Is the clean-cut, confident,
Bright, young executive of to-day.
   No feather-brained romancer,
   Before he'll give an answer,
The facts and all the figures he'll survey!"

   (Emile enters. Joe exchanges a look with him,
   joins him and they listen to Bill together.)

"So bet all you can borrow
On the man of tomorrow—
The bright, young executive of to-day!"

  Joe
   (Explaining to Emile)
We have other important men.

  Bill
But nobody counts as much
As the modern executive type
With the organizational touch!

  Emile
Of course you have the artist—

  Joe
   (To Bill)
How do you rate the artist?

Bill
A screwball and a bohemian.
He's an unreliable type.

Joe
Well, what about the writer?

Emile
How do you rate the writer?

Bill
He goes for walks in the country,
Plays with dogs and smokes a pipe.

Joe
The farmer?

Bill
Just a rube.

Emile
The actor?

Bill
He's a cad.

Joe
The teacher?

Bill
He's a boob.

Joe
The laborer?

Bill
Money-mad.

Emile
Money-mad?

Bill
Money-mad!

Emile
(To Joe)
The laborer, too?

Bill
(Broadminded)
I admit we need all kinds of men—

Joe
(Jumping up with the eagerness of a substitute half-back)
But not one tenth as much
As the peppy executive type
With the organizational touch!

(Joe now sings the refrain as earnestly as Bill and Bill is completely carried away and unaware of any satirical intent)

The hope of the world
    Is the heads-up, on-your-toes,
Bright young executive of today.
You meet him at lunch
In the high-flown Rainbow Room,
Alone on the roof of the R.C.A.!
His luncheon conversation
Is filled with information:
"The Ford Coupe" he'll say, "is here to stay!"

Bill
(Carried away)
I'll say!

Joe
(Very, very vigorously!)
Click your heels and salute, you're
With the man of the future—
The bright young executive of to-day!

(Emile comes to an involuntary salute!)

Bill
(Transported)
He's solid and he's sound,
With both feet on the ground—

Emile
He's not the type to stand around
With one foot off the ground!

(He stands on one foot)

Joe
It's never hard to tell
The man who's rung the bell—
He wears a white carnation
In his tailor-made lapel!

Bill
He doesn't go off half-cocked!
His eye is on the ball!

Joe
And now and then, like mortal men,
He doesn't go off at all!

(Before Bill has time to analyze this one, Joe has barged into the refrain con spirito, as before)

But—
The hope of the world
Is the drive-hard,

    Emile
Crack-the-whip,

    Joe and Emile
Bright young executive of to-day!

    Bill
They all wait to hear
What the sane and sensible,
Bright young executive has to say!

    Joe
He'll tell you that inflation
Will never hurt the nation,
Unless, of course, it comes and then it may!

    Emile
Hooray!

    Joe, Bill and Emile
Click your heels and salute, you're
With the man of the future—

    Joe
The clear-eyed, clean-limbed,

    Bill
Hard-headed,

Emile
      (Proud to have suddenly thought of the word:
Spark-plug!

      (They all take a deep breath and let out:)

      Emile, Joe and Bill
The bright, young executive of to-day!

• • •

COMPARISON OF FINAL VERSION AND DRAFT OF "I'M GONNA WASH THAT MAN RIGHT OUT-A MY HAIR"

Final Version	Draft
	Intro
	If you ask a man right And his answer ain't right, If he don't look right And he don't love right, Then somethin' must be wrong, And nothin' can be wronger than a man who's wrong.
Refrain	*Refrain*
I'm gonna wash that man right out-a my hair,	If the man don't understand you.
I'm gonna wash that man right out-a my hair,	If you fly on separate beams,
I'm gonna wash that man right out-a my hair,	Waste no time
And send him on his way.	Makin' a change Ride the man right off your range, Rub him out-a the roll call And drum him out-a your dreams.
I'm gonna wave that man right out-a my arms,	If his eyes get dull and fishy,

Final Version	Draft

Final Version

I'm gonna wave that man right out-a
   my arms,
I'm gonna wave that man right out-a
   my arms,
And send him on his way.

Draft

When you look for glints and
    gleams,
Waste no time,

Makin' a change,
Ride the man right off your range,
Rub him out-a the roll call
And drum him out-a your dreams!

 If he never buys you flowers
Or a box of chocolate creams,
If he laughs at different comics
And he roots for different teams,
Waste no time
Makin' a switch,
Leave him in a ditch
(Don't matter which ditch)
Rub him out-a the roll call
And drum him out-a your dreams.

Don't try to patch it up,
Tear it up, tear it up!
Wash him out, dry him out,
Push him out, fly him out,
Cancel him and let him go!
Yea, sister!

Don't try to patch it up,
Tear it up, tear it up!
Throw him out, cut him out,
Put him out, shut him out,
Cancel him and let him go!
Yea, sister!
Cancel him and let him go!

I'm gonna wash that man right out-a
   my hair,
I'm gonna wash that man right out-a
   my hair,
I'm gonna wash that man right out-a
   my hair,
And send him on his way!

[Blues:]
If the man don't understand you,

I'm gonna wash that man
    right out-a my hair,
I'm gonna wash that man
    right out-a my hair,
I'm gonna wash that man
    right out-a my hair,
And send him on his way!
Send him on his way!

Don't try to patch it up,

Final Version

If you fly on separate beams,
Waste no time!
Make a change,
Ride that man right off your range,
Rub him out-a the roll call
And drum him out-a your dreams!
Oh-ho!
If you laugh at different comics,
If you root for different teams,
Waste no time,
Weep no more,
Show him what the door is for!
Rub him out-a the roll call
And drum him out-a your dreams.

You can't light a fire when the wood's
    all wet,
You can't make a butterfly strong,
You can't fix an egg when it ain't quite
    good,
And you can't fix a man when he's
    wrong!

You can't put back a petal when it
    falls from a flower,
Or sweeten up a feller when he starts
    turning sour—
Oh no, oh no!

[Dance break]

If his eyes get dull and fishy
When you look for glints and gleams,
Waste no time,
Make a switch,
Drop him in the nearest ditch!
Rub him out-a the roll call

Draft

Tear it up, tear it up!
Wash him out, dry him out,
Put him, fly him out,
Cancel him and let him go!
Yea sister!
Cancel him and . . . let . . .

(Continue directly to final section)

Final Version	*Draft*
And drum him out-a your dreams!	
Oh-ho! Oh-ho!	
I went and washed that man right out-a my hair,	I'm gonna live that man right out-a my life,
I went and washed that man right out-a my hair,	I'm gonna live that man right out-a my life,
I went and washed that man right out-a my hair,	I'm gonna live that man right out-a my life,
And sent him on his way.	And send him on his way.
She went and washed that man right out-a her hair,	I'm gonna live that man right out-a my life,
She went and washed that man right out-a her hair,	I'm gonna live that man right out-a my life,
She went and washed that man right out-a her hair,	I'm gonna live that man right out-a my life,
And sent him on his way.	And send him on his way.
	And send him on his way.

APPENDIX 5

• • •

COMPARISON OF FINAL VERSION AND DRAFT OF "I'M IN LOVE WITH A WONDERFUL GUY"

Final Version

Draft

[Verse]

  I expect every one
Of my crowd to make fun
Of my proud protestations of faith
  in romance,
And they'll say I'm naïve
As a babe to believe
Any fable I hear from a person in
  pants!
Fearlessly I'll face them and argue
  their doubts away,
Loudly I'll sing about flowers and
  spring!
Flatly I'll stand on my little flat
  feet and say,
"Love is a grand and a beautiful
  thing."
I'm not ashamed to reveal
The world-famous feeling I feel.

[Verse]

  I expect every one
Of my crowd to make fun
Of my proud protestations of faith
  in romance,
And you'll say I'm naïve
As a babe to believe
Any fable I hear from a person in
  pants!
Time was when I shared your
  satirical attitude,
Thinking that love could be kept in
  its place,
Till all of a sudden that lyrical
  platitude
Bounced up and hit me—smack in
  the face!
That's how I turned out to be
The happy young woman you see.

[chorus]

[chorus]

I'm as corny as Kansas in August,
I'm as normal as blueberry pie.
No more a smart
Little girl with no heart,
I have me a wonderful guy.

I'm as corny as Kansas in August,
I'm as normal as blueberry pie,
I'm no longer a smart
Little girl with no heart—
I have found me a wonderful guy!

Final Version	Draft
I am in a conventional dither	There's an old fashioned spring in my footstep,
With a conventional star in my eye,	A conventional star in my eye
And, you will note,	And a lump in my throat
There's a lump in my throat	As I breathlessly float
When I speak of that wonderful guy.	To a date with that wonderful guy.
I'm as trite and as gay	I'm as trite and as gay
As a daisy in May	As a daisy in May,
(A cliché coming true!)	I'm another cliché coming true.
I'm bromidic and bright	I'm bromidic and bright
As a moon-happy night	As a moon-happy night
Pouring light on the dew.	Or the dawn's early light on the dew!
I'm as corny as Kansas in August,	I'm as corny as Kansas in August,
High as a flag on the fourth of July!	Or a flag on the fourth of July.
If you'll excuse	I'm in love—you'll excuse the expression—
	I'm in love with a wonderful guy!
An expression I use	
I'm in love,	
I'm in love,	
I'm in love,	
I'm in love,	
I'm in love with a wonderful guy.	
[dance, after which Nellie and nurses sing the last seven lines with extended ending]	

(Dinah and nurses)
She's as normal as school in
   September,
Or an unattached leaf in November
Or a snowflake that falls in
   December
Or an ostrich's tail on a fan.

Final Version   *Draft*

She's as sweet and dumb as
     bumpkin,
Any girl who is that kind of chump,
     kin
Get as plump as a Halloween
     pumpkin,
Sitting home every night with a
     man.

(Nellie)
Sitting home will be all right with
     me—
If my home's on a hill by the sea . . .
(She goes into a second refrain:)
I'm as corny as Kansas in August,
I'm as normal as blueberry pie . . .

(The girls join her in a vocal
     arrangement, finishing out the
     refrain . . .)

ORIGINAL FORM FOR "HAPPY TALK"

Verse: Fella, when you're talkin' to your best girl
            Whatsa gooda talkin' sad?
            Whatsa gooda talkn' 'bout what ain't good?
            Talk about what ain't bad?

Refrain: Talk about a moon
            Floatin' in de sky,
            Lookin' like a lily on a lake;
            Talk about a bird
            Learnin' how to fly,
            Makin' all the music he can make.

            Talk happy
            Talk about a star
            Lookin' like a toy,
            Peekin' t'rough de branches of a tree;
            Talk about a girl
            Talk about a girl
            Countin' all de ripples on de sea.

            Talk happy
                Talk about breakfus, coffee an' toast
                Opposite de one you love de most,
                Dinner an' supper, plen'y to eat,
                Gravy an' potatoes on your meat!

            Talk about a boy
            Sayin' to de girl:
            "Golly, baby! I'm a lucky cuss!"
            Talk about de girl
            Sayin' to de boy:
            "You an' me is lucky to be us!"

Coda: Happy Talk,
          Keep talkin' happy talk,
          Talk about things you like to do.
          You gotta have a dream,
          If you don't have a dream
          How you gonna have a dream come true?
            If you don't talk happy
            An' you never have a dream,
            Den you'll never have a dream come true!

NOTES

• • •

CHAPTER 1: WHO CAN EXPLAIN IT?

1. Frank Rich, "Memorial Day at 'South Pacific,'" *New York Times,* May 25, 2008, http://www.nytimes.com/2008/05/25/opinion/25rich.html.

2. See Studs Terkel, *"The Good War": An Oral History of World War Two* (New York: Pantheon, 1984).

3. Ben Brantley, "An Optimist Awash in the Tropics," *New York Times,* April 4, 2008, "Weekend Arts," 1, 16. Dissenting reviewers were few. Prominent among them was Terry Teachout who, in addition to his *Wall Street Journal* review, wrote for the online *Arts Journal* that *South Pacific* was "a show so reeking of uplift that you can all but feel your pulse slowing to a crawl." He opened his review by stating that "*South Pacific* goes dead in the water every time the characters stop singing and start talking, which is way too often." Terry Teachout, "The Importance of Not Being Earnest," www. Artsjournal.com/aboutlastnight/2008/04/tt_the_importance_of_not_being.

4. Ibid.

5. Harry S. Truman, press conference on civil rights, February 5, 1948. Cited in David McCullough, *Truman* (New York: Simon & Schuster, 1992), 587.

6. Bruce Kirle, *Unfinished Show Business: Musicals as Works-in-Process* (Carbondale, IL: Southern Illinois University Press, 2005), 1.

7. Ibid., 158. Emphasis in the original.

8. Hereafter, act and scene references will be given by number, with the act given first, followed by a period and then the scene number; e.g., act 2, scene 4, becomes 2.4.

9. Hammerstein's addition, and the letter and Hammerstein's response, can be found in the Oscar Hammerstein II Collection, the Library of Congress, box marked "*CORRES* South Pacific." The added passage is in Richard Rodgers and Oscar Hammerstein II, *South Pacific,* vocal score, ed. Albert Sirmay, revised under the supervision of Bruce Pomahac (New York: Williamson Music, 1949), 147–49.

10. Stephen Banfield, *Sondheim's Broadway Musicals* (Ann Arbor: University of Michigan Press,1993), 3.

11. Hugh Fordin, *Getting to Know Him: A Biography of Oscar Hammerstein II* (New York: Ungar Publishing, 1977), 279.

12. Charles Hamm, "The Theatre Guild Production of *Porgy and Bess,*" *Journal of the American Musicological Society* 40 (Fall 1987), 494–532.

13. Geoffrey Block, *Richard Rodgers* (New Haven, CT: Yale University Press, 2003), 139. See also Geoffrey Block, *The Richard Rodgers Reader* (New York: Oxford University Press,2002) and *Enchanted Evenings* (New York: Oxford University Press, 1997).

14. Tim Carter, *Oklahoma! The Making of an American Musical* (New Haven, CT: Yale University Press, 2007), xvi. See also bruce d. mcclung, *Lady in the Dark: Biography of a Musical* (New York: Oxford University Press, 2007).

15. Aldous Huxley, *The Perennial Philosophy* (New York: Harper & Row, 1945), 16.

16. *Richard Rodgers: The Sweetest Sounds,* directed by Roger Sherman (2001; Wellspring Studios, DVD, 2002). First shown on PBS *American Masters,* November 4, 2001.

CHAPTER 2: THE MUSICAL IS THE MESSAGE

1. Oscar Hammerstein II, interviewed by Mike Wallace, *The Mike Wallace Interview*, CBS, March 15, 1958, http://www.hrc.utexas.edu/multimedia/video/2008/wallace/hammerstein_oscar_t.html, 2–3.

2. Richard Rodgers, *Musical Stages: An Autobiography* (New York: Random House, 1975), 261–62.

3. Hammerstein, *Wallace Interview*, 6.

4. Ibid., 7.

5. Meryle Secrest, *Somewhere for Me: A Biography of Richard Rodgers* (New York: Alfred A. Knopf, 2001), 301.

6. Rodgers, *Musical Stages*, 257.

7. Ibid., 229.

8. Ibid., 227.

9. See especially Miles Kreuger, *Show Boat: The Story of a Classic American Musical* (New York: Oxford University Press, 1977); Ethan Mordden, *Make Believe: The Broadway Musical in the 1920s* (New York: Oxford University Press, 1997); John Bush Jones, *Our Musicals, Ourselves: A Social History of the American Musical Theatre* (Hanover, NH: University Press of New England, 2003), 73–78.

10. Stanley Green, ed., *Rodgers and Hammerstein Fact Book: A Record of Their Works Together and with Other Collaborators* (New York: Lynn Farnol Group, 1980), 349–56.

11. For further information on *Free for All*, see Ethan Mordden, *Sing for Your Supper: The Broadway Musical in the 1930s* (New York: Palgrave Macmillan, 2005), 161–62; Green, *Fact Book*, 421–24; and Hugh Fordin, *Getting to Know Him: A Biography of Oscar Hammerstein II* (New York: Ungar Publishing, 1977), 116.

12. Fordin, *Getting to Know Him*, 14.

13. Ibid., 142.

14. "Nazi—in Los Angeles," unidentified memo in the Oscar Hammerstein II Collection, Library of Congress, Box 21 (Correspondence & Misc. by subject).

15. "In Our Own Backyard: Resisting Nazi Propaganda in Southern California 1933–1945," California State University, Northridge, 1989. http://digital-library.csun.edu/backyard.

16. "Historical Context," "Backyard."

17. "Boycott the movies!" "Backyard."

18. Henry Meyers, Memo to Oscar Hammerstein II, November 7, 1936. In the Oscar Hammerstein II Collection, Library of Congress, Box 21 (Correspondence & Misc. by subject).

19. Cited in Fordin, *Getting to Know Him*, 143.

20. Hollywood Anti-Nazi League for the Defense of American Democracy, event pamphlet, January 1937. In the exhibit "In Our Own Backyard: Resisting Nazi Propaganda in Southern California 1933–1945," California State University, 2008. http://digital-library.csun.edu/backyard. Also in the pamphlet are announcements for a banquet in honor of Ernst Toller, an exiled German author, on January 10, and a "giant mass meeting" titled "We Warn America!" on January 12. Hammerstein is mentioned only in connection with DuBois's appearance.

21. See Werner Sollors, "W. E. B. Dubois in Nazi Germany: A Surprising, Prescient Visitor," *Chronicle of Higher Education* 46, no.12 (1999): B4–B5.

22. Fordin, *Getting to Know Him,* 153–59.

23. United States Federal Bureau of Investigation, "Hollywood Anti-Nazi League," file no. 100–6633, declassified June 29, 1999, http://foia.fbi.gov/foiaindex/holly-woodleague.htm, part 1, 1.

24. Ibid., 18.

25. Ibid., 23. The Dies Committee was another name for HUAC during the time it was headed by Martin Dies, Jr. (1938–44).

26. FBI, part 2, 6–7.

27. FBI, part 1, 33.

28. Ibid., 7.

29. FBI, part 2, 7. Emphasis added.

30. FBI, part 1, 12.

31. FBI, part 2, 2. Emphasis added.

32. Ronald Radosh and Allis Radosh, "A Rewrite for Hollywood's Blacklist Saga," *Los Angeles Times,* April 25, 2005, Opinion, http://articles.latimes.com/2005/apr/25/opinion/oe_radosh25.

33. Ibid., 312–13.

34. Rodgers, *Musical Stages,* 149–50.

35. Ibid., 154.

36. Ibid.

37. John Mosher, *The New Yorker,* October 8, 1932; *Time,* October 10, 1932. Cited in Green, *Fact Book,* 133.

38. Lorenz Hart, "Somebody Ought to Wave a Flag," from *The Phantom President.* In *The Complete Lyrics of Lorenz Hart,* ed. Dorothy Hart and Robert Kimball (New York: Alfred A. Knopf, 1986), 179.

39. Rodgers, *Musical Stages,* 155.

40. Ibid., 156.

41. Ibid.

42. Ibid., 176.

43. Andrea Most, *Making Americans: Jews and the Broadway Musical* (Cambridge, MA: Harvard University Press, 2004), 67.

44. Ibid., 71.

45. Ibid., 85.

46. Ibid., 91.

47. Hart, *Lyrics,* 229.

48. Most, *Making Americans,* 90.

49. Ibid., 93.

50. Rodgers, *Musical Stages,* 183.

51. Ibid., 184.

52. Ibid., 187.

53. Garrett Eisler, "Kidding on the Level: The Reactionary Project of *I'd Rather Be Right,*" *Studies in Musical Theatre* 1, no. 1 (2007), 7.

54. Rodgers, *Musical Stages,* 186.

55. Eisler, "Kidding," 7.

56. Ibid., 22.

57. Hart, *Lyrics,* 266.

58. Rodgers, *Musical Stages,* 183, 187.

59. Hammerstein, *Wallace Interview,* 3.

60. Rodgers, *Musical Stages,* 227, 229.

61. John Chapman, *New York Daily News.* In Green, *Fact Book,* 535.

62. Hammerstein, *Wallace Interview,* 4.

63. Ibid.

64. "Third Annual Report of the Writers' War Board," January 1945. In the Oscar Hammerstein II Collection, Library of Congress, Box 21. Emphasis added.

65. Christina Klein, *Cold War Orientalism: Asia in the Middlebrow Imagination, 1945–1961* (Berkeley: University of California Press, 2003), 185.

66. Fordin, *Getting to Know Him,* 283.

67. Oscar Hammerstein II, guest editorial, *Saturday Review of Literature* 33, no. 52 (December 23, 1950), 22–23.

68. Oscar Hammerstein II, "Progress" and "Dear Believer in White Supremacy," in the Oscar Hammerstein II Collection, Library of Congress, Box 21 (Correspondence & Misc. by subject).

69. Hammerstein, *Wallace Interview,* 3.

70. Klein, *Cold War,* 195.

71. Rodgers, *Musical Stages,* 270–71.

72. Klein, *Cold War,* 219.

73. Rodgers, *Musical Stages,* 307.

74. Ibid.

75. Harold Clurman, review of *No Strings,* in *The Nation,* April 14, 1962. In Green, *Fact Book,* 655.

CHAPTER 3: AN ADAPTABLE SOURCE: MICHENER'S *TALES OF THE SOUTH PACIFIC*

1. Much of this chapter is based on a similar chapter in "The Musico-Dramatic Evolution of Rodgers and Hammerstein's *South Pacific,*" my doctoral dissertation, which I defended at The Ohio State University in March 2003. The research for that document heavily informs this work, and passages in later chapters also owe much to the dissertation.

2. James A. Michener, *The World Is My Home: A Memoir* (New York: Random House, 1992), 91. Rodgers and Hammerstein removed the hyphen and made the name two separate words: Bali Ha'i.

3. Quoted in "*South Pacific:* Check Out the Cheese," *Independent Enjoyment,* December 3, 2001, http://enjoyment.independent.co.uk.

4. Two pages of Hammerstein's copy of the novel are reproduced in Laurence Maslon's *South Pacific Companion* (New York: Fireside, 2008), 114. However, that copy, according to Ted Chapin of the Rodgers and Hammerstein Organization, is among William Hammerstein's papers that recently were given to the Library of Congress. They are not catalogued.

5. Wilbur Murra, private correspondence to Kenneth A. Moe, October 2, 1976. Quoted in John P. Hayes, *James A. Michener: A Biography* (Indianapolis: Bobbs-Merrill, 1984), 60.

6. James A. Michener, private correspondence to John P. Hayes, December 15, 1971. Quoted in Hayes, *Michener*, 61.

7. Michener, *World*, 8.

8. Ibid., 20.

9. Ibid.

10. Ibid., 28.

11. Ibid., 265.

12. See Appendix 1, "The Structure of *Tales of the South Pacific*," for a chart of the book's structure.

13. See Hugh Fordin, *Getting to Know Him: Oscar Hammerstein II: A Biography* (New York: Random House, 1977), 259–62; Richard Rodgers, *Musical Stages: An Autobiography* (New York: Random House, 1975), 258–59.

14. Lawrence Grobel, *Talking with Michener* (Jackson, MS: University of Jackson Press, 1999), 241. The other "stories," all contained within long novels, include one about King David and the hoopoe bird in *The Source*, the tale of the dinosaur diplodocus from *Centennial*, and the factual account of Admiral Lord Nelson's search for a wife of means in *Caribbean* (241).

15. Geoffrey Block provides further insight into the issue of Cable and class in his chapter on *South Pacific*. See *Richard Rodgers* (New Haven, CT: Yale University Press, 2003), 161.

16. Michener, *World*, 266.

17. Marilyn S. Severson, *James A. Michener: A Critical Companion* (Westport, CT: Greenwood, 1996), 18.

18. Michener, *World*, 266.

19. James A. Michener, *Tales of the South Pacific* (New York: Macmillan, 1947; New York: Fawcett Crest, 1973), 10. All citations are from the Fawcett Crest paperback.

20. George J. Becker, *James A. Michener* (New York: Ungar Publishing, 1983), 30–31.

21. Michener, *Tales*, 222.

22. Ibid., 304, 326.

23. Edward Said, *Culture and Imperialism* (New York: Vintage, 1994), xxiv–xxv. Emphasis in the original.

24. Christina Klein, *Cold War Orientalism: Asia in the Middlebrow Imagination, 1945–1961* (Berkeley: University of California Press, 2003), 120.

25. Michener, *Tales*, 118.

26. Ibid., 138, 139.

27. Ibid., 180.

28. Ibid., 183.

29. Ibid., 191.

30. Ibid., 192, 196, 197, 207.

31. Ibid., 194–95.

32. Fordin, *Getting to Know Him,* 259.

33. Ibid., 260.

34. Michener, *World,* 290.

35. Ibid.

36. Ibid., 291.

37. Maslon, *South Pacific Companion,* 101.

38. Rodgers, *Musical Stages,* 258–59.

39. Ibid., 259.

40. Fordin, *Getting to Know Him,* 261.

41. Oscar Hammerstein II, "Notes on Michener's *Tales of the South Pacific,*" Oscar Hammerstein II Collection, Library of Congress, box marked "South Pacific."

42. Oscar Hammerstein II, "Note on Lyrics," in *Lyrics by Oscar Hammerstein II* (Milwaukee: Hal Leonard Books, 1985), 9. In addition to Hammerstein's account, many popular histories of American musical theater mention Hammerstein's use of the play's opening stage directions as the source for his memorable lyrics.

43. Michener, *Tales,* 1.

44. Oscar Hammerstein II and Joshua Logan, *South Pacific,* in *6 Plays by Rodgers and Hammerstein* (New York: Random House, 1953), 276.

45. Ibid., 287.

46. Ibid., 189.

47. A. Grove Day, *James Michener,* 2nd edition (Boston: Twayne, 1977), 39.

48. See Maslon, *South Pacific Companion,* 111.

49. Michener, *Tales,* 59.

50. Hammerstein and Logan, *South Pacific,* 347.

51. Michener, *Tales,* 79.

52. Hammerstein and Logan, *South Pacific,* 353.

53. Day, *Michener,* 43.

54. Ibid., 50.

55. Rodgers, *Musical Stages,* 259.

56. Michener, *World,* 292–93.

57. Ethan Mordden, *Rodgers and Hammerstein* (New York: Harry N. Abrams, 1995), 116. The combined qualities of seriousness and levity in pairs of couples that are often treated as generic "types" suggest the dangers of misreading dimensional characters as mere character types in Rodgers and Hammerstein's work.

CHAPTER 4: FALSE STARTS: THE DISAPPEARANCE OF BILL HARBISON AND DINAH CULBERT

1. James A. Michener, *Tales of the South Pacific* (New York: Macmillan, 1947; New York: Fawcett Crest, 1973), 10.

2. Ibid., 50–51.

3. Ibid., 56.

4. Ibid.

5. Ibid., 59–60.

6. Ibid.

7. Ibid., 62.

8. Ibid., 67. Geoffrey Block provides a reading of this scene that, to me, seems unsubstantiated. He assumes that Nellie has sex with Harbison, writing, "By the time Nellie meets Emile, she has been seduced and abandoned—damaged goods." (See *Richard Rodgers* [New Haven, CT: Yale University Press, 2003], 128.) However, Michener's description of the scene is straightforward: Nellie is willing to have sex with Harbison, but she will not do so until she learns of his feelings and his marital status. Even if they had had sex, it would have been consensual, and Nellie would not have been seduced. She knew exactly what she was doing.

9. Ibid., 65–66.

10. Ibid., 119.

11. Ibid.

12. Ibid., 316.

13. Ibid., 317.

14. See Appendix 2, "Scene Breakdown for *South Pacific*."

15. Oscar Hammerstein II, draft for 1.1. In the Oscar Hammerstein II Collection (uncatalogued), Library of Congress, Washington, D.C., box marked "*CORRES* South Pacific (2)."

16. Oscar Hammerstein II, draft for 1.4 [*sic*], in the Oscar Hammerstein II Collection, Library of Congress, Washington, D.C., box marked "South Pacific."

17. Michener noted in a *New York Times* article after the show's opening that "Lieutenant Harbison is cleaned up and promoted to a commander." James A. Michener, "Happy Talk: Tribute to Writers of 'South Pacific,'" *New York Times*, July 3, 1949. Quoted in Block, *Richard Rodgers*, 139.

18. See Michener, *Tales*, 132–33.

19. Hammerstein, draft for 1.4 [*sic*].

20. Hammerstein retained Billis's shy discussion about his laundry, although in altered form. In 1.3 of the final version, Billis has the discussion with Nellie. The soldiers overhear it and tease him about it. See Oscar Hammerstein II and Joshua Logan, *South Pacific*, in 6 *Plays by Rodgers and Hammerstein* (New York: Random House, 1953), 290–91.

21. Joshua Logan, *Josh: My Up and Down, In and Out Life* (New York: Delacorte, 1976), 233–34.

22. The insertion of dance music for the actual hair washing, according to Logan, occurred during the New Haven tryouts. Logan realized that Martin was upstaging herself, and the number, by singing and washing at the same time. Logan, *Josh*, 235, 239. The published script indicates that Nellie starts washing her hair at the top of the number and, after the first four lines of the song, "struts around splashing soap out of her hair." Hammerstein and Logan, *South Pacific*, 311. The score, however, indicates that Nellie washes her hair during the orchestral dance break, indicating Logan's revised staging. Richard Rodgers and Oscar Hammerstein II, *South Pacific*, vocal score, ed. Albert Sirmay, revised under the supervision of Bruce Pomahac (New York: Williamson Music, 1949), 66.

23. For a comparison of the early lyrics and the final version, see Appendix 3.

24. For the final music and lyrics of "I'm Gonna Wash That Man Right Out-a My Hair," see Rodgers and Hammerstein, vocal score, 60–69. The "blues" section is on pp. 62–64 (rehearsals 2–4).

25. Hammerstein, draft for 1.4 [*sic*].

26. Approximately ten years later, Hammerstein told the creators of the musical *Gypsy* that "Rose's Turn," the final big number for star Ethel Merman that had been written and staged without a big finish, needed musical closure because the audience felt the need to applaud the star. Someone, perhaps the director Josh Logan, seems to have given him the same advice for "I'm Gonna Wash That Man Right Out-a My Hair." See, among other sources, Arthur Laurents, *Original Story: A Memoir of Broadway and Hollywood* (New York: Applause Theatre Books, 2000), 395.

27. See Block, *Richard Rodgers,* 143–44.

28. Logan, *Josh,* 239. See also Block, *Richard Rodgers,* 136.

29. Hammerstein, draft for 1.4 [*sic*].

30. For a comparison of the song's early lyrics and its final version, see Appendix 5.

31. Hammerstein, draft for 1.4. [*sic*]. Between the time of the research for this work and its completion, many, although not all, of the previously unpublished lyrics for *South Pacific* found among Hammerstein's papers in the Library of Congress and other places have been collected and published in *The Complete Lyrics of Oscar Hammerstein II,* ed. Amy Asch (New York: Alfred A. Knopf, 2008). The cut lyrics from "I'm in Love with a Wonderful Guy" are on page 339.

32. See Logan, *Josh,* 222; 235–36. In her autobiography, Mary Martin remembers hearing the song well after her first meeting with Rodgers and Hammerstein and their first performance of completed songs for her. Among the songs Martin recalls hearing at the first meeting with Rodgers and Hammerstein were the "Twin Soliloquies" and "Some Enchanted Evening." Mary Martin, *My Heart Belongs* (New York: William Morrow, 1976), 160. Rodgers recalls playing for Martin the five songs the team had completed in July 1948, but he does not list the songs. Richard Rodgers, *Musical Stages: An Autobiography* (New York: Random House, 1975), 260.

33. See Logan, *Josh,* 233–34.

34. Hammerstein, draft for 1.1.

35. Ibid.

36. Ibid.

37. Hammerstein had a working farm near Doylestown, Pennsylvania, where he did much of his writing. See Hugh Fordin, *Getting to Know Him: A Biography of Oscar Hammerstein II* (New York: Ungar Publishing, 1977), 176–77; and Logan, *Josh,* 221.

38. Hammerstein, draft for 1.1.

39. Rodgers, *Musical Stages,* 221. This also suggests why the early drafts for "I'm in Love with a Wonderful Guy" do not fit the music we know for the song; Rodgers could simply have altered the words, or asked Hammerstein to do so, to fit the waltz melody he so memorably provided for the lyrics.

40. Ibid.

41. See David Riesman, in collaboration with Reuel Denney and Nathan Glazer, *The Lonely Crowd: A Study of the Changing American Character* (New Haven, CT: Yale University Press, 1959); C. Wright Mills, *White Collar: The American Middle Classes* (New York: Oxford University Press, 1956); and William H. Whyte Jr., *The Organization Man* (New York: Simon & Schuster, 1956).

42. See C. Wright Mills, "The Competitive Personality," *Partisan Review* 13, no. 4 (September–October 1946), 433–41; also in *Power, Politics and People: The Collected Essays of C. Wright Mills,* ed. Irving Louis Horowitz (New York: Oxford University Press, 1963), 263–73. All citations are from the 1963 Oxford University Press collected essays.

43. Mills, "Competitive," 269.

44. Also see Whyte, *Organization,* 143.

45. Mills, "Competitive," 268. In *White Collar,* Mills pursues this grim assessment of the American middle class.

46. Ibid., 268–69. In his later book, Mills expands on his observation about the old guard executive not being particularly bright. Mills: "It is often hard to say, with any success, whether the new entrepreneur lives on his own wits, or upon the lack of wits in others." Mills, *White Collar,* 95.

47. Hammerstein, draft for 1.1.

48. Ibid.

49. Mills, "Competitive," 369.

50. Ibid. On the same page as this sentence, Mills also writes, "For the bright, young, educated man, these fields ['business services'] offer limitless opportunities, if he only has the initiative and the know-how."

51. Ibid., 270.

52. Ibid., 273. Earlier in the article, Mills writes that the new entrepreneur "serves them [the powers that be] by 'fixing things,' between one big business and another, between big business and government, and between business as a whole and the public," 269.

53. William H. Whyte Jr., "The Class of '49," *Fortune,* June 1949; in *The Essential William H. Whyte,* ed. Albert LaFarge (New York: Fordham University Press, 2000), 13.

54. Ibid., 12.

55. In his recent review of a collection of essays and speeches by Susan Sontag, the author Pankaj Mishra writes that Sontag "grew up on the high idea of European literature and thought upheld by the *Partisan Review,* the primary magazine of New York liberal intellectuals in the 1940s and 1950s." Pankaj Mishra, review of *At the Same Time: Essays and Speeches by Susan Sontag,* in *New York Times,* March 11, 2007, Book Review, 14. Hammerstein worked with some of those "liberal intellectuals" when he was active with the Writers' War Board; his interest in a journal of and/or about their work would not be surprising. And in the finished scene, Hammerstein uses European culture as an indicator of feelings deeper than those found in American wartime popular music; his exploitation of that idea allows the musical expression of Nellie's emotional depth and her eventual discovery of it.

56. Irving Louis Horowitz, "Introduction," in *Power, Politics and People,* 4.

57. Ibid., 9.

58. At the end of the number, Hammerstein's stage directions for Harbison state, "Coming to and abruptly becoming the efficient executive, which he undoubtedly is." Hammerstein, draft for 1.1.

59. David Halberstam, *The Fifties* (New York: Villard, 1993), 528–29.

60. The only indication of Harbison's character in the final script is one stage direction before his first line describing him as "a brusque man." Hammerstein and Logan, *South Pacific*, 297.

61. Hammerstein, draft for 1.1.

62. See Appendix 2.

63. Hammerstein, draft for 1.1.

64. Fordin, *Getting to Know Him*, 263.

65. Logan, *Josh*, 220, 222. See also Block, *Richard Rodgers*, 133–34. Fordin also suggests that "Twin Soliloquies" and "Some Enchanted Evening" were completed early in the process.

66. Ibid., 222. See also Fordin, *Getting to Know Him*, 262.

67. Ibid., 221. See also Fordin, *Getting to Know Him*, 263.

68. Fordin, *Getting to Know Him*, 263.

69. The rank of commandant is used only in the Marine Corps and the Coast Guard; the United States Navy has no such rank. In the Marine Corps, the commandant is the highest-ranking officer of the entire corps and is a member of the Joint Chiefs of Staff. He would not have been commanding a relatively obscure island base in the South Pacific (www.defenselink.mil/specials/insignias/officers.html).

70. See Hammerstein and Logan, *South Pacific*, 306, 318–20, 350–58. Plans to rescue de Becque from the island—Cable is killed during the mission—remain inconclusive in the final script as well, although the mission is successful and the U.S. forces land on the island where the two men had been hiding (362–63).

71. In 1.8 of the final version, Captain Brackett, the island commander, asks de Becque to be part of the mission and de Becque refuses. After admitting that he cares more about his future with Nellie "than anything else in the world," de Becque adds, "I cannot afford to risk it" and declines the mission. See Hammerstein and Logan, *South Pacific*, 319.

72. Geoffrey Block thoroughly discusses the changes in the earlier part of 1.1, from the January 1949 rehearsal script to the final version, in *Rodgers*, 139–43.

73. Hammerstein and Logan, *South Pacific*, 280.

CHAPTER 5: YOU'VE GOT TO BE CAREFULLY REWRITTEN: THE DISTILLATION OF RACIAL INTOLERANCE

1. Tammy R. Kernodle, "Arias, Communists, and Conspiracies: The History of William Grant Still's *Troubled Island*." *Musical Quarterly* 83, no. 4 (1999), 487–508.

2. Ronald Taylor, *Kurt Weill: Composer in a Divided World* (Boston: Northeastern University Press, 1991), 321–22.

3. Ibid.

4. Ibid., 324.

5. Kurt Weill, letter to Olin Downes, November 14, 1949. Quoted in Taylor, *Kurt Weill*, 324.

6. "An Appeal to the World," NAACP petition to the United Nations, 1947. Quoted in Mary A. Dudziak, *Cold War Civil Rights: Race and the Image of American Democracy* (Princeton: Princeton University Press, 2000), 44.

7. Wendell Willkie, quoted in David M. Bixby, "The Roosevelt Court, Democratic Ideology and Minority Rights: Another Look at *United States v. Classic*" *Yale Law Journal* 90 (March 1981), 741.

8. Michael Bess, *Choices under Fire: Moral Dimensions of World War II* (New York: Alfred A. Knopf, 2006), 21.

9. Ibid., 33. The placement of Japanese Americans in wartime detention camps, which was ordered by President Roosevelt in early 1942, was a controversial act on the part of the United States government and a problematic moment in the nation's past. See Bess, *Choices*, 33–36.

10. Paul Robeson, quoted in Dudziak, *Cold War*, 62.

11. Howard Zinn, *Postwar American: 1945–1971* (Indianapolis: Bobbs-Merrill, 1973), 171.

12. Dudziak, *Cold War*, 13.

13. Ibid., 14.

14. Hugh Fordin, *Getting to Know Him: A Biography of Oscar Hammerstein II* (New York: Ungar Publishing, 1977), 271. The song is often incorrectly referred to as "You've Got to Be Taught," but its title in the score and the script is "You've Got to Be Carefully Taught." In his autobiography, Rodgers refers to it simply as "Carefully Taught." Richard Rodgers, *Musical Stages: An Autobiography* (New York: Random House, 1975), 261.

15. Wolcott Gibbs, "What a Wonderful War," *New Yorker* 25, no. 8 (April 16, 1949), 30.

16. John Mason Brown, "For the Fairest," *Saturday Review of Literature* 32, no. 18 (April 30, 1949), 30.

17. A clipping of this article is found in the Oscar Hammerstein II Collection, Library of Congress, Box 21 (Correspondence & Misc. by subject), hereafter Box 21.

18. Bess, *Choices*, 33.

19. James A. Michener, *Tales of the South Pacific* (New York: Macmillan, 1947; New York: Fawcett Crest, 1973), 118.

20. John Egerton, *Speak Now against the Day: The Generation before the Civil Rights Movement in the South* (New York: Alfred A. Knopf, 1994), 206.

21. Ibid., 5.

22. Sidney S. McMath, interviewed by John Egerton, *Documenting the American South*, interview A-352, September 8, 1990, "Southern Oral History Program Collection," http://www.docsouth.unc.edu/A352/A352.html, 11, 17.

23. Oscar Hammerstein II and Joshua Logan, *South Pacific*, in *6 Plays by Rodgers and Hammerstein* (New York: Random House, 1953), 326–32.

24. Oscar Hammerstein II, rehearsal script for *South Pacific*, January 1949, Oscar Hammerstein II Collection, Library of Congress, box marked "South Pacific Scripts."

25. Michener, *Tales*, 138.

26. Ibid. Hammerstein dropped the capitalization of the preposition "de" in de Becque's name.

27. Rich, "Memorial Day."

28. Elsewhere in his interview with John Egerston, Sid McMath comments that even in 1949 and 1950, "the notion that any real substantive change

along racial lines was going to come in the south just hadn't sunk into people's minds. . . . They never realized that, and it didn't sink in really, until the Central High School incident [in 1957]." Egerston notes with surprise that this is after *Brown v. Board of Education,* and McMath concurs that even *Brown* did not cause the message to "sink in." (The Central High School incident occurred when nine African American students tried, in accordance with the law, to attend Central High School, a previously all-white school. They were not allowed to enter, and Governor Orval Faubus deployed the Arkansas National Guard to ensure that they stayed outside. Eventually, President Dwight Eisenhower sent federal troops to accompany the students into the school and enforce integration.) McMath interview, 14.

29. After a character gains this knowledge, of which he or she has previously been ignorant or somehow mistaken, his or her fortunes reverse, and the action of the plot continues on an irreversible and tragic course.

30. Hammerstein and Logan, *South Pacific,* 344.

31. Ibid., 346.

32. Ibid., 349.

33. Ibid., 346.

34. Graham Wood, "The Development of Song Forms in the Broadway and Hollywood Musical of Richard Rodgers, 1919–1943" (PhD diss., University of Minnesota, 2000). Wood's complete discussion of these forms is on pages 74–163 of his dissertation. Wood also finds particular representative uses for each song type.

35. Although each statement of the motive includes a pick-up, and because each pick-up is the same note as the subsequent downbeat, the pick-ups are not included as part of the motive.

36. Richard Rodgers and Oscar Hammerstein II, *South Pacific,* vocal score, ed. Albert Sirmay, revised under the supervision of Bruce Pomahac (New York: Williamson Music, 1949), 147–49. The draft for the insert is in the Oscar Hammerstein II Collection, Library of Congress, box marked "*CORRES* South Pacific."

37. This subject, and de Becque's response to it, is explored in greater detail in the discussion of gender and *South Pacific.*

38. For more specific information about this rehearsal script, see Geoffrey Block, *Richard Rodgers* (New Haven, CT: Yale University Press, 2003), 139–46.

39. Sketch for 2.4, in the Oscar Hammerstein II Collection, Library of Congress, box marked "*CORRES* South Pacific."

40. Over underscoring of "I'm in Love with a Wonderful Guy," Nellie says, "Come back so I can tell you something. I know what counts now. You. All those other things—the woman you had before—her color . . . (She laughs bitterly) What piffle! What a pinhead I was! Come back so I can tell you." Hammerstein and Logan, *South Pacific,* 359.

41. "Report," 17.

42. Review of Hortense Powdermaker's *Probing Our Prejudices.* The Oscar Hammerstein II Collection, Library of Congress, Box 21. Emphasis added.

43. From the Oscar Hammerstein II Collection, Library of Congress, box marked "*CORRES* South Pacific (2)."

44. Ibid. The reprise of a number to indicate an often ironic change in character or situation is not unique to *South Pacific*, of course. In *Oklahoma!*, for instance, "People Will Say We're in Love" becomes "Let People Say We're in Love," indicating a change in Laurie and Curley's acceptance of their feelings.

45. Ibid. Joshua Logan writes about his suggestion to replace "Now Is the Time," although he mistakenly refers to it as a song that came late in the show, when it was actually first sung in act 1. Still, he seems to have been the first to notice the problem with the song: "If Cable and Emile were going on a mission to save Allied lives, why didn't they get a goddamn move on instead of standing and singing, 'Now is the time to act, no other time will do'?" Joshua Logan, *Josh: My Up and Down, In and Out Life* (New York: Delacorte, 1976), 232.

46. Richard Rodgers Collection, Library of Congress, Box 16, folder 13. Also in the Oscar Hammerstein II Collection, Library of Congress, box marked "CORRES South Pacific." See also *The Complete Lyrics of Oscar Hammerstein II*, ed. Amy Asch (New York: Alfred A. Knopf, 2008), 342.

47. "This Nearly Was Mine" is discussed further in chapter 6.

48. The song was reinstated in the 1958 film version. The short speech was not. In the 2002 London production, directed by Trevor Nunn, the song was also reinstated, as was some of the accompanying scene. It is included in the 2008 Broadway revival.

49. The Oscar Hammerstein II Collection, Library of Congress, box marked "South Pacific Scripts."

50. Ibid.

51. The phrase "her hair is blonde and curly" later shows up in the lyrics of "Honey Bun."

52. Ibid.

53. Ibid.

54. "How Writers Perpetuate Stereotypes: A Digest of Data Prepared for the Writers' War Board by the Bureau of Applied Social Research of Columbia University" (New York: Writers' War Board, 1945), 1. A copy of this report is in the Oscar Hammerstein II Collection, Library of Congress, Box 21.

55. Ibid., 12. Months before this report came out, the WWB presented a meeting titled "The Myth That Threatens America." One of several "presentations," as the program called them, was a skit by Hammerstein called "Ol' Man Author." Hammerstein wrote new lyrics for four weary characters, set to the tune of "Ol' Man River." Each character was a stereotype complaining, "We are as old as the Mississippi / Stereotyped as inferior men." In the skit, Hammerstein berates authors for continuing to write characters who are racial and cultural stereotypes. Oscar Hammerstein II, "Ol' Man Author," January 11, 1945. In the Oscar Hammerstein II Collection, Library of Congress, Box 21.

56. Ibid.

57. Ibid.

58. This recalls Hammerstein's problematic evocation of African American dialect in *Show Boat* (1927) and especially *Carmen Jones* (1943).

59. John W. Dower, *War without Mercy: Race and Power in the Pacific War* (New York: Pantheon, 1986), 14.

60. This is a theme of Dower's well-documented book, a fascinating investigation of its special aspect of the war in the Pacific.

61. The offensive language was removed from the film.

62. Rodgers and Hammerstein, vocal score, 145.

CHAPTER 6: NELLIE AND THE BOYS: SITUATING GENDER IN *SOUTH PACIFIC*

1. Stacy Wolf, *A Problem Like Maria: Gender and Sexuality in the American Musical*(Ann Arbor: University of Michigan Press, 2002), 58.

2. Oscar Hammerstein II and Joshua Logan, *South Pacific*, in 6 *Plays by Rodgers and Hammerstein* (New York: Random House, 1953), 364. This phrase is further explored later in the chapter.

3. James A. Michener, *Tales of the South Pacific* (New York: Macmillan, 1947; New York: Fawcett Crest, 1973), 10–11.

4. Hammerstein and Logan, *South Pacific,* 290.

5. Ibid.

6. Ibid., 296.

7. Ibid., 353.

8. Meryle Secrest, *Somewhere for Me: A Biography of Richard Rodgers* (New York: Alfred A. Knopf, 2001), 294.

9. In *The King and I,* the King's many children are of multiple wives, all of who are simultaneously married to him.

10. However, *Me and Juliet* (1953), *Pipe Dream* (1955), *Cinderella* (created for television in 1957), and *Flower Drum Song* (1958) do not follow this path. An argument might be made that *Pipe Dream* bears some resemblance to the older man–younger woman model—Doc is older and better educated than Suzy, although he does not have much power within his down-on-its-heels social group—but otherwise the model is not consistent in later works.

11. See Richard M. Goldstein, "'I Enjoy Being a Girl': Women in the Plays of Rodgers and Hammerstein," *Popular Music and Society* (Spring 1989), 1–8.

12. The scene descriptions in the script of *Oklahoma!* indicate the farm as Laurey's domain: "The Front of Laurey's Farmhouse," "A Grove on Laurey's Farm," and "The Back of Laurey's House." In 2.2, after Jud physically threatens her, Laurey temporarily overcomes her fear of him and fires him on the spot. Oscar Hammerstein II, *Oklahoma!,* in *Six Plays by Rodgers and Hammerstein* (New York: The Modern Library, 1953), 4, 69.

13. Ibid., 69, 70. As for Laurey's economic stability, by the time she and Curly are in their middle to late thirties, their land will be the Dust Bowl.

14. This transformation of Curly, in turn, indicates the eventual resolution of the conflict between the farmers and the cowboys memorably described in the opening number of act 2, "The Farmer and the Cowman."

15. Ibid., 71.

16. Ibid., 76. These lyrics had special resonance in 1943, when Americans were fighting on two fronts to protect the "land" and its inhabitants.

17. Oscar Hammerstein II, *Carousel,* in *Six Plays by Rodgers and Hammerstein* (New York: The Modern Library, 1953), 118.

18. Ibid., 140.

19. Like the lyrics of the title song of *Oklahoma!,* the ending of *Carousel* is especially moving when read in the context of the war and the immediate postwar period. The promise of "You'll Never Walk Alone," the song sung at Billy's death and reprised at the show's end, and the message of a love able to transcend death comforted many women whose husbands or loved ones never returned from the war.

20. Oscar Hammerstein II, *Allegro,* in *Six Plays by Rodgers and Hammerstein* (New York: The Modern Library, 1953), 224.

21. Ethan Mordden, *Rodgers and Hammerstein* (New York: Harry N. Abrams, 1995), 104. To demonstrate this "vision" in *Allegro,* Mordden quotes the song "Come Home," which Joe imagines being sung to him by his dead mother: "You will find a world of honest friends who miss you, / You will shake the hands of men whose hands are strong, / And when all their wives and kids run up and kiss you, / You will know that you are back where you belong."

22. For an excellent critical assessment of *Allegro,* see Mordden, *Rodgers and Hammerstein,* 87–105.

23. Betty Friedan, *The Feminine Mystique* (New York: W. W. Norton, 1963).

24. Ibid., 338.

25. Ibid., 41.

26. Ibid.

27. See Susan Hartmann, *The Home Front and Beyond: American Women in the 1940s* (New York: Twayne, 1982). Hartmann observes that "by the late 1940s, women found significantly fewer screen models for female strength, self-sufficiency, and satisfying experiences beyond domestic and romantic life" (202). She uses two films starring Barbara Stanwyck among her examples; in 1944's *Double Indemnity,* Stanwyck is a scheming, controlling, and powerful figure who exploits men for her own gain; in 1948's *Sorry Wrong Number,* on the other hand, she is the helpless victim—literally, a bedridden invalid—of her husband's plot to have her murdered.

28. Friedan, *Feminine Mystique,* 44. A 1993 article by the historian Joanne Meyerowitz reassessed Friedan's seminal work. Meyerowitz notes, "With a somewhat different sample and a somewhat different interpretive approach, I come to different conclusions about postwar mass culture than did Friedan and her followers. Friedan's widely accepted version of the 'feminine mystique,' I suggest, is only one piece of the postwar cultural puzzle. The [nonfiction articles in] popular literature I sampled did not simply glorify domesticity or demand that women return to or stay at home. . . . In this literature, domestic ideals co-existed in ongoing tension with an ethos of individual achievement." Joanne Meyerowitz, "Beyond the Feminine Mystique: A Reassessment of Postwar Mass Culture, 1946–1958," *Journal of American History* 79 (March 1993), 1458.

29. Evelyn Steele, *Wartime Opportunities for Women* (New York: E. P. Dutton, 1943), 61. Steele was the editorial director of Vocational Guidance Research, a group associated with the Office of War Information (OWI). Her bibliography indicates that the literature for women on vocational opportunities was extensive and was published by independent publishers—Harpers; Harcourt, Brace & Co.; etc.—by government organizations—the Public Affairs Committee, the OWI, etc.—and by

various industries—the Boeing School of Aeronautics and the Nursing Information Bureau, among others.

30. Ibid., 82.

31. Hartmann, *Home Front,* 32.

32. Steele, *Wartime,* 90.

33. Ibid., 5. Additional insight into the wartime and, especially, postwar employment of women is found in James T. Patterson, *Grand Expectations: The United States, 1945–1974* (New York: Oxford University Press, 1996), 31–38.

34. Ibid., 165–67. Regarding daycare: "A Day Care section has been set up by the War Manpower Commission in the Office of Defense Health and Welfare Services to work out the entire problem of safeguarding the children of the women who go into war production jobs" (166). Regarding pregnancy: "The Women's Bureau and Children's Bureau of the U.S. Department of Labor, in consultation with medical specialists and industrial women, have recommended as a general policy that provisions for maternity care and leave should not jeopardize a woman's job nor her seniority privileges" (166).

35. "To pay women less than men for the same work undermines the whole pay structure, causing employers to take women on as 'cheap labor' and precipitating male unemployment in normal times" (ibid., 165).

36. Leila Rupp, *Mobilizing Women for War: German and American Propaganda, 1939–1945* (Princeton, NJ: Princeton University Press, 1978), 175.

37. Ibid., 4. Later in her book, Rupp argues, "Public images, unlike basic beliefs about women's nature, can change quickly in response to economic need. The economic role and the popular image of women may change drastically in the course of a modern war, but basic ideas about women's proper sphere, characterized by cultural lag even in the case of long-term economic developments, change little" (174).

38. Ibid., 138, 178.

39. Nell Giles, "What about the Women," *Ladies' Home Journal* 61 (June 1944), 22–23, quoted in Rupp, *Mobilizing Women,* 161.

40. Maureen Honey, *Creating Rosie the Riveter: Class, Gender, and Propaganda during World War II* (Amherst: University of Massachusetts Press, 1984), 2.

41. Hartmann, *Home Front,* 25.

42. "Whether by force or by choice, women did leave the labor force as the war ended. By 1946 the female labor force had declined from its wartime peak of 19,170,000 to 16,896,000. Women's share of the civilian labor force decreased from 35.4 percent in 1944 to 28.6 percent in 1947; and the proportion of all women in the job market fell from 36.5 percent to 30.8 percent. Even at their low point, however, these figures were higher than those for 1940, and by 1947 they had begun to climb again as the long-term trend in female employment reasserted itself" (Hartmann, *Home Front,* 24).

43. Maria Diedrich and Dorothea Fischer-Hornung, *Women and War: The Changing Status of American Women from the 1930s to the 1950s* (New York: Berg, 1990), 9. See also William Chafe, *The Paradox of Change: American Women in the 20th Century* (New York: Oxford University Press, 1991). Chafe likewise maintains that the war, while not stirring up an immediate revolution in the lives of American women,

"may eventually have helped to create a context in which another generation could attempt a revolution" (33). He also observes that "although a Women's Advisory Commission was appointed as an adjunct to the War Manpower Commission, all the decisions were made in a group composed entirely of men" (24).

44. Honey, *Creating Rosie*, 7.

45. Andrea Most, *Making Americans: Jews and the Broadway Musical* (Cambridge, MA: Harvard University Press, 2004), 165–66.

46. Stacy Wolf notes, "Her [Nellie's] lack of understanding of race parallels her lack of romantic experience" (*Problem Like Maria*, 59).

47. Michener, *Tales*, 63.

48. Hammerstein and Logan, *South Pacific*, 277–79. See also Wolf, *Problem Like Maria*, 58.

49. Lloyd Shearer, "Mary Martin: The Star Who Loves Everybody," *Parade* (n.d.), n.p. In Wolf, *Problem Like Maria*, 57.

50. Hammerstein and Logan, *South Pacific*, 364.

51. Ibid., 366.

52. Honey, *Creating Rosie*, 7. Of course, the end of *South Pacific* predates the end of World War II; but, for the purposes of the story and the romance between Nellie and de Becque, the war figuratively ends with de Becque's return.

53. Honey, *Creating Rosie*, 216.

54. Ibid.

55. Wolf, *Problem Like Maria*, 60; Most, *Making Americans*, 182. Wolf makes much of what she sees as Nellie's "avoidance of heterosexuality" (59). Arguably, however, Nellie avoids any kind of sexuality at all.

56. Most, *Making Americans*, 182.

57. Richard Rodgers, *Musical Stages: An Autobiography* (New York: Random House, 1975), 260. Actually, Nellie and de Becque sing together at the end of act 1, after they have been drinking and are feeling playful. The duet is less romantic than comic, although it is also affectionate.

58. Most, *Making Americans*, 178.

59. Hammerstein and Logan, *South Pacific*, 329.

60. Most, *Making Americans*, 177.

61. Richard Rodgers and Oscar Hammerstein II, *South Pacific*, vocal score, ed. Albert Sirmay, revised under the supervision of Bruce Pomahac (New York: Williamson Music, 1949), 18–19. For an extended discussion of this scene and the development of "A Cockeyed Optimist," see Geoffrey Block, *Richard Rodgers* (New Haven, CT: Yale University Press, 2003), 139–43; and James Lovensheimer, "The Musico-Dramatic Evolution of Rodgers and Hammerstein's *South Pacific*" (PhD diss, Ohio State University, 2003), 115–17.

62. Hammerstein and Logan, *South Pacific*, 276.

63. Stacy Wolf consistently, and incorrectly, refers to "Twin Soliloquies" as the 'Dual Soliloquy.'" See Wolf, *Problem Like Maria*, 57–63.

64. Michener, *Tales*, 130.

65. Rodgers and Hammerstein, vocal score, 20.

66. Michener, *Tales*, 130.

67. Rodgers and Hammerstein, vocal score, 20.

68. See Rodgers and Hammerstein, vocal score, 5, 46–50. Of course, as the leading tone of the D major scale, the C# in the introduction is diatonic; it is the unstable major-seventh relation with the tonic that gives it a sense of chromatic tension before the conjunct descent to the dominant. The third pitch in the opening gesture of "Bali Ha'i," which is the downbeat, is a raised subdominant, which creates a tritone with the tonic, played in the bass, and which is also the root of a diminished-seventh chord played on beat one. This chromaticism creates a sense of the setting's "exotic" quality, which is explored in a later discussion.

69. Scott McMillin also observes this, noting that the two characters "share a melody even though they think they are ruminating to themselves." Scott McMillin, *The Musical as Drama* (Princeton: Princeton University Press, 2006), 89.

70. Rodgers and Hammerstein, vocal score, 21.

71. Joshua Logan, *Josh: My Up and Down, In and Out Life* (New York: Delacorte, 1976), 285.

72. Ibid., 283.

73. Ibid., 284.

74. Another successful example—the use of the music to "My Girl Back Home" when the audience learns of Cable's death—lost much of its effect when the song was cut from the show. The music nonetheless remained as underscoring.

75. In his biography of Hammerstein, Hugh Fordin comments, "The use of leitmotifs in musical plays—an innovation of Jerry Kern in *Show Boat*—was here brought to full development by [the orchestrator] Russell Bennett and Trude Rittman." He makes no mention of Logan's contribution to this element of the show, which may have grown in relation to the director's hindsight. Hugh Fordin, *Getting to Know Him: A Biography of Oscar Hammerstein II* (New York: Ungar Publishing, 1977), 278.

76. McMillin, *Musical as Drama*, 130.

77. Rodgers and Hammerstein, vocal score, 72–76. In addition to Block's observations of musical "family resemblances" in this scene and throughout the score, Edward Green also has analyzed the opening scene in terms of its taut musical construction. Borrowing Arnold Schönberg's term "developing variation," Green provides keen insight into the scene's internal musical unification. See Edward Green, "What Gives Musical Theatre *Musical* Integrity? An Analysis of the Opening Scene of *South Pacific*." In *Journal of Dramatic Theory and Criticism* 21 no. 1 (Fall 2006), 75–93.

78. Additional information about the development of this scene, in addition to that in chapter 4 of this work, can be found in Block, *Richard Rodgers*, 143–44; and in Lovensheimer, "Musico-Dramatic Evolution," 143–74. Both works, with differing degrees of detail, explain Rodgers and Hammerstein's long process of arriving at "Some Enchanted Evening" as the central musical component of the scene.

79. Most, *Making Americans*, 179.

80. See Rodgers and Hammerstein, vocal score, 60–69. However, most of this discussion can be successfully demonstrated simply by listening to the song on the original cast recording.

81. "The word [ride], which was current in early jazz and the swing era, carries connotations, variously, of inventiveness, freedom of delivery, and *swinging rhythmic momentum.*" Barry Kernfeld, editor, *The New Grove Dictionary of Jazz* (New York: St. Martin's Press, 1988; reprinted 1991), 1046. Emphasis added. The term is related to the practice, starting in the late 1930s, of executing the central beat in a jazz band on the large cymbal known as the "ride" cymbal.

82. Hammerstein and Logan, *South Pacific*, 313.

83. Ibid., 308.

84. Most, *Making Americans*, 173. See also 153–54, 171–72, 174.

85. Block, *Richard Rodgers*, 144.

86. Most, *Making Americans*, 179.

87. Ibid., 336.

88. David. H. J. Morgan, "Theater of War: Combat, the Military, and Masculinities," in *Theorizing Masculinities*, ed. Harry Brod and Michael Kaufman (Thousand Oaks, CA: Sage, 1994), 165.

89. Christina S. Jarvis, *The Male Body at War: American Masculinity during World War II* (Dekalb, IL: Northern Illinois University Press, 2004), 4, 188.

90. Hammerstein and Logan, *South Pacific*, 364.

91. Ibid.

92. Suzanne Clark, *Cold Warriors: Manliness on Trial in the Rhetoric of the West* (Carbondale, IL: Southern Illinois University Press, 2000), 1.

93. Robert R. Dean, *Imperial Brotherhood: Gender and the Making of Cold War Policy* (Amherst, MA: University of Massachusetts Press, 2001), 66.

94. Ibid., 4–5.

95. Ibid., 64. Dean further notes, "Under Truman's administration between January 1947 and January 1953, more than four hundred State Department employees, from ambassadors and senior foreign service officers to clerks and secretaries, were fired or forced to resign for real or imagined homosexuality—a rate approaching twice that of those dismissed for communist 'sympathy' or other offenses" (*Imperial Brotherhood*, 66).

96. Michener, *Tales*, 123, 130–31, 136.

97. In act 1, scene 2, of *Oklahoma!*—the smokehouse scene between Jud and Curly—the two men refer to "that f'ar [fire] on the Bartlett farm . . . [that] burnt up the father and daughter." Jud adds, "That warn't no accident." The suggestion is that Jud was the arsonist–murderer. Hammerstein, *Oklahoma!*, 25.

98. Hammerstein, sketch for 1.7, Oscar Hammerstein II Collection, Library of Congress, box marked "South Pacific."

99. Block finds a similarity between this and Jud's "accidental" death in *Oklahoma!* (See Block, *Richard Rodgers*, 144.) It is also reminiscent of Harry Beaton's "accidental" death in *Brigadoon* (1947).

100. Hammerstein and Logan, *South Pacific*, 358.

101. William S. Graebner, *The Age of Doubt: American Thought and Culture in the 1940s* (Boston: Twayne, 1991), 91.

102. As far as the musical is concerned, the population of the island is made up almost entirely of American officers, sailors, and Marines. Very few indigenous people appear in the musical, and most of them are on Bali Ha'i.

103. Hammerstein and Logan, *South Pacific*, 308.

104. James Gilbert, *Men in the Middle: Searching for Masculinity in the 1950s* (Chicago: University of Chicago Press, 2005), 191.

105. Rodgers and Hammerstein, vocal score, 23. The remaining quotes from the song are from the vocal score; "Some Enchanted Evening" is on pages 23–27.

106. Graham Wood, "The Development of Song Forms in the Broadway Musicals of Richard Rodgers, 1919–1943" (PhD diss., University of Minnesota, 2000), 116.

107. Block, *Richard Rodgers*, 146. According to Joshua Logan, Rodgers referred to the song as "a big bass waltz" (*Josh*, 232).

108. Hammerstein and Logan, *South Pacific*, 348.

109. Mordden, *Rodgers and Hammerstein*, 120.

110. Dean, *Imperial Brotherhood*, 151.

111. Michael Kimmel, "Masculinity as Homophobia: Fear, Shame, and Silence in the Construction of Gender Identity," in *Theorizing Masculinities*, ed. Harry Brod and Michael Kaufman (Thousand Oaks, CA: Sage, 1994), 132.

112. Kathy Ferguson, *The Man Question: Visions of Subjectivity in Feminist Theory* (Berkeley: University of California Press, 1993), 159. Emphasis in the original.

113. Michener, *Tales*, 174, 179, 383.

114. Hammerstein and Logan, *South Pacific*, 289.

115. Logan, *Josh*, 231.

116. Michener's sailors and Marines talk about Hollywood's misrepresentation of island women, noting that the actual women look nothing like Dorothy Lamour, whose sarong-wrapped figure was Hollywood's most famous representation (192). Twelve years earlier, in his legendary *The Cradle Will Rock*, Marc Blitzstein parodied the then-popular Hawaiian and island music styles in the number "Honolulu."

117. Susan McClary, *Feminine Endings: Music, Gender, and Sexuality* (Minneapolis: University of Minnesota Press, 1991), 58.

118. Rodgers, *Musical Stages*, 262.

119. Hammerstein and Logan, *South Pacific*, 295.

120. Ibid., 296–300.

121. Ibid., 323.

122. Cable makes his initial entrance at the *conclusion* of "There Is Nothin' Like a Dame"; he is not a part of the number.

123. Hammerstein and Logan, *South Pacific*, 323.

124. Ibid.

125. Curiously, with the exception of a brief comic bit when a sailor is "caught" naked in Billis's shower, all the sailors in the 2008 revival keep their shirts on throughout the production.

126. Logan, *Josh*, 241–42. The story is a wonderful example of postwar masculine conflict; the man claims he was not looking at the men's physiques—that would imply homosexuality—yet he quickly notes how great the men's physiques used to look.

127. Jarvis, *Male Body*, 35.

128. Ibid., 186.

129. K. A. Cuordileone, *Manhood and American Political Culture in the Cold War* (New York: Routledge, 2005), xx.

130. See Logan, *Josh*, 233.

131. Richard Rodgers Collection, Library of Congress, Box 16, folder 18. See also *The Complete Lyrics of Oscar Hammerstein II*, ed. Amy Asch (New York: Alfred A. Knopf, 2008), 344.

132. Richard Rodgers Collection, Library of Congress, Box 16, folder 18. Geoffrey Block mistakenly comments, "No one seems to know what 'My Friend' sounded like, and if a manuscript ever existed, it is now unknown" (145).

133. Logan, *Josh*, 233.

134. Geoffrey Block, in the most recent discussion of *South Pacific*, writes, "Logan mistitles 'Suddenly Lovely' as 'Suddenly Lucky,' an error that set in motion decades of confusion." Block, *Richard Rodgers*, 277, note 46. In her collection of Hammerstein's lyrics Asch supports the conclusion, also reached in the research for this work, that the existence of both sets of lyrics in Hammerstein's papers demonstrates that both titles, in addition to two different sets of lyrics, were considered during the creative process. Asch further notes that "Suddenly Lucky," the first set of lyrics, was first performed at a Hammerstein Centennial event on Broadway in 1995 (343).

135. Oscar Hammerstein II Collection, Library of Congress, box marked "South Pacific." See also Hammerstein, *Complete Lyrics*, 343.

136. Logan, *Josh*, 233.

137. Several sources cite the origin of the melody as a song discarded from *Allegro*. See Stephen Citron, *The Wordsmiths: Oscar Hammerstein 2nd and Alan Jay Lerner* (New York: Oxford University Press, 1995), 199; Hugh Fordin, *Getting to Know Him: Oscar Hammerstein II: A Biography* (New York: Random House, 1977), 279; William G. Hyland, *Richard Rodgers* (New Haven, CT: Yale University Press, 1998), 180; or Rodgers, *Musical Stages*, 260.

138. Rodgers and Hammerstein, vocal score, 93–97.

139. Hammerstein and Logan, *South Pacific*, 339.

140. Oscar Hammerstein II, sketch for 2.11, Oscar Hammerstein II Collection, Library of Congress, box marked "CORRES South Pacific (2)."

141. Cable dies in Michener's novel, too, but, as earlier revealed, he dies under quite different circumstances.

142. Hammerstein and Logan, *South Pacific*, 337.

143. Kirle, *Show Business*, 127.

CHAPTER 7: CULTURE CLASH: COLONIALISM AND *SOUTH PACIFIC*

1. Richard Rodgers Collection, Library of Congress, Box 16, folder 5.

2. Oscar Hammerstein II and Joshua Logan, *South Pacific*, in *6 Plays by Rodgers and Hammerstein* (New York: Random House, 1953), 273.

3. Everett R. Clinchy, letter to Oscar Hammerstein II, September 11, 1949. In the Oscar Hammerstein II Collection, Library of Congress, Box 21 (Correspondence & Misc. by subject).

4. Sketch for 2.4. In the Oscar Hammerstein II Collection, Library of Congress, box marked "South Pacific 2."

5. James A. Michener, *The World Is My Home: A Memoir* (New York: Random House, 1992), 149.

6. James A. Michener, *Tales of the South Pacific* (New York: Macmillan, 1947; New York: Fawcett Crest, 1973), 169–73.

7. Hammerstein and Logan, *South Pacific*, 283.

8. Michener, *Tales*, 172.

9. Bill Ashcroft, *Post-Colonial Transformation* (London: Routledge, 2001), 42, 56.

10. Sketches for "Bloody Mary." In the Oscar Hammerstein II Collection, Library of Congress, box marked "South Pacific 2." The implication in the sketch that Mary is Chinese is inconsistent with later versions of the score and the book, which repeatedly and consistently refer to her as Tonkinese.

11. Michener, *World*, 291.

12. Hammerstein and Logan, *South Pacific*, 293.

13. Ethan Mordden, *Rodgers and Hammerstein* (New York: Harry N. Abrams, 1995), 115.

14. Richard Rodgers, *Musical Stages: An Autobiography* (New York: Random House, 1975), 262.

15. Hammerstein and Logan, *South Pacific*, 297.

16. Andrea Most, *Making Americans: Jews and the Broadway Musical* (Cambridge, MA: Harvard University Press, 2004), 158.

17. Hammerstein and Logan, *South Pacific*, 322–24. Most mistakenly comments that Rodgers and Hammerstein made Liat "far younger" than Michener (159), but they actually borrowed the phrase "perhaps seventeen" straight from the story (Hammerstein and Logan, 322; Michener, *Tales*, 185).

18. Michener, *Tales*, 201.

19. Ibid., 215.

20. Richard Rodgers and Oscar Hammerstein II, *South Pacific*, vocal score, ed. Albert Sirmay, revised under the supervision of Bruce Pomahac (New York: Williamson Music, 1949), 123–30.

21. Hammerstein and Logan, *South Pacific*, 338.

22. "Happy Talk," draft in the Oscar Hammerstein II Collection, Library of Congress, "South Pacific box 2." Appendix 6 demonstrates the original form of "Happy Talk."

23. Hammerstein and Logan, *South Pacific*, 339.

24. Ibid.

25. Michener, *Tales*, 126.

26. Notes from dress rehearsal, Boston, March 15, 1949, in the Oscar Hammerstein II Collection, Library of Congress, box marked "South Pacific."

27. Michener, *Tales*, 202. The rights and status of indigenous peoples and indentured servants were complex, but among the first steps toward achieving either was the "rejection of non-Christian legal and religious principles." D. K. Fieldhouse, *Colonialism, 1879–1945: An Introduction* (London: Weidenfeld & Nicolson, 1981), 36.

28. Ibid., 38.

29. Michener, *Tales*, 122, 126.

30. Jules Harmand, quoted in Philip D. Curtin, ed. *Imperialism* (New York: Qalker, 1972), 294–95.

31. Michener, *Tales,* 134.

32. Christina Klein, *Cold War Orientalism: Asia in the Middlebrow Imagination, 1945–1961* (Berkeley: University of California Press, 2003), 163. Klein notes that the United States had bases on, and/or political control of, the large islands of Japan and the outlying island chains; Okinawa; the Philippines; South Korea; China, until the Communist takeover of 1949; and the Caroline, Marshall, and Marianna islands, some of which were later used as nuclear-test sites (163).

33. Edward Said, *Culture and Imperialism* (New York: Alfred A. Knopf, 1993; New York: Vintage, 1994), 289–90.

34. Klein, *Cold War,* 9.

35. Dwight Macdonald, *Against the American Grain: Essays on the Effects of Mass Culture* (1962; reprint, New York: Da Capo, 1983), 39.

36. Klein, *Cold War,* 7.

37. Ibid., 168.

38. Ibid., 175.

39. James A. Michener, *The Voice of Asia* (New York: Random House, 1951), 4–5.

40. John P. Hayes, *James A. Michener: A Biography* (Indianapolis: Bobbs-Merrill, 1984), 91.

41. Michener, *World,* 97. Michener comments that he "even at age seven . . . preferred *Rigoletto* to coon songs or the ridiculing of Jewish immigrants" (98). His extended discussion of his musical taste is on pages 95–107.

42. Hammerstein and Logan, *South Pacific,* 360–63.

CHAPTER 8: STILL DREAMING OF PARADISE

1. Stephen Sondheim, "Opening Doors," *Merrily We Roll Along,* Original Broadway Cast Recording, RCAD1 5840.

2. Author's notes from *Stephen Sondheim, A Life in the Theater: An Onstage Conversation with Frank Rich,* Avery Fisher Hall, New York, January 18, 2009. (The newsletter of the Rodgers and Hammerstein Organization is titled *Happy Talk.*)

3. For a detailed discussion of this excision, see Geoffrey Block, *Richard Rodgers* (New Haven, CT: Yale University Press, 2003), 160.

4. Geoffrey Block provides a substantial discussion of the changes made in the film version. Ibid., 146–59.

5. Sally Cragin, "'South Pacific' Star Finds Show Is Just Right for Difficult Times," *Boston Globe,* December 5, 2001, D7.

6. Ted Chapin, "*South Pacific* in Concert from Carnegie Hall," in booklet accompanying *Rodgers and Hammerstein's South Pacific in Concert from Carnegie Hall,* DVD, directed by Walter Bobbie (Burbank, CA: Rhino Entertainment, 2006).

7. "Building a House: An Interview with Michael Yeargan and Bartlett Shert," *Lincoln Center Review* 45–46 (Spring 2008), 19, 20.

8. "Remembering *South Pacific,*" *Lincoln Center Review* 45–46 (Spring 2008), 33.

BIBLIOGRAPHY

• • •

ARCHIVAL SOURCES

The uncatalogued Oscar Hammerstein II Collection at the Library of Congress was the source for all sketches, drafts, correspondence, rehearsal scripts, rehearsal notes, and other unpublished materials used for this study. The boxes with material specific to *South Pacific* are marked with the show's title, or an abbreviation of it, and were made available through the generous cooperation of Mark Eden Horowitz. Additional materials have been added to the collection since the research for this study was made, and while those materials have been somewhat inventoried through the diligent efforts of Amy Asch, they are not catalogued and are unavailable for inspection as of this writing.

The fully catalogued Richard Rodgers Collection is more easily available in the Performing Arts Reading Room of the Library of Congress. The materials for *South Pacific* include pencil drafts of many of the completed songs, including those cut from the show during rehearsals and tryouts, in addition to sketches for songs left incomplete, and are found in Box 16 of the collection.

Materials regarding the Hollywood Anti-Nazi League are in the California State University online exhibit "In Our Own Backyard: Resisting Nazi Propaganda in Southern California 1933–1945," http://digital-library.csun.edu/backyard. Other materials concerning the league are provided online by the United States Federal Bureau of Investigation, "Hollywood Anti-Nazi League," file no. 100-6633, declassified June 29, 1999, http://foiaindex/hollywoodleague.htm.

PUBLISHED SCRIPT AND SCORE

Hammerstein, Oscar, and Joshua Logan. *South Pacific.* In *Six Plays by Rodgers and Hammerstein.* New York: Random House, 1953.

Rodgers, Richard, and Oscar Hammerstein II. *South Pacific.* Vocal score. Edited by Albert Sirmay. New York: Williamson Music, 1949.

SECONDARY SOURCES

Ashcroft, Bill. *Post-Colonial Transformation.* London: Routledge, 2001.

Banfield, Stephen. *Sondheim's Broadway Musicals.* Ann Arbor: University of Michigan Press, 1993.

Becker, George J. *James A. Michener.* New York: Ungar Publishing, 1983.

Bess, Michael. *Choices under Fire: Moral Dimensions of World War II.* New York: Alfred A. Knopf, 2006.

Bixby, David M. "The Roosevelt Court, Democratic Ideology and Minority Rights: Another Look at *United States v. Classic.*" *Yale Law Journal* 90, no. 5 (March 1981).

Block, Geoffrey. *Enchanted Evenings.* New York: Oxford University Press, 1997.

———. *Richard Rodgers.* New Haven, CT: Yale University Press, 2003.

———. *The Richard Rodgers Reader*. New York: Oxford University Press, 2002.

Brown, John Mason Brown. "For the Fairest." *Saturday Review of Literature* 32, no. 18 (April 30, 1949): 30.

"Building a House: An Interview with Michael Yeargan and Bartlett Sher." *Lincoln Center Review* 45–46 (Spring 2008): 19–20.

Carter, Tim. *Oklahoma! The Making of an American Musical*. New Haven, CT: Yale University Press, 2007.

Chafe, William. *The Paradox of Change: American Women in the 20th Century*. New York: Oxford University Press, 1991.

Chapin, Ted. "*South Pacific* in Concert from Carnegie Hall." In booklet accompanying *Rodgers and Hammerstein's South Pacific in Concert from Carnegie Hall*. DVD. Directed by Walter Bobbie. Burbank: Rhino Entertainment, 2006.

Citron, Stephen. *The Wordsmiths: Oscar Hammerstein 2nd and Alan Jay Lerner*. New York: Oxford University Press, 1995.

Clark, Suzanne. *Cold Warriors: Manliness on Trial in the Rhetoric of the West*. Carbondale, IL: Southern Illinois University Press, 2001.

Cuordileone, K. A. *Manhood and American Political Culture in the Cold War*. New York: Routledge, 2005.

Curtin, Philip D., ed. *Imperialism*. New York: Walker, 1972.

Day, A. Grove. *James Michener*. 2nd edition. Boston: Twayne, 1977.

Dean, Robert R. *Imperial Brotherhood: Gender and the Making of Cold War Policy*. Amherst, MA: University of Massachusetts Press, 2001.

Diedrich, Maria, and Dorothea Fischer-Hornung. *Women and War: The Changing Status of American Women from the 1930s to the 1950s*. New York: Berg, 1990.

Dower, John W. *War without Mercy: Race and Power in the Pacific War*. New York: Pantheon, 1986.

Dudziak, Mary A. *Cold War Civil Rights: Race and the Image of American Democracy*. Princeton: Princeton University Press, 2000.

Egerton, John. *Speak Now against the Day: The Generation before the Civil Rights Movement in the South*. New York: Alfred A. Knopf, 1994.

Eisler, Garrett. "Kidding on the Level: The Reactionary Project of *I'd Rather Be Right*." *Studies in Musical Theatre* 1, no. 1 (2007): 7–24.

Ferguson, Kathy. *The Man Question: Visions of Subjectivity in Feminist Theory*. Berkeley: University of California Press, 1993.

Fieldhouse, D. K *Colonialism, 1879–1945: An Introduction*. London: Weidenfeld & Nicolson, 1981.

Fordin, Hugh. *Getting to Know Him: A Biography of Oscar Hammerstein II*. New York: Ungar Publishing, 1977.

Friedan, Betty. *The Feminine Mystique*. New York: W. W. Norton, 1963.

Gibbs, Wolcott. "What a Wonderful War." *New Yorker* 25, no. 8 (April 16, 1949): 30.

Gilbert, James. *Men in the Middle: Searching for Masculinity in the 1950s*. Chicago: University of Chicago Press, 2005.

Giles, Nell. "What about Women." *Ladies' Home Journal* 61 (June 1944): 22–23.

Goldstein, Richard M. "'I Enjoy Being a Girl': Women in the Plays of Rodgers and Hammerstein." *Popular Music and Society* (Spring 1989): 1–8.

Graebner, William S. *The Age of Doubt: American Thought and Culture in the 1940s.* Boston: Twayne, 1991.

Green, Edward. "What Gives Musical Theatre *Musical* Integrity? An Analysis of the Opening Scene of *South Pacific.*" *Journal of Dramatic Theory and Criticism* 21, no. 1 (Fall 2006): 75–93.

Green, Stanley, ed. *Rodgers and Hammerstein Fact Book: A Record of Their Works Together and with Other Collaborators.* New York: Lynn Farnol Group, 1980.

Grobel, Lawrence. *Talking with Michener.* Jackson, MS: University of Jackson Press, 1999.

Halberstam, David. *The Fifties.* New York: Villard, 1993.

Hamm, Charles. "The Theatre Guild Production of *Porgy and Bess.*" *Journal of the American Musicological Society* 40 (Fall 1987): 494–532.

Hammerstein, Oscar. *The Complete Lyrics of Oscar Hammerstein II.* Edited by Amy Asch. New York: Alfred A. Knopf, 2008.

———. "Editorial." *Saturday Review of Literature* 33, no. 52 (December 23, 1950): 22–23.

———. Interview by Mike Wallace. *The Mike Wallace Interview.* CBS. March 15, 1958. http://www.hrc.utexas.edu/multimedia/video/2008/wallace/Hammerstein_oscar_t.html.

———. *Lyrics by Oscar Hammerstein II.* Milwaukee, WI: Hal Leonard Books, 1985.

———. *Oklahoma!, Carousel,* and *Allegro.* In *Six Plays by Rodgers and Hammerstein.* New York: Random House, 1953.

Hart, Lorenz. *The Complete Lyrics of Lorenz Hart.* Edited by Dorothy Hart and Robert Kimball. New York: Alfred A. Knopf, 1986.

Hartmann, Susan. *The Home Front and Beyond: American Women in the 1940s.* New York: Twayne, 1982.

Hayes, John P. *James A. Michener: A Biography.* Indianapolis: Bobbs-Merrill, 1984.

Honey, Maureen. *Creating Rosie the Riveter: Class, Gender, and Propaganda.* Amherst: University of Massachusetts Press, 1984.

Horowitz, Irving Louis, ed. *Power, Politics and People: The Collected Essays of C. Wright Mills.* New York: Oxford University Press, 1963.

Huxley, Aldous. *The Perennial Philosophy.* New York: Harper & Row, 1945.

Hyland, William G. *Richard Rodgers.* New Haven, CT: Yale University Press, 1998.

Jarvis, Christina S. *The Male Body at War: American Masculinity during World War II.* Dekalb: Northern Illinois University Press, 2004.

Jones, John Bush. *Our Musicals, Ourselves: A Social History of the American Musical Theatre.* Hanover, NH: University Press of New England, 2003.

Kernfeld, Barry. "Ride." In *The New Grove Dictionary of Jazz.* Edited by Barry Kernfeld. New York: St. Martin's Press, 1988.

Kernodle, Tammy R. "Arias, Communists, and Conspiracies: The Distillation of William Grant Still's *Troubled Island.*" *Musical Quarterly* 83, no. 4 (1999): 487–508.

Kimmel, Michael. "Masculinity as Homophobia: Fear, Shame, and Silence in the Construction of Gender Identity." In *Theorizing Masculinities.* Edited by Harry Brod and Michael Kaufman. Thousand Oaks, CA: Sage, 1944.

Kirle, Bruce. *Unfinished Show Business: Musicals as Works-in-Process.* Carbondale: Southern Illinois University Press, 2005.

Klein, Christina. *Cold War Orientalism: Asia in the Middlebrow Imagination, 1945–1961.* Berkeley: University of California Press, 2003.

Kreuger, Miles. *Show Boat: The Story of a Classic American Musical.* New York: Oxford University Press, 1977.

Laurents, Arthur. *Original Story: A Memoir of Broadway and Hollywood.* New York: Applause Theatre Books, 2000.

Logan, Joshua. *Josh: My Up and Down, In and Out Life.* New York: Delacorte, 1976.

Lovensheimer, James. "The Musico-Dramatic Evolution of Rodgers and Hammerstein's *South Pacific.*" PhD diss, The Ohio State University, 2003.

Macdonald, Dwight. *Against the American Grain: Essays on the Effects of Mass Culture.* 1962. Reprint, New York: Da Capo, 1983.

Martin, Mary. *My Heart Belongs.* New York: William Morrow, 1976.

Maslon, Laurence. *The South Pacific Companion.* New York: Fireside, 2008.

McClary, Susan. *Feminine Endings: Music, Gender, and Sexuality.* Minneapolis: University of Minnesota Press, 1991.

McClung, Bruce D. *Lady in the Dark: Biography of a Musical.* New York: Oxford University Press, 2007.

McCullough, David. *Truman.* New York: Simon & Schuster, 1992.

McMath, Sidney S. Interviewed by John Egerton. *Documenting the American South.* Interview A-352 (September 8, 1990). Pages 11–17 of http://www.docsouth.unc.edu/A352/A352.html.

McMillin, Scott. *The Musical as Drama.* Princeton: Princeton University Press, 2006.

Meyerowitz, Joanne. "Beyond the Feminine Mystique: A Reassessment of Postwar Mass Culture, 1946–1958." *Journal of American History* 79 (March 1993): 1455–82.

Michener, James A. *Tales of the South Pacific.* 1947. Reprint, New York: Fawcett Crest, 1973.

———. *The Voice of Asia.* New York: Random House, 1951.

———. *The World Is My Home: A Memoir.* New York: Random House, 1992.

Mills, C. Wright. "The Competitive Personality." *Partisan Review* 13, no. 4 (September–October 1946): 433–41.

———. *White Collar: The American Middle Classes.* New York: Oxford University Press, 1956.

Mishra, Pankjaj. Review of *At the Same Time: Essays and Speeches by Susan Sontag. New York Times,* March 11, 2007, Book Review, 14.

Mordden, Ethan. *Make Believe: The Broadway Musical in the 1920s.* New York: Oxford University Press, 1997.

———. *Rodgers and Hammerstein.* New York: Harry Abrams, 1995.

———. *Sing for Your Supper: The Broadway Musical in the 1930s.* New York: Palgrave Macmillan, 2005.

Morgan, David H. J. "Theatre of War: Combat, the Military, and Masculinities." In *Theorizing Masculinities.* Edited by Harry Brod and Michael Kaufman. Thousand Oaks, CA: Sage, 1994.

Most, Andrea. *Making Americans: Jews and the Broadway Musical.* Cambridge, MA: Harvard University Press, 2004.

Patterson, James T. *Grand Expectations: The United States, 1945–1974.* New York: Oxford University Press, 1996.

"Remembering *South Pacific*." *Lincoln Center Review* 45–46 (Spring 2008): 33.

Richard Rodgers: The Sweetest Sounds. DVD. Directed by Roger Sherman. Wellspring Studios, 2002.

Riesman, David, in collaboration with Reuel Denney and Nathan Glazer. *The Lonely Crowd: A Study of the Changing American Character*. New Haven, CT: Yale University Press, 1959.

Rodgers, Richard. *Musical Stages: An Autobiography*. New York: Random House, 1975.

Rupp, Leila. *Mobilizing Women for War: German and American Propaganda, 1939–1945*. Princeton: Princeton University Press, 1978.

Said, Edward. *Culture and Imperialism*. New York: Vintage, 1994.

Secrest, Meryle. *Somewhere for Me: A Biography of Richard Rodgers*. New York: Alfred A. Knopf, 2001.

Severson, Marilyn S. *James A. Michener: A Critical Companion*. Westport, CT: Greenwood, 1996.

Sollors, Werner. "W. E. B. Dubois in Nazi Germany: A Surprising, Prescient Visitor." *Chronicle of Higher Education* 46, no. 12 (1999): B4–B5.

Steele, Evelyn. *Wartime Opportunities for Women*. New York: E. P. Dutton, 1943.

Taylor, Ronald. *Kurt Weill: Composer in a Divided World*. Boston: Northeastern University Press, 1991.

Terkel, Studs. *"The Good War": An Oral History of World War Two*. New York: Pantheon, 1984.

Whyte, William H. "The Class of '49." In *The Essential William H. Whyte*. Edited by Albert LaFarge. New York: Fordham University Press, 2000.

———. *The Organization Man*. New York: Simon and Schuster, 1956.

Wolf, Stacy. *A Problem Like Maria: Gender and Sexuality in the American Musical*. Ann Arbor: University of Michigan Press, 2002.

Wood, Graham. "The Development of Song Forms in the Broadway and Hollywood Musicals of Richard Rodgers, 1919–1943." PhD diss., University of Minnesota, 2000.

Zinn, Howard. *Postwar America: 1945–1971*. Indianapolis: Bobbs-Merrill, 1973.

INDEX

• • •

Page numbers in bold indicate pictures.

liberal views, 33
liberals
    Babes in Arms, 26
    FBI scrutiny, 21
    and Hammerstein, 33, 77–78, 225n55
    and leftists, 14–15
    Partisan Review, 225n55
    Rodgers and Hart, 28
Library of Congress, 8, 220n4
Lincoln Center, 1–3, 12, 185–86, 217n3
Lippmann, Walter, 31
live-wires, 73, 76–77
"Lobeck, the Asiatic," 179
Loesser, Frank, 9
Logan, Joshua
    as co-writer for *South Pacific*, 80
    directorial techniques, movie, 183, 187
    excisions, 3
    Gypsy, 224n26
    and Hammerstein, 72, 79–80
    "I'm Gonna Wash That Man Right
        Out-a My Hair," 65, 68, 223n22,
        224n26
    "I'm in Love with a Wonderful Guy," 71,
        224n32
    and Michener, 56
    Mr. Roberts, 80
    nudity king, 153–54
    pictured, **48**, **69**, **123**
    Richard Rodgers: The Sweetest Sounds,
        12
    Rittman transitions, 130–31, 234n75
    Rodgers, Hammerstein and Michener,
        46–47
    "Suddenly Lucky/Lovely," 237n134
    "There Is Nothing Like a Dame," 150
    "Younger Than Springtime," 155–56
Lonely Crowd, 75
Los Angeles Civic Light Opera, **89**
Los Angeles Philharmonic Auditorium, 19
Los Angeles Times, 22
Lost in the Stars, 83
"Love Is Sweeping the Country," 25
Love Me Tonight, 23–24
loyalty tests, 31

Luna, Barbara, **123**, **124**
lyric binary, 94–95, 133–34, 146–47, 156–57

Macdonald, Dwight, 178
MacDonald, Jeanette, 23
MacMillan, Louis, **109**
Macmillan publishers, 38
Madama Butterfly, 49, 171
Majestic Theater, **132**
"Mamma, Look Sharp," 188
Mamoulian, Rouben, 23
March, Frederic, 17
Marie Clément, 170–71
Martin, Mary
    Annie Get Your Gun, 49
    and Ezio Pinza, **88**, **90**
    "Honey Bun," **112**
    as Honey Bun, 180
    "I'm Gonna Wash That Man Right Out-
        a My Hair," **66**, **68**
    musical theater singer, 123
    as Nellie, 120, **121**
    original cast recording, 2, **189**
    playbill, **132**
    rehearsals, **124**
    and Rodgers, 224n32
masculinity
    and Cable, 12, 142–44, 150, 152
    Cold War ideals, 143
    and de Becque, 12, 175
    gender constructs, 158–60
    hyper-masculinity, 108
    and the male body, 154
    in postwar America, 141–44
    South Pacific (movie), 154
    and violence, 148
    in WWII, 155
Maslon, Laurence, 10–12, 46, 48, 220n4
Mauceri, John, 9
May Wine, 17
McCarthyism, 5, 15, 143
McClary, Susan, 150–51
McClung, Bruce D., 10
McCormick, Myron, **110**
McEntire, Reba, 185–86

McKenna, Kenneth, 47–48
McMath, Sidney S., 87–88, 227–28n28
Me and Juliet, 114, 230n10
Merman, Ethel, 49, 224n26
Merrily We Roll Along, 183
Messner, Barbara R., 104
Metro-Goldwyn-Mayer, 17, 25, 47
Meyerowitz, Joanne, 231n28
Meyers, Henry, 19
Michener, James A., See also *Tales of the South Pacific* (book)
   and Buck, 179
   Hammerstein manuscript, 32
   Hawaii, 41
   Hayes biography, 179
   indentured servants and planters, 164–65
   and Logan, 56
   personal courage, 41
   pictured, **109**
   popular song styles, 179–80
   Pulitzer Prize, 39
   on racial intolerance, 85
   Richard Rodgers: The Sweetest Sounds, 12
   and Rodgers, 168
   and Rodgers and Hammerstein, 46–57
   symphonic music, 180
   Talking with Michener, 221n14
   and tolerance, 41
   The World Is My Home memoir, 35
   World War II, 37–39
middlebrow, 8, 178
Middleton, Ray, **72**
Mielziner, Jo, 47–48
Militant Christian Patriots, 18
military, 4
military bases, 177–78
"The Milk Run" (story), 40, 52, 191
Mills, C. Wright, 75–77, 225n55
miscegenation, 14–16, 45–46, 115
Mishra, Pankaj, 225n55
Miss Saigon, 171
Mister Roberts, 153
Molnar, Ferenc, 35
Molotov-Ribbentrop Pact, 20

Mordden, Ethan, 57, 114, 148, 168, 222n42, 231n21
Morgan, David H. J., 141
Mosher, John, 24
Most, Andrea
   "I'm in Love with a Wonderful Guy," 139
   Liat (fictional), 238n17
   Making Americans, 25–26
   musical dynamic, 132
   on Nellie, 119–20, 138, 140–41, 146
   nuclear family, 122–23
   Rodgers and Hart, 28
   stereotyping during WWII, 170
   vocal separation in *South Pacific* (play), 123–24
The Most Happy Fellow, 9
movie industry, 17–23
Mr. Roberts, 80
Murra, Wilbur, 37
musical examples
   "*Dites-moi*," **126**
   Finale Ultimo, **141**
   "I'm Gonna Wash That Man Right Out-a My Hair," **133**, **134**, **135**
   "I'm in Love with a Wonderful Guy," **139**
   "Some Enchanted Evening," **131**, **137**
   "Twin Soliloquies," **129**
Musical Stages: An Autobiography, 224n32, 224n39
musical theater
   American postwar expansionism, 178
   development of, 15–16
   dialogue, 25
   gender identity, 160
   integration conscious, 16
   leit-motifs, 234n75
   racial intolerance in postwar America, 82
   research on, 8–9
   rock 'n roll, 188
   soliloquies, 127–30
   South Pacific as musical icon, 187
"Mutiny" (story), 41, 51, 191